# THE ALL NEW CHICKEN COOKBOOK

## 200+ CHICKEN RECIPES FOR THE AIR FRYER, INSTANT POT, SLOW COOKER, AND MORE!

Christine Pittman

© 2019 More Cheese Please Productions, LLC. All rights reserved.

No part of this book may be reproduced or transmitted in any form or by any means, electronic, mechanical or manual, including photocopying, recording, or by any information storage and retrieval system, without expressed written permission from the author.

ISBN: 978-1-7343405-0-1

Edited by Christine Pittman.
Interior designed by Garnishing Co.
Cover designed by Brombosz Consulting LLC.
Cover photo by Jill Silverman Hough.

First printing edition 2019.

*To Jeremy and Emily.*

*You two amaze and inspire me with your intelligence and sense of fun every day. I'm so grateful to have you in my life, and I'm really grateful that you both like chicken!*

# Table of Contents

Introduction ......................................................... vi

Chicken Basics ....................................................... 1

15-Minute Soups ..................................................... 27

Air Fryer Chicken ................................................... 41

Pressure Cooker Chicken ............................................. 72

Slow Cooker Chicken ................................................ 101

One-Pot or Pan Dinners ............................................. 131

Grilling Chicken ................................................... 175

Wings and Buffalo Things ........................................... 194

World Flavors ...................................................... 223

Chicken Classics and More .......................................... 255

About the Author ................................................... 302

Acknowledgements ................................................... 303

Contributors ....................................................... 304

# Introduction

**Welcome to The New Chicken Cookbook!**

Get excited because starting right now your chicken dinners are going to be ready quicker and taste better than ever before. That's because so many of the recipes in this book are devoted to new faster methods of cooking. This includes cooking in some of the most popular kitchen gadgets of today, like the electric pressure cooker and air fryer.

The electric pressure cooker and air fryer haven't just changed the way I cook, they've changed the pattern of my entire daily life. That includes what I put on my grocery list, how I prep meals, the amount of time I allot for making a meal, and what's on my counter. It even extends to after cooking when I wipe down the exteriors of my new appliances.

In short, my whole kitchen life has shifted, and yours will too.

I'll start off by saying I'm not really a gadget person. When I first began seeing the pressure cooker craze on the internet, I mostly ignored it. After it stuck around for a while, I became curious and finally made the purchase.

I was surprised by how much I liked my electric pressure cooker. I was even more surprised by how much I used it. It became my go-to gadget for weekly meal prep, soups, stews, hard boiled eggs, grains, legumes, and all sorts of things.

That same sequence repeated itself when the air fryer frenzy began. I actually bought myself an air fryer early on but didn't open the box for months. It seemed too complicated and I thought I didn't have time to figure it out. But then I did it. And wow! I use my air fryer daily now. Multiple times a day, in fact.

I use my air fryer and my pressure cooker so much that I rarely need to turn on my oven!

I'm not the only one either. I've noticed a shift among my readers. If you aren't familiar with who I am, I have a culinary media company with two recipe websites at its center. They are COOKtheSTORY.com and TheCookful.com. Combined, these sites have over 2 million visitors per month. That's a lot of people so I'm able to see a lot of trends based on their interests. I use that info to forecast the future directions of the home-cooking world.

Lately, I've seen a new trend among my readers. They're gravitating toward electric pressure cooker and air fryer recipes. They also seem to spend a lot of time looking at the basics. Those simple "How to Cook Chicken Breasts in the Air Fryer" kinds of recipes. I noticed this a while ago, but only started making sense of it recently.

Here's my theory. In the past few years, the way we cook has fundamentally changed. That's due in part to these two new gadgets. Cooks can no longer just turn to their old cookbooks or established knowledge anymore. They need to research and find new cooking times and preparation instructions, and they have to learn all the tips and tricks that go along with them. Cooks are therefore looking for *current* recipes. That's more than just about finding new dishes to make. It's also about relearning the basics. They need this new information, and they need it now.

That's why I decided to write this cookbook. Its subject matter is the beloved standby, chicken. However, its approach isn't like anything you've seen in past chicken cookbooks. It crucially focuses on how we cook chicken *today.*

This cookbook contains all of the basics for cooking chicken in the air fryer and electric pressure cooker. From whole chickens to breasts to wings — we've got it all here. In addition, we recognize that the older methods are not gone forever. There are times when you will still need to know how to roast a whole chicken in the oven, or how to panfry chicken thighs. That's why we've included all the old school basics for more standard chicken-cooking as well.

What you'll get from these pages is a complete chicken resource. It features all the traditional cooking methods and classic dishes, while also focusing on new methods and new types of recipes.

I'm going to take a moment now to walk you through the book. That way you'll know what you're going to find and what you should expect.

As mentioned, we cover the chicken basics. That's the focus of Chapter 1. You'll find traditional cooking methods like roasting a chicken and making chicken gravy. You'll also find details on carving a chicken, as well as some more general information about cooking chicken.

Chapter 2 is called "15-Minute Chicken Soups." As the title implies, it features homemade soups that are ready in 15 minutes or less. That's from start to finish and includes chopping and prep time! You'll get all the comfort of homemade soup for dinner, but in a fraction of the time. Who knew that homemade soup could fit so perfectly into modern life? You'll also learn great time-saving techniques here. That means you can begin to invent 15-minute soups of your own.

Chapter 3 is about that wonderful new gadget, the air fryer. It contains all of your air fryer chicken basics, like how to roast a whole chicken. It also goes into detail on how to cook chicken breasts, wings, thighs, drumsticks, and leg quarters. In addition, this third chapter has a wealth of delicious recipes like Air Fryer Chicken Cordon Bleu, Air Fryer Chicken Fajitas, Air Fryer Lemon Chicken, Air Fryer Fried Chicken, and Air Fryer Chicken Quesadillas.

The electric pressure cooker takes over in Chapter 4 with some pressure cooker chicken basics followed by a slew of innovative meal ideas. You're going to love making Pulled Chicken and Chicken Shawarma in your pressure cooker, along with Honey Bourbon Chicken, and so much more!

Chapter 5 is all about the old reliable slow cooker. There are classics in there like Coq au Vin and Chicken with 40 Cloves of Garlic, alongside some awesome new ideas like Chicken Burger Dip and Chicken Stroganoff.

For Chapter 6, we turn to a big trend that has been staying strong. That's the One Pot/One Pan meal. You'll find over 30 chicken recipes here that use only one pot or pan to make an entire dinner. Using only one pan makes cleanup a breeze. It also means that you'll only have one thing happening at a time while you cook, which can be really soothing after a long day.

If you love to grill chicken, you'll find everything you need to know in Chapter 7. There's a recipe for a whole grilled chicken, a quicker spatchcocked grilled chicken, and, most importantly, a recipe for grilling chicken breasts that are juicy every time. Yes, really!

I'm particularly excited about Chapter 8. Here, we've focused on a flavor profile that has overtaken the chicken world: Buffalo Chicken Wings. There are a bunch of wing recipes in this chapter. My specialty is the oven-baked crispy wings. You've got to try those out! In addition to learning how to bake and fry wings, there's a recipe for making your own boneless wings. I'm also going to walk you through how to make a quick wing breading. And, you're going to discover a whole bunch of recipes featuring that tangy, rich, and spicy favorite, Buffalo wing sauce. Buffalo Chicken Poutine, anyone?

Chapter 9 brings in some older and newer flavor profiles from around the world. Head to this chapter when you want to give your chicken a little jolt. I especially love the recipes for Chicken Vindaloo and Chicken Goulash Pasta.

Finally, in Chapter 10 we're going to cover a whole bunch of classic chicken recipes, like Chicken and Dumplings, Chicken Meatloaf, and The Best Chicken Burger. We'll also look at a bunch of other exciting ideas that we just couldn't leave out of this book. Check out the Chicken Parmesan

Baked Pasta and the Avocado Chicken Salad (it uses mashed avocado instead of mayo!). These are classic chicken recipes with a twist.

Altogether, we've brought you over 200 recipes that cover all the chicken basics, the classic chicken dishes you crave, convenient new ways of cooking chicken, and the exciting new appliances that make chicken dinners easier than ever. It's all chicken, but in a way that you've never seen or tasted before.

Enjoy!

Christine

# CHAPTER 1
# CHICKEN BASICS

How to Brine Chicken
How to Roast Chicken Perfectly
How to Cook a Whole Chicken From Frozen
How to Carve a Chicken
How to Cook Chicken Breasts Perfectly
How to Cook Chicken Breasts from Frozen
How to Make Breaded Chicken Cutlets
Baked Chicken Cutlets
How to Cook Chicken Thighs Perfectly
How to Cook Ground Chicken
One-Ingredient Meatballs
How to Poach Chicken Breasts
How to Cut Chicken Wings
How to Make Chicken Gravy
How to Make Gravy without Drippings
Ground Chicken in Gravy
Homemade Condensed Cream of Chicken Soup
Best Chicken Marinade

# How to Brine Chicken

*Chicken breasts can be dry, but they don't have to be. There are a few techniques in this book to help keep breast meat moist but this is my favorite. You brine them. A brine is a simple salt and water mixture that penetrates into meat making it moister after cooking. Your brine can also serve as a marinade if you add other flavorful ingredients, like peppercorns, to the mix. Note that you can't use the drippings from brined meat to make gravy (it will be way too salty). Don't worry though. Turn to page 22 to learn how to make gravy without drippings.*

**Ingredients:**
8 cups cold water
12 Tbsp. Diamond Crystal kosher salt, 8 Tbsp. Morton's kosher salt, or 6 Tbsp. fine or table salt
4 Tbsp. brown or white sugar (optional)
8 chicken breasts or 1 whole chicken

1. In a large nonreactive container or pot big enough to fit your chicken and liquid, combine the water, salt, and sugar (if using), stirring to dissolve the salt and sugar.

2. Add the 8 chicken breasts or 1 whole chicken, and any optional flavor ingredients you'd like to add, like peppercorns or minced garlic. The chicken should be entirely submerged. If not, use a narrower container, or you can make more brine mixture.

3. Cover and refrigerate for 4-6 hours for chicken breasts, 8-12 hours for a whole chicken.

4. Remove chicken from the brine, pat it dry and proceed with your recipe. Do not add extra salt to the recipe you make since the chicken will already be well seasoned. If roasting the chicken, do not use drippings from the chicken for making gravy.

# How to Roast Chicken Perfectly

There's nothing like perfectly roasted chicken. All that tender, juicy meat. And oh the crispy skin. To achieve both of those things, juicy meat and crispy skin, is a bit of a balancing act. For this recipe, you roast the chicken slowly so that the meat is nice and juicy. Then you let the chicken rest for a good 30 minutes so that the juices redistribute throughout the meat, making it even juicier. And then, finally, you put the chicken back into the oven at a really high temperature for a short time to crisp the skin. No need for the bird to rest after the last time in the oven. You want to serve it immediately while the skin is crispiest.

**Yield:** 4 servings

**Prep Time:** 30 minutes

**Cook Time:** 1 hour, 30 minutes

**Total Time:** 2 hours

**Ingredients:**
1 (4-6 lb.) whole chicken
Salt
Pepper
Low-sodium chicken stock

1. Take your chicken out of the fridge and remove the giblets from inside. Discard giblets or save for alternate use.
2. Place chicken into roasting pan and let it rest at room temperature for 30 minutes.
3. Preheat oven to 300°F.
4. Truss the drumsticks tightly together with butcher's twine.
5. Tuck the wings underneath the chicken: Grab a wing tip and pull it backwards then bend and tuck the wing under the chicken.

# How to Roast Chicken Perfectly
*Continued from previous page*

6. Season the top of the chicken with salt and pepper. Approximately 1/4 teaspoon of salt and 1/8 teaspoon of pepper.

7. Pour 1/2 inch of stock into the bottom of a roasting pan.

8. Roast the chicken uncovered until internal temperature is 160°F. After an hour, if much of the stock has evaporated add more.

9. Check chicken temperature after 20 minutes per pound (so for a 4 pound turkey, check after 80 minutes). Test temperature in both breast and thigh, being sure to not touch bone.

10. Take the chicken out once it reaches 160°F. Transfer to another pan or cutting board. Use juices to make gravy, if desired. Let chicken sit for 30 minutes. Do not cover it during the resting time.

11. Preheat oven to 500°F.

12. Place the chicken into a clean, empty roasting pan or onto a baking sheet, then put it into the hot oven for 10-15 minutes until the skin is well browned and crisp.

13. Take it out of the oven.

14. Carve and serve immediately.

# How to Cook a Whole Chicken From Frozen

*Cooking a chicken from frozen, while safe, is never as good as cooking it from fresh. It doesn't end up as juicy and it doesn't cook as evenly. However, there are times when I've found myself with insufficient time to both defrost and cook a chicken. If I want a roast chicken anyhow, this is what I do.*

**Yield:** 4 servings

**Prep Time:** 5 minutes

**Cook Time:** 2 hours

**Total Time:** 2 hours, 5 minutes

**Ingredients:**
1 (4 lb.) frozen chicken
1/2 lemon (optional)
1/2 small onion (optional)
2 sprigs fresh rosemary (optional)
2 sprigs fresh thyme (optional)
1 Tbsp. olive oil
1/2 tsp. coarse salt
1/4 tsp. coarse black pepper

1. Preheat oven to 350°F. Put a rack in a large roasting pan. Put the chicken breast-side-up on top of it. If there are giblets inside of the chicken, see if you can remove them. If not, it's okay. Proceed with the remaining steps. If you can access the inside cavity of the chicken, put the lemon, onion, rosemary and thyme inside, if using. If you cannot access the cavity, it's okay. Proceed with remaining steps.

2. Drizzle the top of the chicken with the olive oil. Sprinkle with salt and pepper. Put in oven uncovered and roast for 90 minutes. If there are still giblets in the chicken, remove them when you can using tongs and wearing oven mitts (you should be able to after 30-60 minutes). If you wanted to add lemon, onion, rosemary, and/or thyme to the chicken cavity but couldn't before, you should be able to now. Return chicken to oven and continue to roast.

3. Increase oven temperature to 450°F to help brown skin. Roast until drumsticks loosen easily when jiggled and all meat is cooked to 165°F according to an instant read thermometer inserted into various places in the chicken (breast and thigh are best), 15-30 minutes.

4. Transfer chicken to a carving board. Let rest 10-15 minutes. Carve. If there is any pink or red meat, return those pieces to the oven, or microwave them for 1 minute at a time until white.

# How to Carve a Chicken

*The key to carving a chicken is a sharp knife and the right cutting board. Do use a nice sharp boning or carving knife. Either will work fine. And get a cutting board that has a deep groove all around the edge. The groove catches any juices that drip out of your chicken, keeping them from dripping onto the counter and making a slippery mess. The groove also helps gather those juices so you can pour them into your gravy, because you definitely don't want to miss out on all that!*

You will need:

- A whole roasted chicken

- A sharp boning or carving knife

- A carving fork or regular dinner fork

- A cutting board with a groove around the edge

**Step 1:** Using your knife, cut in-between the thigh and breast and follow your cut. Using your hands pull the thigh and leg loose from the chicken body and repeat with the other side.

**Step 2:** Next, cut between the thigh and leg bone. To find where to cut, move the leg and watch where it hinges. Cut there. Repeat on other piece.

**Step 3:** Locate the breast bone in the middle of the breast and cut on both sides of the bone.

**Step 4:** Use your boning knife to slowly cut the breast from the ribs using short strokes from the tip of the blade. Slice the breast. Remove second breast and slice as well.

**Step 5:** Disconnect the wing from the chicken. Repeat on the opposite side.

**Step 6:** Transfer chicken pieces and slices to a large plate or platter to serve.

# How to Cook Chicken Breasts Perfectly

*It's probably obvious that the thicker half of a chicken breast (where it's more rounded in shape) takes longer to cook than the thinner half (where it tapers to a point). What's less obvious is that there's something we can do to fix that. How? Even out the thickness of the chicken breast by pounding the thicker side down a little bit. That's what I've done in this recipe.*

**Yield:** 4 servings

**Prep Time:** 5 minutes

**Cook Time:** 10 minutes

**Total Time:** 15 minutes

**Ingredients:**
4 (7-8 oz.) boneless skinless chicken breasts
3/4 tsp. salt
3/4 tsp. pepper
1 Tbsp. olive oil

1. Preheat the oven to 400°F.

2. Flatten the chicken breasts if needed: Put one breast into a large ziptop bag but keep it unzipped. Use a flat mallet or heavy rolling pin to hit the chicken breast at the thickest part. Continue to do so, moving around a bit, until the chicken is of an even thickness of approximately 3/4-inch. Remove chicken from bag and repeat one at a time with remaining breasts. Sprinkle both sides of the chicken with the salt and pepper.

3. Preheat a large oven-safe skillet (large enough to hold the chicken without crowding) over medium-high heat.

4. Add the oil. Swirl it around to coat the skillet.

5. Add the chicken and cook undisturbed until well browned on the underside, 4 to 5 minutes.

6. Turn the chicken and place the skillet in the oven until the chicken is cooked through to 165°F as read on an instant read thermometer, 6 to 8 minutes.

7. Remove the skillet from the oven (be careful—it will be very hot).

8. Transfer the chicken to plates and let rest for about 5 minutes before serving.

# How to Cook Chicken Breasts from Frozen

*It's absolutely safe to cook chicken straight from frozen as long as you follow a few rules. First, only do this for chicken pieces that have been individually frozen. It won't work if the chicken was frozen in clumps. You either need to buy them individually frozen or lay them on a tray in a single layer to freeze them yourself. After they're frozen gather them into a bag. They might stick together a little bit in the bag but a gentle knock of the bag against the counter should dislodge them. Second, cook the chicken for 1.5X the amount of time as it usually takes. Fresh chicken breasts usually need 20-25 minutes to cook at 350°F, so frozen chicken breasts will need 30-40 minutes. Third, use an instant read thermometer to check if the chicken has reached a safe temperature. It needs to be at 165°F in the thickest part. Insert the thermometer into the thickest part of all of the breasts to make sure they're done. Note that this recipe is for breaded chicken breasts. You can leave them plain instead, just season with salt and pepper before cooking, or brush them with your favorite BBQ sauce.*

**Yield:** 4 servings

**Prep Time:** 10 minutes

**Cook Time:** 30 minutes

**Total Time:** 40 minutes

**Ingredients:**

1/3 cup dry breadcrumbs (panko crumbs turn out way better, if you have them)
1 Tbsp. cooking oil (olive oil, vegetable oil, etc.)
1/2 tsp. salt
1/4 tsp. pepper
1/4 tsp. garlic powder
4 frozen boneless skinless chicken breasts that have been frozen individually
4 tsp. mustard (yellow or dijon)

1. Preheat oven to 425°F. Lightly oil a baking sheet.
2. In a small bowl combine the breadcrumbs, oil, salt, pepper, and garlic powder. Set aside.
3. Put the chicken breasts on the prepared baking sheet. Spread or brush 1 teaspoon of mustard onto each breast. Sprinkle with the breadcrumbs, pushing down to help them adhere to the mustard.
4. Bake until chicken is 165°F according to an instant read thermometer, 30-40 minutes.

# How to Make Breaded Chicken Cutlets

*Making chicken cutlets is a wonderful technique to learn because it can then be used as the basis for other dishes, like Chicken Parmesan, or chicken topped with just about anything.*

**Yield:** 4 servings

**Prep Time:** 30 minutes

**Cook Time:** 10 minutes

**Total Time:** 40 minutes

**Ingredients:**
- 4 (6 oz.) boneless skinless chicken breasts
- 1 and 1/2 cups plain dry breadcrumbs
- 1 tsp. dried thyme
- 1/2 lemon, zested
- 1/2 tsp. salt
- 1/4 tsp. pepper
- 1/2 cup all-purpose flour
- 2 eggs
- Vegetable oil

**Step 1:** Put a chicken breast between two sheets of plastic wrap.

**Step 2:** Use a flat meat mallet to pound it to 1/4-inch thick. Repeat with remaining chicken breasts.

**Tip:** Once a breast is flattened, leave it between its plastic wrap to keep it separated from the others. This is especially helpful if you're doing a lot of cutlets because you can stack them without them sticking together. Then use new plastic wrap for each breast.

**Step 3:** In a large shallow bowl, combine breadcrumbs, thyme, lemon zest, salt and black pepper. Into another shallow bowl, crack eggs and beat to combine. Into another shallow bowl, add flour.

**Step 5:** Preheat oven to 400°F. Dredge a chicken piece in flour, coating lightly on all sides.

**Step 6:** Put chicken into the eggs, coating it fully.

# How to Make Breaded Chicken Cutlets
*Continued from previous page*

**Step 7:** Place it onto the breadcrumb mixture. Use your fingers to mound breadcrumbs on top of chicken piece then press down to adhere crumbs to the chicken. Flip and repeat. Place chicken on a large plate. Repeat with the rest of the chicken pieces. Set a wire rack over a baking sheet.

**Step 8:** In a large skillet add enough vegetable oil to cover the bottom completely by about 1/8 inch. Heat skillet over medium until very hot and shimmering. Add two chicken breasts in a single layer and cook until brown underneath, about 2-3 minutes. Flip and brown on the other side.

**Step 9:** Transfer to rack. Repeat this cooking step with the other two breasts.

**Step 10:** Transfer chicken, rack and baking sheet to the oven and bake until cooked through and firm, about 8-10 minutes.

# Baked Chicken Cutlets

*These baked chicken cutlets use the same method as the fried cutlets in the previous recipe but they require less fat and no frying. The reason they brown is because there's a bit of oil mixed right in with the breadcrumbs. Because of this, each little crumb has a touch of oil which toasts it to a golden brown. The Parmesan in the crumb mixture gets toasted too which adds some extra crunch and flavor.*

**Yield:** 4 servings

**Prep Time:** 10 minutes

**Cook Time:** 25 minutes

**Total Time:** 35 minutes

**Ingredients:**
4 (6 oz.) boneless skinless chicken breasts
1 and 1/4 cups plain breadcrumbs
1/4 cup finely shredded Parmesan cheese
2 Tbsp. vegetable oil
1 tsp. dried thyme
1/2 tsp. salt
1/4 tsp. pepper
2 egg whites
2 tsp. Dijon mustard

1. Preheat oven to 400°F.
2. Pound chicken breasts to equal 1/4-inch thickness.
3. In small shallow bowl or pie plate, combine breadcrumbs, Parmesan cheese, vegetable oil, thyme, salt and ground pepper.
4. In another shallow bowl combine egg whites and Dijon mustard.
5. Dredge chicken in egg mixture then the breadcrumb mixture.
6. Place chicken on a wire rack set on a baking sheet.
7. Repeat with remaining chicken and then bake until cooked through and crispy, about 20-25 minutes.

Photo: Jill Silverman Hough

# How to Cook Chicken Thighs Perfectly

*While I know that white meat is leaner and thus better for me, I'm always partial to dark, and especially to thighs. They're so meaty, juicy, and full of flavor. If you get them with the skin on, like in the picture, you also get bronzed, crackling skin. I really like cooking chicken thighs using this method. They're started on the stovetop and then transferred to the oven. The stovetop gives them a good blast of direct heat for color and crunch, and then the oven surrounds them in less direct heat to finish them off more evenly. I garnished these ones with some fresh rosemary but they'd also be great with thyme, basil, or even plain.*

**Yield:** 6 servings

**Prep Time:** 15 minutes

**Cook Time:** 20 minutes

**Total Time:** 35 minutes

**Ingredients:**
2 Tbsp. olive oil
2 egg whites
3/4 cup panko bread crumbs
1/3 cup finely shredded
   Parmesan cheese
1 tsp. Italian seasoning
1/2 tsp. salt
1/4 tsp. pepper
2 lbs. boneless skinless chicken breasts, pounded to 1/2-inch thickness and cut into tenders

1. Preheat the oven to 400°F.
2. Sprinkle both sides of the chicken with the salt and pepper.
3. Preheat a large oven-safe skillet (large enough to hold the chicken without crowding) over medium-high heat.
4. When the skillet is good and hot, add the oil.
5. When the oil is good and hot, add the chicken skin-side-down and cook undisturbed until well browned, 4 to 5 minutes. Turn the chicken and place the skillet in the oven until the chicken is cooked throughout, 6 to 8 minutes.
6. Remove the skillet from the oven (be careful—it will be very hot). Transfer the chicken to plates and let rest for about 5 minutes before serving.

# How to Cook Ground Chicken

*You can add extra flavor and moisture to ground chicken by sautéing aromatic vegetables before adding the raw chicken. I typically use two aromatic vegetables for one pound of ground chicken. Aromatics to choose from are a small onion (chopped), 1 clove garlic (minced), 2 ribs celery (finely chopped), 2 carrots (peeled and finely chopped), and 1 green bell pepper (finely chopped). Eight ounces of sliced button mushrooms are also a nice addition. Simply add these ingredients to some heated oil and sauté until soft before adding the chicken to the skillet.*

**Yield:** 4 servings

**Prep Time:** 5 minutes

**Cook Time:** 8 minutes

**Total Time:** 13 minutes

**Ingredients:**
2 tsp. cooking oil
1 small onion, chopped (optional)
1 clove garlic, minced (optional)
1 lb. ground chicken
1/2 tsp. salt
1/4 tsp. pepper
1/4 tsp. garlic powder (optional)

1. Heat the oil in a large skillet over medium heat.
2. Optional: Add the onion and cook, stirring occasionally until softened, 3-4 minutes.
3. Optional: Add the garlic and cook, stirring constantly for 30 seconds.
4. Add the ground chicken, salt, and pepper. Add the garlic powder, if using.
5. Use wooden spoon to break up chicken into crumbles. Continue to cook, stirring occasionally and breaking up bigger clumps when you spot them, until chicken is white all the way through, 6-7 minutes.
6. Transfer chicken to a clean plate immediately so that chicken stops cooking and doesn't dry out.

# One-Ingredient Chicken Meatballs

*To make these sausage meatballs you simply take the meat from inside of the sausage casings, roll it into balls, and cook it. It doesn't get easier than that! Note that instructions are given for panfrying and for baking. You can alternatively plop the meatballs raw into soup to simmer them until cooked through.*

**Yield:** 4 servings

**Prep Time:** 5 minutes

**Cook Time:** 20 minutes

**Total Time:** 25 minutes

**Ingredients:**
1 lb. raw Italian chicken sausage links

1. If following baking directions, heat oven to 400°F.

2. Using a sharp knife, slice open the casing of each sausage link. Use your hands to squeeze out 1/3 of the link and roll into a ball. Repeat with remaining sausage until you have used up all of the sausage meat.

3. To panfry: Heat a skillet over medium heat. Add meatballs to the pan, turning until all sides are browned and the meatballs are cooked through, about 20 minutes.

4. To bake: Arrange meatballs in a single layer on a baking sheet. Bake until cooked through to 165°F as read on an instant read thermometer, about 20 minutes. Turn on the broiler. Set meatballs 6-8 inches from the broiler element. Broil until a nice crust forms on top, 2-4 minutes. Flip and broil on the other side.

Photo: Jill Silverman Hough

# How to Poach Chicken Breasts

*It matters which pot you use when poaching chicken breasts. The chicken breasts need to fit in the pot in a single layer. It's ok if they overlap a little bit but they shouldn't overlap much. This is so that all the chicken breasts are at the same place in the pan so that they cook evenly. I've listed a variety of aromatics that you can optionally add to your poaching liquid. They all will add subtle flavor to the chicken, and also to the liquid if you're planning to use that for making soup.*

**Yield:** 4 servings

**Prep Time:** 2 minutes

**Cook Time:** 15 minutes

**Total Time:** 17 minutes

**Ingredients:**
4 skinless chicken breasts (bone-in or boneless)
1 tsp. salt
1 cup white wine (optional)
Optional Aromatics: 1 small onion (peeled and halved), 2 cloves garlic (peeled), 2 ribs celery (cut in half), 2 carrots (peeled and cut in half), 10 peppercorns, a handful of fresh herbs (parsley, basil, dill, thyme, or rosemary), a bay leaf.

1. Arrange the chicken in a pot large enough that they fit in a single layer. If they overlap a little bit, that's fine.
2. Sprinkle salt over chicken. Add white wine, if using. Add any aromatics that you're using.
3. Add enough cool tap water to cover the chicken by 1 inch.
4. Heat on the stove over high heat until it reaches a boil. If you'll be using the liquid for another purpose, skim off any foam that has risen to the top.
5. Reduce heat to low. Cover and simmer until chicken is cooked through to 165°F as read on an instant read thermometer placed in the middle of a breast, 9-14 minutes depending on the thickness of the chicken.
6. Remove chicken from poaching liquid. Let rest for 5 minutes before slicing chicken or using in a recipe.
7. Discard the aromatics. Use the liquid for making a soup or sauce, or discard.

# How To Cut Chicken Wings

*By Stephanie Manley*

*Fresh chicken wings are usually sold uncut, and this is the cheapest way to buy them. However, you can absolutely leave them whole to make any of the wing recipes in this book, and there are a lot of them! If you prefer your wings to look the way they do in restaurants, cut into drumettes and wingettes, then these are the instructions for you. Note that we have removed the wing tip and told you to save it for another use, like making stock, because it isn't sufficient on its own as a wing. If you have no use for the wing tips and you don't want to waste them, you can leave the wing tips attached to the wingette (that is, skip steps 2 and 3). They get nice and crispy, even if they don't have much meat on them.*

**Yield:** 2 pounds

**Prep Time:** 2 minutes

**Total Time:** 2 minutes

**Ingredients:**
2 lbs. whole chicken wings

**Step 1:** Flip the wing over (nicer, plumper side down) so that you can easily see the joints.

**Step 2:** Identify the wing tip, which is the short end that tapers to a point. Locate the joint where it attaches to the center part, the wingette, of the wing.

**Step 3:** Cut it cleanly with one cut right through the joint. Set the tips aside to make stock.

**Step 4:** Find the other joint.

**Step 5:** Place the knife at the high ridge on the joint between the wingette and the drumette. Push your knife through. If you have a lot of resistance, wiggle the knife just a bit and when you feel less resistance push the knife down.

# How to Make Chicken Gravy

*There are four keys to making good gravy. First, you need the right thickness. The ratio of flour to liquid used here yields a gravy of medium thickness, not too gloopy and not too thin. Second, you need flavorful liquid. Using the drippings from a roast is the best. The drippings are the liquid that escape from the meat while it cooks. These collect in the roasting pan. If you don't have enough drippings, you can make up the amount using stock. Third, you need to separate the drippings into fat and flavored water. My prefered method is to use a gravy separator. It's a large measuring cup with a spout affixed to the base of the cup such that it pours the liquid out from the bottom, rather than pouring the fat that has risen to the top. Reserve the fat to mix with flour at the beginning of your gravy-making process. Then the liquid gets blended in later. Finally, seasoning properly is essential. Season your gravy at the very end right before serving. This is because liquid evaporating out of the gravy as you simmer it concentrates the gravy and can make it overly seasoned. Waiting to season until the end resolves this problem. Season with salt and pepper for certain. You can also add garlic powder. Beyond that, I like poultry seasoning, which is a blend of sage, thyme, rosemary, marjoram, pepper, and sometimes nutmeg. If you don't have the blend on hand you can instead use 1 or more of those items on their own.*

**Yield:** 6 servings

**Prep Time:** 5 minutes

**Cook Time:** 10 minutes

**Total Time:** 15 minutes

**Ingredients:**
3 cups drippings (fat removed) from a roast chicken
Low-sodium chicken stock (if needed)
4 and 1/2 Tbsp. fat rendered from a roast chicken
Unsalted butter (if needed)
4 and 1/2 Tbsp. all-purpose flour
Salt, pepper, and seasonings

1. Measure your drippings into a liquid measuring cup. If there is less than 3 cups, use the stock to make up the difference.
2. Melt the fat in a medium pot over low heat. If you don't have enough fat, make up the difference using butter. Remove from heat once melted.
3. Whisk flour into fat.
4. Drizzle 1/2 cup drippings/stock into the flour mixture. Whisk until smooth. Whisk in another 1/2 cup. Repeat until all drippings are used.
5. Bring to a boil over medium-high heat. Reduce heat to low and simmer 1 minute. Taste and add salt, pepper, and seasonings.
6. Strain through a fine-mesh sieve.

# How to Make Gravy without Drippings

*I first developed this recipe when I brined a turkey and then couldn't use the drippings from roasting it because they were too salty. I then realized that this recipe is also great for if you're deep-frying turkey because you don't get drippings then either. And then I realized that this recipe is great for when I have leftover boring cooked chicken in the fridge and I want a comforting, warm sauce to pour over it. You'd be correct if you guessed that I now make this all the time. Note that the recipe does call for wine. If you don't want to use wine, that's fine. Just use extra chicken stock instead, but then also add a couple drops of Worcestershire sauce for a bit of deep tang.*

**Yield:** 4 servings

**Prep Time:** 15 minutes

**Total Time:** 15 minutes

**Ingredients:**
4 Tbsp. unsalted butter
1 small onion, chopped
2 cloves garlic, peeled and halved
1/4 cup all-purpose flour
1/4 cup white wine
1/2 tsp. poultry seasoning
1/8 tsp. salt
1/8 tsp. pepper
2 cups low-sodium chicken stock

1. In a large skillet heat the butter over medium heat. Let it melt and get slightly brown. Add the onion and halves of garlic. Cook stirring often until everything is browning a bit but nothing is burnt.

2. Remove from heat. Whisk in the flour. Return to heat and whisk and cook the flour mixture until it is lightly brown.

3. Add the wine and stir to bring up any brownings that are stuck to the pan. Remove from heat. Whisk in the poultry seasoning, salt, and pepper.

4. Whisk in the chicken stock 1/4 cup at a time, whisking to keep everything smooth as you go. Heat over medium heat to a simmer, stirring often.

5. Strain gravy through a fine mesh sieve. Taste and add more salt and pepper if desired before serving.

# Ground Chicken in Gravy

*This is a versatile recipe that is more about technique than it is about the ingredients used. What you're doing is sautéing some chicken with onions (you could also add diced carrots, celery, bell peppers, and/or mushrooms). Then you sprinkle everything with flour, stir, and then add in stock. The sprinkling and stirring with other ingredients distributes the flour evenly so that it doesn't clump up when you add the liquid.*

**Yield:** 6 servings

**Prep Time:** 10 minutes

**Cook Time:** 20 minutes

**Total Time:** 30 minutes

**Ingredients:**
1 Tbsp. cooking oil
1 small onion, finely chopped
1 clove garlic, minced
1 and 1/2 lbs. ground chicken or chopped chicken breasts or thighs
1 tsp. salt
1/2 tsp. pepper
2 Tbsp. all-purpose flour
1 cup low-sodium chicken stock
2 tsp. Worcestershire sauce (optional)

1. In medium sauté pan, on medium-high heat, heat oil. Add the onions and cook stirring occasionally until soft, about 5-6 minutes. Add garlic and stir for 30 seconds.

2. Add the chicken, salt, and pepper. Stir occasionally until cooked through, about 7-8 minutes. Drain excess fat, if any.

3. Sprinkle chicken with flour. Stir until incorporated.

4. Slowly stir in the stock and Worcestershire sauce, if using.

5. Bring mixture to a boil, then reduce heat to a simmer, stirring occasionally until very thick, 2-3 minutes. Taste and season with salt and pepper, if desired.

# Homemade Condensed Cream of Chicken Soup

*If you want to make a recipe that calls for canned condensed soup but you don't have any on hand, or if you don't want to use processed soup, you can make a batch of this instead. One batch makes 2 and 1/2 cups which is approximately the amount you would get from two 10.5 ounce cans of condensed soup. You can halve or double the recipe to make whatever amount you need. To use it in a casserole, use 1 and 1/4 cup of condensed mixture whenever a recipe calls for one can of condensed soup. To eat this as a soup, mix condensed soup with equal amounts milk, heat and serve.*

**Yield:** 2.5 cups

**Prep Time:** 3 minutes

**Cook Time:** 5 minutes

**Total Time:** 8 minutes

**Ingredients:**
6 Tbsp. unsalted butter, cut into pieces
6 Tbsp. all-purpose flour
1 cup non-fat milk
1 cup low-sodium chicken stock
1/4 tsp. salt (or more to taste)
1/4 tsp. garlic powder
1 cup finely chopped cooked chicken

1. In a medium pot over medium heat melt butter.
2. Remove from heat. Whisk in flour until it forms a smooth paste.
3. Drizzle in milk a bit at a time while whisking, making sure it stays smooth.
4. Drizzle in the stock a bit at a time while whisking, making sure it stays smooth.
5. Return to medium-high heat. Stir until it comes to a boil and thickens.
6. Remove from heat. Stir in chicken.

# Best Chicken Marinade

*By Allie Doran*

*What makes this marinade so good? The balsamic vinegar and lemon juice add flavor and acidity. This helps break down the chicken so that it's more tender and juicy. Worcestershire and soy sauce add salt and depth. Honey adds a touch of sweetness, just enough for some flavor. Then there's garlic in there too. I like to smash garlic with the side of my knife and then roughly chop it. This releases the oil from the garlic, resulting in tastier chicken. Italian seasoning, salt, and pepper round out the flavor profile, making this a truly delicious marinade for chicken.*

**Yield:** 8 servings

**Prep Time:** 5 minutes

**Total Time:** 5 minutes

**Ingredients:**
1/3 cup olive oil
1/4 cup balsamic vinegar
1 lemon, juiced
1 Tbsp. soy sauce
4–5 dashes Worcestershire sauce
3 garlic cloves, smashed and chopped
2 tsp. Italian seasoning
3/4 tsp. salt
1/2 tsp. pepper

1. Add all of the ingredients into a bowl or jar with a lid. Whisk or shake together.

2. Pour the marinade over chicken in a bowl with a lid or a ziptop bag. Marinate covered in the refrigerator for at least 1 hour and up to 4 hours. This recipe marinates up to 2 pounds of chicken.

# CHAPTER 2
# 15-MINUTE SOUPS

Chicken Noodle Soup
Chicken Dumpling Soup
Chicken Enchilada Soup
Chicken Tortilla Soup
Mexican Lime Soup
Chicken Lasagna Soup
Fettucine Alfredo Soup
Italian Wedding Soup
Greek Lemon Soup
Mulligatawny Soup

# Chicken Noodle Soup

*This chicken noodle soup tastes like it's been simmering on the stove all day even though it only takes 15 minutes. The reason is that the butter and the use of chicken thighs instead of breasts gives it a rich, schmaltzy flavor. There are some great time-saving tips hidden in this recipe as well. First, the liquid is heated in the microwave while other ingredients are being prepped. Second is the use of carrot matchsticks, sometimes called shredded carrots, which are bought already peeled and in matchstick form from the grocery store. Finally, using fine egg noodles, or another noodle with a very short cooking time, puts soup on the table lickety split.*

**Yield:** 4 servings

**Total Time:** 15 minutes

**Ingredients:**
- 7 cups low-sodium chicken stock
- 1 Tbsp. vegetable or olive oil
- 1 Tbsp. unsalted butter
- 2 cups carrot matchsticks (sometimes packaged as shredded carrots), roughly chopped
- 1 small onion, chopped
- 1 clove garlic, minced
- 1/2 tsp. salt
- 1/4 tsp. pepper
- 1 bay leaf
- 3 boneless skinless chicken thighs, chopped into 1/2-inch pieces
- 2 cups uncooked thin/fine egg noodles

1. Pour the chicken stock into a large microwave-safe bowl and microwave it on high for 6 minutes.
2. Meanwhile, put a large pot over medium heat. Add the oil and butter. Once heated, add the carrots and onion. Stir and cook for 3 minutes.
3. Add the garlic, salt, pepper, and bay leaf. Stir and cook for 30 seconds.
4. Carefully add the hot stock to the pot. Stir. Cover and increase heat to high.
5. When the stock comes to a boil, stir in the chicken. Bring it back to a boil and then reduce heat to a simmer. Cook until chicken is cooked through, about 1 minute.
6. Increase the heat to high and add the fine egg noodles. When it comes back to a boil, reduce to a simmer and cook until noodles are al dente, about 3 minutes. Remove bay leaf.
7. Taste and add more salt and pepper if desired.

# Chicken Dumpling Soup

*The dumplings in this soup are the same ones that my mom used to make when I was a kid. She'd drop them into homemade soups, but also into packaged powdered soups while they were simmering. Such a fun and tasty homemade twist to otherwise processed food! Note that the dumplings aren't the fluffy puffy dumplings from Southern Chicken and Dumplings. They're a bit more like free-form spaetzle or rough noodles. They're a touch dense and very hearty, perfect for a cold winter day.*

**Yield:** 5-6 servings

**Total Time:** 15 minutes

**Ingredients:**
6 cups low-sodium chicken stock
1 Tbsp. olive oil
1 Tbsp. unsalted butter
2 cups carrot matchsticks (sometimes packaged as shredded carrots), roughly chopped
1 medium onion, chopped
3 boneless skinless chicken thighs, cut into 1/2-inch pieces
Salt
1 cup all-purpose flour
1/4 tsp. baking powder
2 eggs
a small handful of fresh parsley leaves, chopped
4-6 Tbsp. milk
6 Tbsp. whipping cream

1. Pour the stock into a large microwave-safe bowl and microwave on high for 6 minutes.

2. Meanwhile, warm the olive oil and butter in a large pot over medium-high heat. Once heated, add the carrot matchsticks and onion. Stir and cook until softened a bit, 3-4 minutes.

3. When the microwave is done, add the stock to carrots and onions. Also add the chicken and 1/2 teaspoon of salt. Stir and cover. Increase heat to high. When it comes to a boil, reduce to a simmer.

4. While the stock is coming to a boil, in a small bowl combine the flour, baking powder, and 1/4 teaspoon of salt. Add the eggs and whisk to combine. Add the parsley and then enough of the milk to make a stiff wet dough.

5. Stir the soup and get it to a really low simmer. Drop the dough into the soup by the teaspoonful, dropping them all around the pot so they're far apart and less likely to stick together. Don't stir for 30 seconds, then stir gently.

6. Increase heat to a stronger simmer, cover and cook, stirring occasionally until dumplings are cooked through, 3-4 minutes.

7. Turn off the heat and add the whipping cream.

# Chicken Enchilada Soup

Masa harina, a type of fine corn flour, is used to thicken this soup, and to give it a sweet, toasted corn flavor. The toppings for the soup are tortilla chips, green onions, and shredded cheese. But you can also add diced tomatoes, avocado, and/or some sour cream.

**Yield:** 4-5 servings

**Total Time:** 15 minutes

**Ingredients:**
4 cups low-sodium chicken stock
1 Tbsp. vegetable or olive oil
1 medium onion, chopped
2 boneless skinless chicken breasts, cut into 1/2-inch cubes
1 tsp. salt
1/2 tsp. ground cumin
1/2 cup masa harina (corn flour)
1 (14 oz.) can crushed tomatoes
1 (10 oz.) can enchilada sauce
1 (4 oz.) can diced green chilies (optional), drained
2 cups shredded cheddar cheese, divided
2 green onions, chopped
10 tortilla chips

1. Measure the stock into a microwave-safe bowl and put it in the microwave on high for 6 minutes.
2. Heat oil in a large pot over medium heat. Add the onion and stir occasionally until starting to soften, 2 minutes.
3. Increase heat to medium-high and add the chicken along with the salt and cumin. Stir and cover. Cook stirring occasionally until chicken is white on all sides, about 2 minutes.
4. Once the chicken has whitened all over, sprinkle it with the masa harina and then stir.
5. Slowly stir in the hot stock. Increase heat to high and stir well.
6. Add the crushed tomatoes, enchilada sauce, and green chilies, if using. Stir.
7. When it comes to a simmer, remove from heat and add 1 and 1/2 cups of the cheese. Stir to melt.
8. Ladle soup into bowls. Top with the remaining cheese, green onions, and tortilla chips.

# Chicken Tortilla Soup

*The salsa in this soup gives it a lot of flavor with very little effort. Other than that, most of the flavor and texture comes from the toppings that you add at the end. Using cold, fresh toppings is a great technique for making quick meals. While a few simple ingredients are cooking, you chop up some fresh veggies and shred some cheese. Then when dinner is ready to serve, add your toppings and dig in!*

**Yield:** 4-5 servings

**Total Time:** 15 minutes

**Ingredients:**
4 cups low-sodium chicken stock
1 (28 oz.) can petite diced tomatoes
1 cup medium-heat low-sodium chunky salsa
3/4 lb. chicken breast cutlets, cut into 1/4" strips
1 (15.25 oz.) can low-sodium black beans, drained
20 tortilla chips
4 oz. cheddar cheese, shredded
2 green onions, chopped
1 avocado, chopped
1/4 cup fresh cilantro leaves

1. Put a large pot on the stove over high heat. Pour in the chicken stock, diced tomatoes, and salsa. Cover and let it come to a boil.

2. When the stock comes to a boil, add the chicken. Reduce heat to a low simmer until the chicken is cooked through, 2-3 minutes.

3. Add the black beans and heat through for 30 seconds.

4. To serve: Put two tortilla chips into each bowl. Crush slightly with a spoon. Ladle soup over top. Top with shredded cheese, green onions, avocado, cilantro, and another couple of crushed tortilla chips.

# Mexican Lime Soup

*Sopa de Lima is a traditional soup from the Yucatan penninsula. It has a bold lime flavor and a bit of heat. This is a good recipe for learning to prep ingredients in stages while other ingredients are cooking. Try chopping the onion while the oil heats and then add it to the pot. Mince the habanero just after adding the onion and then add it too. Mince the garlic while the onion and habanero cook. Chop the tomatoes and the chicken while the soup comes to a boil. Juice and cut the limes, and prep the toppings, while the chicken cooks. It might take you a couple extra minutes here and there when you first try this staggered method but it's a huge time-saver once you're in the habit of doing it.*

**Yield:** 4 servings

**Total Time:** 15 minutes

**Ingredients:**
6 cups low-sodium chicken stock
1 Tbsp. vegetable or olive oil
1 small onion, chopped
1 habanero pepper, seeded and minced
2 cloves garlic, minced
1 tsp. oregano
1/2 tsp. salt
1/4 tsp. cinnamon
a pinch of ground cloves
3/4 lb. tomatoes (about 2 medium), finely chopped
3 boneless skinless chicken thighs, cut in 1/4 " slices
2-3 limes
1/3 cup cilantro leaves, roughly chopped
1 avocado, chopped
8 tortilla chips

1. Pour the chicken stock into a large microwave-safe bowl and microwave it on high power for 6 minutes.

2. Meanwhile, heat the oil in a large pot over medium heat. Add the onion and habanero. Cook until softened a bit, 2 minutes.

3. Add the garlic, oregano, salt, cinnamon, and cloves. Stir and cook for 30 seconds.

4. Add the hot stock. Cover and increase heat to high. When soup reaches a boil, reduce it to a simmer.

5. Add the tomatoes and the chicken. Cover and cook until the chicken is no longer pink inside, 2-3 minutes.

6. While the chicken cooks, juice 1-2 of the limes to yield 1/4 cup of juice. Cut the remaining lime(s) into wedges.

7. Once the chicken is cooked, remove the soup from the heat. Stir in the lime juice. Ladle soup into bowls and serve garnished with the lime wedges, cilantro, avocado, and tortilla chips.

# Chicken Lasagna Soup

*Here's a way to get all of the cheesy, garlicky flavors of lasagna without the long cooking time. The best part is the ricotta, garlic, and basil mixture that you dollop into the soup before serving. It's so creamy and flavorful!*

**Yield:** 6 servings

**Total Time:** 15 minutes

**Ingredients:**
6 oz. broken lasagna noodles or 10 oz. fresh cheese ravioli
1 Tbsp. olive oil
1 lb. ground chicken
Salt
Pepper
1/2 tsp. dry oregano leaves
2 cloves garlic, minced
2 handfuls fresh parsley, divided
4 cups low-sodium chicken stock
3 cups tomato sauce
1 big handful fresh basil leaves, chopped
1 and 1/2 cups ricotta cheese
1/4 cup grated Parmesan cheese
1/4 tsp. garlic powder
3/4 cup shredded mozzarella cheese

1. Fill a medium pot with hot tap water. Put the lid on and heat it to boiling over high heat. Cook the pasta in the boiling water according to package directions. Drain.

2. Meanwhile, heat olive oil in a large pot over medium-high heat. Add the ground chicken, 1/2 teaspoon salt, 1/4 teaspoon pepper, and dry oregano. Use wooden spoon to mix it and break it up. Cook stirring occasionally until chicken is white on the outside, 2-3 minutes.

3. To the chicken add the garlic, half of the parsley, the stock, and tomato sauce. Stir. Increase heat to high and cover. Stir occasionally until it reaches a simmer. Turn heat to low.

4. Meanwhile, put the basil in a medium bowl with the ricotta, remaining parsley, Parmesan, garlic powder, 1/4 teaspoon of salt, 1/4 teaspoon of pepper. Stir. Taste. Add more salt and pepper if desired.

5. Divide the pasta among soup bowls. Top with the soup. Then to each bowl add a scoop of the ricotta mixture and a good sprinkle of shredded mozzarella. Garnish with additional basil leaves, if desired.

# Fettucine Alfredo Soup

*This soup uses a really simple thickening method. You begin sautéing an ingredient, in this case it's chicken. Then you sprinkle it with flour and stir. As you stir, the flour gets evenly distributed over the chicken. Then you slowly add in the liquid. Because the flour was evenly and smoothly distributed, it mixes with the liquid to form a lump-free sauce or soup-base. Anytime you want to thicken a soup or sauce, you can sauté some vegetables or meat, add flour, stir, and then slowly add liquid.*

# Fettucine Alfredo Soup

*Continued from previous page*

**Yield:** 6 servings

**Total Time:** 15 minutes

**Ingredients:**
4 cups low-sodium chicken stock
4 Tbsp. unsalted butter
2 boneless skinless chicken breasts, cut into 1/4-inch slices
4 Tbsp. all-purpose flour
2 cloves garlic, minced
1/2 tsp. salt
1/4 tsp. pepper
1 (9 oz.) package of fresh fettuccine noodles
5 oz. shredded Parmesan cheese, divided
1 cup shredded mozzarella cheese

1. Measure stock into a large microwave-safe bowl. Microwave on high for 5 minutes.

2. Meanwhile, put the butter in a large pot over medium heat to melt. Add the chicken to the melted butter. Cook stirring occasionally until it is white on the outside.

3. Add the garlic and the flour to the chicken and stir.

4. When the stock is done heating, add 1/4 cup slowly to the chicken mixture. Stir. Add another 1/4 cup and stir. Repeat until you've added about half of it. Then stir in the rest of the stock at once. Stir in the salt and pepper.

5. Increase heat to high and bring the soup up to a boil. Add the fettuccine noodles and reduce heat to a simmer. Cook noodles until cooked through (read package directions. It's usually 2-3 minutes), stirring occasionally.

6. Remove pot from heat. Stir in three-quarters of the Parmesan cheese and all of the mozzarella.

7. Ladle soup into bowls and garnish with remaining Parmesan cheese.

# Italian Wedding Soup

*This soup contains my favorite meatball hack – 1 ingredient meatballs! What you do is get some fresh Italian sausage links (in this case chicken ones, because this is a chicken book, you know?). Then you squeeze the raw seasoned meat out of the casings, pinching a meatball-sized amount out at a time, and roll it into balls. Meatballs formed! You can panfry them, oven-bake them, or, you can put them in soup, like I did here.*

**Yield:** 4 servings

**Total Time:** 15 minutes

**Ingredients:**
4 cups low-sodium chicken stock
1 cup water
1/2 tsp. salt
1 Tbsp. olive oil
1 small onion, chopped
1 lb. fresh mild chicken Italian sausage links (about 5 links)
3/4 cup dry orzo or other small, quick-cooking pasta
2 cups fresh spinach
2 oz. shredded Parmesan cheese

1. Measure the stock and water into a large microwave-safe bowl. Add the salt. Microwave on high for 5 minutes.

2. While the stock is heating put a large pot over medium heat. Add the olive oil. Then add the onion. Stir.

3. Use your fingers to squeeze and form 3/4-inch balls of chicken sausage meat out from the casings. Let them fall directly into the pan of onions. Stir gently now and then as you make all the sausage balls. Discard casings. Stir gently and cover pot.

4. When the stock has finished heating, add it to the large pot with the sausage. Stir. Cover and increase heat to high.

5. When the stock reaches a simmer add the orzo. Let it come to a boil. Reduce heat to a heavy simmer. Stir occasionally until the pasta is al dente, about 6 minutes.

6. When the noodles are cooked (the sausage will be cooked by now as well), taste and add extra salt if desired.

7. Put a handful of spinach into each of 4 soup bowls. Ladle hot soup on top of spinach. Garnish with the Parmesan.

# Greek Lemon Soup

*This traditional soup, called Avgolemono, uses eggs as a thickening ingredient, in the same way that a hollandaise sauce is thickened with egg. When trying to thicken a soup or sauce with egg, it's important to heat the eggs slowly so that they don't turn into cooked scrambled eggs. Here, we dilute the eggs with some lemon juice and then slowly add hot water to them to start the heating. Then the egg and hot water mixture gets added to the soup to thicken it.*

**Yield:** 4 servings

**Total Time:** 15 minutes

**Ingredients:**
5 cups low-sodium chicken stock
2 Tbsp. cornstarch
1/3 cup cold water
2 lemons
2 large eggs
1/2 of a cooked rotisserie chicken (about 2 cups of shredded meat)
1/2 tsp. salt
3/4 cup acini di pepe pasta (tiny tiny tubes)

1. Pour the chicken stock into a large pot over high heat. Cover and let it come to a boil.

2. Meanwhile, in a small bowl dissolve the cornstarch in the cold water. Juice the lemons until you have 1/3 cup juice. Add it to the cornstarch mixture.

3. Crack the eggs into a medium bowl. Use an egg beater on medium to whip eggs until frothy, 1-2 minutes. Stir the cornstarch-lemon mixture into the eggs.

4. Once the stock is simmering, add the salt to the stock. Stir. Remove 1 cup of hot stock and set aside.

5. Add the pasta to the simmering stock in the pot. Bring it back to a boil over high. Stir. Reduce to a simmer. Stir occasionally until al dente, 5-6 minutes.

6. While stirring the eggs constantly, slowly drizzle the hot cup of stock that you set aside into the egg mixture.

7. When pasta is al dente, do not drain it. Instead, add the chicken. Stir. Heat through 30 seconds.

8. Turn off heat. While stirring continuously, drizzle in the egg mixture.

9. Put heat on low and stir constantly for a minute.

10. Serve. If the soup sits for a while before serving, it will thicken more. Add hot water to thin it. Do not ever let the soup come to a boil after you've added the eggs or the eggs could set and scramble, giving the soup a curdled appearance.

# Mulligatawny Soup

*This chicken soup is sweet, sour, and rich all at once. All that delicious flavor comes from curry powder, butter, sour apple, and cream.*

**Yield:** 4 servings

**Total Time:** 15 minutes

**Ingredients:**

4 cups low-sodium chicken stock
2 Tbsp. unsalted butter
2 medium onions, chopped
4 cloves garlic, minced
2 Tbsp. all-purpose flour
1 Tbsp. curry powder
1/2 tsp. salt
2 chicken breasts, cut into 1/2" cubes
1 large granny smith apple, chopped
1 (8.8 oz.) package cooked rice (about 2 cups cooked rice)
1 tsp. sugar
1/2 cup half and half
1/4 cup fresh cilantro leaves for garnish

1. Measure the stock into a large microwave-safe bowl. Microwave it on high for 5 minutes.

2. Meanwhile, melt the butter over medium-low heat in a large pot. Add the onions and cook, stirring occasionally until softened, 2-3 minutes.

3. To the onions add the garlic, flour, curry powder, and salt. Stir.

4. When the stock is done heating, stir the onions continuously while slowly drizzling in half of the stock. Then pour in the rest of the stock.

5. Increase the heat to high, cover the pot, and bring the soup up to a boil. Reduce heat to a simmer.

6. Once the soup is simmering, add the chicken to the pot and cook for 2 minutes. Add the apple, rice, and sugar. Cook for 1 minute.

7. Once chicken is cooked through (cut a piece in half and make sure it is no longer pink inside), remove soup from heat and add the half and half. Serve the soup garnished with cilantro leaves.

# CHAPTER 3
# AIR FRYER CHICKEN

Air Fryer Whole Chicken
Air Fryer Chicken Breasts
Air Fryer Chicken Thighs
Crispiest Air Fryer Chicken Breasts
Air Fryer Stuffed Chicken Breasts
Air Fryer Chicken Drumsticks
Air Fryer Chicken Leg Quarters
Air Fryer Buffalo Wings
Air Fryer Honey Garlic Chicken Wings
Air Fryer Fried Chicken
Air Fryer Chicken Tenders
Air Fryer Chicken Parm
Air Fryer BBQ Chicken
Air Fryer Lemon Chicken
Air Fryer Chicken Cordon Bleu
Air Fryer Chicken Dinner with Potatoes and Green Beans
Air Fryer Chicken Fajita Dinner
Air Fryer Chicken Fajita Kebabs
Air Fryer Chinese Chicken
Air Fryer Cheesy Chicken Quesadillas
Air Fryer Chicken Egg Rolls
Air Fryer Chicken Burgers
Air Fryer Chicken Sandwich

# Air Fryer Whole Chicken

A whole chicken cooked in the air fryer ends up super-juicy with crisp skin. I start the chicken cooking breast-side-down so that the juices from the back and dark meat trickle down to the breast. Then the chicken is flipped over to finish cooking and crisp up at the end. Note that not all whole chickens will fit in all air fryers. If you have a 5-quart air fryer, you can fit a 4 pound chicken. If you have a 4-quart, you can fit a 3 pound chicken . If your air fryer is smaller than 4 quarts, you probably can't do a whole chicken. But don't worry since we have recipes for chicken pieces in this book coming right up, and those will definitely fit.

**Yield:** 3 servings

**Prep Time:** 5 minutes

**Cook Time:** 42 minutes

**Total Time:** 47 minutes

**Ingredients:**
3 to 4 lb. whole chicken
2 Tbsp. olive oil
1/2 tsp. salt
1/4 tsp. pepper
1/4 tsp. garlic powder

1. Preheat air fryer to 360°F.
2. Take chicken out of the refrigerator. Remove giblets and discard or save for other use.
3. In small bowl combine olive oil, salt, pepper, and garlic powder. Rub all over chicken, inside and out.
4. Put chicken in air fryer basket breast-side-down. Cook 30 minutes.
5. Flip chicken. Cook another 12-22 minutes, until internal temperature on an instant read thermometer reads 165°F in the chicken thigh, being careful not to touch bone.

# Air Fryer Chicken Breasts

*Chicken breasts cook really quickly in the air fryer and turn out golden brown on the outside and tender on the inside. This is a great way to do some quick food prep for the week ahead. If you want to add a sauce (like BBQ or honey mustard) brush it onto the tops of the chicken breasts right after you flip them over.*

**Yield:** 3 servings

**Prep Time:** 5 minutes

**Cook Time:** 15 minutes

**Total Time:** 20 minutes

**Ingredients:**
3 (8 oz.) boneless skinless chicken breasts*
1 Tbsp. olive oil
1/4 tsp. salt
1/4 tsp. pepper
1/4 tsp. garlic powder

1. Remove chicken breasts from refrigerator.
2. Preheat air fryer to 400°F.
3. Coat chicken on all sides with olive oil.
4. Sprinkle on all sides with salt, pepper, and garlic powder.
5. Put chicken in air fryer basket, rounder-side-down. Cook 10 minutes.
6. Flip chicken and cook until 165°F on an instant read thermometer, 5-8 more minutes.
7. Remove from basket and let rest at least 2 minutes before serving.

*\*If using chicken breasts that are on the bone (with or without skin) oil and season them as instructed. Then put the chicken breasts into the air fryer skin-side down (or rounded-side-down) and cook for 15 minutes. Flip them over and cook until they reach 165°F on an instant read thermometer, about 12-15 minutes more.*

# Air Fryer Chicken Thighs

*Chicken thighs are dark meat and as such they're juicier and more flavorful than chicken breasts. They're typically sold with the skin and bone on or with the skin and bone removed. Whichever way you get them, they'll be browned and crisp on the outside and juicy in the middle when you cook them in the air fryer.*

**Yield:** 3 servings

**Prep Time:** 5 minutes

**Cook Time:** 15 minutes

**Total Time:** 20 minutes

**Ingredients:**
1 and 3/4 lbs. (about 6) boneless skinless chicken thighs*
1 Tbsp. olive oil
1/4 tsp. salt
1/4 tsp. pepper
1/4 tsp. garlic powder

1. Remove chicken thighs from refrigerator.
2. Preheat air fryer to 400°F.
3. Coat chicken on all sides with olive oil.
4. Sprinkle on all sides with salt, pepper, and garlic powder.
5. Put chicken in air fryer basket, rounder-side-down. Cook 10 minutes.
6. Flip chicken and cook until 165°F on an instant read thermometer, 5-7 more minutes.
7. Remove from basket and let rest at least 2 minutes before serving.

*For bone-in thighs (with or without skin) follow the instructions above exactly except after you first put the thighs into the air fryer, cook them for 15 minutes. Then flip and cook until the interior is 165°F as read on an instant read thermometer, which will take another 10-15 minutes.

# Crispiest Air Fryer Chicken Breasts

*By Allie Doran*

*This chicken gets extra crispy without using any oil because the panko breadcrumbs are crunchy to start with, and because we put the chicken on a rack so that hot air circulates around it and is able to better crisp things up. If you don't have a rack, you can put the chicken right in the tray. It just won't get quite as crisp, especially on the bottom.*

**Yield:** 4 servings

**Prep Time:** 10 minutes

**Cook Time:** 22 minutes

**Total Time:** 32 minutes

**Ingredients:**
1 lb. boneless skinless chicken breast
1 cup all-purpose flour
1 tsp. salt, divided
1 tsp. pepper, divided
1 egg
1 cup panko breadcrumbs
Cooking spray

1. Remove the chicken breasts from the packaging and pound them into an even thickness. If your air fryer has a metal rack, set it in the tray. Cooking the chicken on the rack promotes crispy chicken.

2. Whisk together flour, 1/2 teaspoon of the salt, and 1/2 teaspoon of the pepper. Pour it out onto a plate.

3. Crack the egg into a bowl and beat it lightly.

4. Mix the panko breadcrumbs together with the remaining salt and pepper. Pour that out onto an additional plate.

5. Dip the chicken breasts into the flour mixture, then the egg, and then the panko mixture until all of the pieces are coated. Spray the pieces with cooking spray on both sides.

6. Lay the chicken on the rack in your air fryer if you're using one.

7. Slide the tray into the air fryer, and turn the dial to 350°F. Set the timer for 22 minutes.

8. The chicken should have an internal temperature of 165°F before serving and it will be golden brown and delicious.

Photo: Ilona Orzechowska

# Air Fryer Stuffed Chicken Breasts

*By Ilona Orzechowska*

*This recipe can be doubled or quadrupled, so long as you have room in your air fryer. When checking the internal temperature of the chicken, make sure that your thermometer is inserted only into the chicken and not in the stuffing.*

# Air Fryer Stuffed Chicken Breasts
*Continued from previous page*

**Yield:** 1 serving

**Prep Time:** 10 minutes

**Cook Time:** 25 minutes

**Total Time:** 35 minutes

**Ingredients:**
1 boneless skinless chicken breast
1/4 tsp. salt
1/4 tsp. garlic powder
1/4 tsp. dry basil
2 slices cheddar cheese
1 strip cooked bacon, or use a slice of ham
2 slices tomato
2 toothpicks (optional)
Cooking spray

1. Preheat air fryer to 350°F.

2. Cut chicken breast horizontally with a sharp knife to make a pocket, making sure not to cut through the whole way.

3. In a small bowl combine salt, garlic powder, and dry basil. Season chicken on both sides evenly.

4. Inside of the pocket you created, layer 1 slice of cheddar cheese, bacon, tomato slices, then another slice of cheese.

5. Use toothpicks to secure the pocket closed (optional).

6. Spray the chicken breast with cooking spray.

7. Place the chicken breast in the air fryer basket and cook for 20 minutes. Check to see if the meat is cooked through using an instant read thermometer. It should read 165°F. Cook for another 3 – 5 minutes more if needed.

# Air Fryer Chicken Drumsticks

*You can use either skin-on or skin-off drumsticks for this recipe. The cooking times and preparations remain the same. But know that if you have the skin on, you're in for a treat since it gets so crispy and delicious in the air fryer.*

*Note: If you have skin-on drumsticks but want to remove the skin, it's possible to do so. You can do it while they're raw. I like to use a pair of kitchen scissors to cut the skin apart at the joint end of the bone, which makes it easier to pull off the meat. Even easier though is to cook the drumsticks with the skin on and then remove it when it has crisped up. This works for all kinds of skin-on chicken pieces. The only problem is that the crispy skin is very hard to resist eating as you pull it off the meat. Mmmm.*

**Yield:** 3 servings

**Prep Time:** 5 minutes

**Cook Time:** 20 minutes

**Total Time:** 25 minutes

**Ingredients:**
2 lbs. (about 5–6) chicken drumsticks with skin*
1 Tbsp. olive oil
1/4 tsp. salt
1/4 tsp. pepper
1/4 tsp. garlic powder

1. Remove chicken drumsticks from refrigerator.
2. Preheat air fryer to 400°F.
3. Coat chicken on all sides with olive oil.
4. Sprinkle on all sides with salt, pepper, and garlic powder.
5. Put chicken in air fryer basket. Cook 10 minutes.
6. Flip chicken and cook until 165°F on an instant read thermometer, 10–12 more minutes.
7. Remove from basket and let rest at least 2 minutes before serving.

*For skinless chicken drumsticks, use the exact same method. Nothing needs to be changed.

# Air Fryer Chicken Leg Quarters

*Chicken leg quarters are often on sale in bulk for a very cheap price at my grocery store. I bring them home, pop them into the air fryer, and then I have luscious chicken meat to use in all kinds of ways. I like the leg quarter meat in sandwiches, on salads, in soups, in pasta dishes – really you can use it anywhere you'd use rotisserie chicken meat. Oh, or you can just eat the leg quarter as is, fresh out of the air fryer with all its juicy dark chicken meat and crispy, salted skin. So good!*

**Yield:** 2 servings

**Prep Time:** 5 minutes

**Cook Time:** 30 minutes

**Total Time:** 35 minutes

**Ingredients:**
2 chicken leg quarters with skin* (one pound each)
1 Tbsp. olive oil
1/4 tsp. salt
1/4 tsp. pepper
1/4 tsp. garlic powder

*\*For skinless chicken leg quarters, use the exact same method. Nothing needs to be changed except put them in rounded-side-down (that's the side that would have had the skin on it if it had skin).*

1. Remove chicken leg quarters from refrigerator.
2. Preheat air fryer to 400°F.
3. Coat chicken on all sides with olive oil.
4. Sprinkle on all sides with salt, pepper, and garlic powder.
5. Put chicken in air fryer basket, skin-side-down. Cook 20 minutes.
6. Flip chicken and cook until 165°F on an instant read thermometer, 10-12 more minutes.
7. Remove from basket and let rest at least 2 minutes before serving.

# Air Fryer Buffalo Wings

*The air fryer is the perfect way to make a small batch of crispy wings. If you want to make a bigger batch (like for Game Day!) check out the Wings chapter later in this book. There's a wonderful recipe there for oven-baked crispy wings that are great to make for a crowd.*

**Yield:** 2 servings

**Prep Time:** 5 minutes

**Cook Time:** 30 minutes

**Total Time:** 35 minutes

**Ingredients:**
5 whole chicken wings, cut into 10 wing pieces
1 Tbsp. olive oil
1/4 tsp. salt
1/4 tsp. pepper
1/4 tsp. garlic powder
1/3 cup Buffalo sauce, homemade or store-bought

1. Remove chicken wings from refrigerator.
2. Preheat air fryer to 360°F.
3. Coat chicken on all sides with olive oil.
4. Sprinkle on all sides with salt, pepper, and garlic powder.
5. Put chicken in air fryer basket, uglier-side-up. Cook 12 minutes.
6. Flip chicken wings and cook for another 12 minutes.
7. Increase temperature to 400°F and cook until crisp and internal temperature on an instant read thermometer is 165°F, 5-6 more minutes.
8. Put the Buffalo sauce into a medium bowl.
9. Remove chicken from basket and put in the bowl with the sauce. Toss to coat.

# Air Fryer Honey Garlic Chicken Wings

*By Emily Dingmann*

*We've discovered a delicious secret to crispy wings: Potato starch! Potato starch is traditionally used in Korean Fried Chicken and it gives an incredibly crunchy crust to the wings. There are two main reasons that the starch results in crispy foods. The simplest reason (and all we really need to know here) is that starch absorbs water, then when it's cooked, the starch molecules are "locked into place", which results in a rigid structure, aka the crunchy coating.*

**Yield:** 8-10 pieces

**Prep Time:** 5 minutes

**Cook Time:** 20 minutes

**Total Time:** 25 minutes

**Ingredients:**
1 and 1/2 lbs. chicken wings
2 Tbsp. soy sauce
1/4 cup potato starch
3 cloves garlic
1 Tbsp. unsalted butter
3 Tbsp. honey
1 tsp. red pepper flakes (less if you don't want it spicy)
Salt

1. Toss wings with soy sauce and set aside.

2. Preheat air fryer for a few minutes. Put the potato starch in a large ziptop plastic bag and add wings to bag. Shake until wings are evenly coated with potato starch. Grease air fryer basket with a bit of oil and arrange wings in basket, shaking off any excess potato starch and being careful not to crowd the basket. Cook in batches if necessary.

3. Cook at 360°F for 12 minutes. Flip over and cook for another 12 minutes. Turn temperature up to 400°F and cook another 5-6 minutes to crisp.

4. Meanwhile combine garlic and butter in a small microwave-safe bowl. Microwave for 30 seconds to melt. Stir in honey and season with the red pepper flakes and a pinch of salt. Toss wings in sauce.

# Air Fryer Fried Chicken

*By Emily Dingmann*

*Marinading chicken in buttermilk is not only done because it's tradition. It adds tons of flavor and also tenderizes the chicken.*

**Yield:** 4 servings

**Prep Time:** 4 hours, 5 minutes

**Cook Time:** 20 minutes

**Total Time:** 4 hours, 25 minutes

**Ingredients:**
1 and 1/2 lbs. bone-in chicken thighs or drumsticks
1 cup buttermilk
3/4 cup all-purpose flour
4 Tbsp. corn starch
1 tsp. paprika
1/4 tsp. cayenne pepper
1 tsp. salt + some for sprinkling
Cooking spray

1. Combine chicken and buttermilk together in a bowl. Refrigerate for at least four hours, or up to 24 hours.

2. Take chicken out at least a half hour before cooking.

3. Whisk together flour, corn starch, cayenne pepper, and 1 teaspoon of the salt in another large bowl.

4. Line air fryer with foil and then preheat to 380°F.

5. Dredge chicken through flour mixture. Repeat with all pieces of chicken.

6. Spray chicken pieces with cooking spray. Arrange in a single layer in air fryer.

7. Cook chicken for 15 minutes and then increase heat to 400°F and cook an additional 5-7 minutes, or until chicken reaches an internal temperature of 165°F (larger pieces will take longer).

8. Remove chicken and let rest for 2 minutes on a wire drying rack. Sprinkle with salt before serving.

# Air Fryer Chicken Tenders

*By Jamie Silva*

*Chicken tenders in the air fryer are done in just 10 minutes and they're deliciously crispy, moist, and ready for dipping.*

**Yield:** 4

**Prep Time:** 10 minutes

**Cook Time:** 20 minutes

**Total Time:** 30 minutes

**Ingredients:**
1/4 cup panko bread crumbs
1/2 tsp. salt
1/2 tsp. paprika
1/4 tsp. pepper
1/4 tsp. garlic powder
1/4 tsp. onion powder
1 lb. chicken tenderloins
1 egg

1. Heat air fryer to 400°F. Lightly oil the basket.

2. In a bowl, stir together panko, salt, paprika, pepper, garlic powder, and onion powder. In another bowl, whisk egg.

3. Dredge the chicken first in egg then in the bread crumb mixture, making sure each tender is well coated. Place them in the air fryer. Do not overcrowd, only cook 3-4 at a time.

4. Cook for 10 minutes, flipping once at 5 minutes. Repeat with remaining chicken tenders until they have all been cooked through. Serve with your favorite sauce.

Photo: Traci Devito

# Air Fryer Chicken Parmesan

*By Traci Devito*

Chicken Parmesan is the perfect thing to cook in the air fryer. You cook and brown the chicken cutlets in the air fryer. Then you top them with marinara sauce and cheese and put them back in until the cheese is melted and the chicken is heated through. It's as convenient as it is delicious!

# Air Fryer Chicken Parmesan

*Continued from previous page*

**Yield:** 4 servings

**Prep Time:** 10 minutes

**Cook Time:** 12 minutes

**Total Time:** 22 minutes

**Ingredients:**
4 (6 oz.) boneless skinless chicken breasts
1 and 1/4 cups plain breadcrumbs
1/4 cup grated Parmesan cheese
2 Tbsp. vegetable oil
1 tsp. dried thyme
1/2 tsp. salt
1/4 tsp. pepper
2 egg whites
2 tsp. Dijon mustard
Cooking spray
1/4 cup marinara sauce
4 oz. mozzarella cheese, shredded

1. Preheat air fryer to 360°F.
2. Pound chicken breasts to 1/4-inch thickness.
3. In small shallow bowl, combine the breadcrumbs, Parmesan cheese, vegetable oil, thyme, salt, and pepper.
4. In another shallow bowl, combine the egg whites and Dijon mustard.
5. Dredge chicken in egg mixture and then the breadcrumb mixture.
6. Place breaded chicken pieces in the air fryer and spray the tops with cooking spray. Cook for 6 to 8 minutes, then turn. Top each with 1 tablespoon sauce and 1 ounce mozzarella cheese and cook for 3 to 4 minutes longer, or until internal temperature of the chicken reaches 165°F. If using a smaller air fryer, you will need to cook in batches. Keep first batch warm in an oven set to 250°F.

# Air Fryer BBQ Chicken

*By Traci Devito*

*Making BBQ chicken in the air fryer is a great alternative to the grill. What we're doing here is cooking the chicken in seasonings until it's nearly cooked through. Then we add sauce and put it back in to finish cooking and to let the sauce begin to caramelize.*

**Yield:** 4 servings

**Prep Time:** 4 minutes

**Cook Time:** 21 minutes

**Total Time:** 25 minutes

**Ingredients:**
- 3 and 1/2 lbs. bone-in chicken pieces with skin
- 1 Tbsp. smoked paprika
- 1 tsp. onion powder
- 1 tsp. salt
- 1/2 tsp. pepper
- 1/8 tsp. cayenne pepper
- 1 cup barbeque sauce (homemade or store-bought)

1. Remove the chicken from the refrigerator.
2. Preheat air fryer to 375°F.
3. In a small bowl, combine the smoked paprika, onion powder, salt, pepper and cayenne. Rub the spice mixture all over the chicken to coat.
4. Place chicken in the air fryer skin-side-down. Cook for 18 minutes, until chicken is golden brown.
5. Transfer chicken to a plate and brush with barbeque sauce.
6. Wipe off excess chicken fat from air fryer basket.
7. Return chicken to the air fryer and cook, skin-side-up, until chicken reaches an internal temperature of 165°F on an instant read thermometer, about 3 minutes. Larger pieces may require longer cooking time.

# Air Fryer Lemon Chicken

*To get a lemony flavor onto chicken, I used to marinate it, and I still do sometimes. But if I want the lemon flavor quicker, I cook the chicken with slices of lemon under it and over it. As the chicken and lemon cook, the juices from the lemon flavor the chicken. It ends up being like lemon-marinated chicken but without the time it takes to actually let the chicken marinate.*

**Yield:** 2 servings

**Prep Time:** 5 minutes

**Cook Time:** 15 minutes

**Total Time:** 20 minutes

**Ingredients:**
2 boneless skinless chicken breasts
1/2 tsp. garlic powder
1/2 tsp. dry rosemary
1/4 tsp. salt
1/8 tsp. pepper
Cooking spray
1 whole lemon
1/4 tsp. sugar

1. Set the air fryer temperature to 350°F.
2. In a small bowl combine the garlic powder, rosemary, salt, and pepper. Sprinkle over chicken.
3. Spritz chicken on all sides with cooking spray.
4. Slice lemon into 8 slices. Arrange 4 slices in the air fryer basket. Put each chicken breast over two slices of lemon. Top chicken with another two slices of lemon each. Sprinkle tops with sugar.
5. Cook until chicken reaches 165°F, using an instant read thermometer to check the temperature, about 15-20 minutes.

Photo: Lauren Keating

# Air Fryer Chicken Cordon Bleu

*By Lauren Keating*

*Pounding the chicken breasts makes them thinner, which helps for rolling and tucking the meat around the filling. These are great served by themselves but are also delicious with a light gravy-type sauce. Try making the "Gravy without Drippings" recipe from the Basics chapter but stir in some sour cream right before serving.*

# Air Fryer Chicken Cordon Bleu

*Continued from previous page*

**Yield:** 2 servings

**Prep Time:** 5 minutes

**Cook Time:** 30 minutes

**Total Time:** 35 minutes

**Ingredients:**
4 boneless skinless chicken breasts
4 slices ham
4 slices Swiss cheese
1/4 cup all-purpose flour
1 egg, beaten
1/4 cup seasoned bread crumbs
Cooking spray

1. Preheat oven to 400°F.
2. Using a meat mallet, pound the chicken breasts until they're 1/4-inch thick.
3. Season the chicken with salt and pepper, then layer each breast with one slice of ham and one slice of cheese.
4. Starting on the long side, tightly roll the chicken around the filling and secure with a toothpick.
5. Put the flour on a large plate. Put the egg into a medium bowl. Put the breadcrumbs on a large plate.
6. Lightly coat the chicken with flour, then dip it into the egg.
7. Roll the chicken in breadcrumbs to coat thoroughly. Spray the chicken with cooking spray and place seam-side-down in the basket of your air fryer.
8. Cook for 12 minutes, or until 165°F on an instant read thermometer.
9. Let rest 5 minutes and then remove toothpicks before serving.

# Air Fryer Chicken Dinner with Potatoes and Green Beans

*By Allie Doran*

*For this recipe, the whole meal is cooked in the air fryer, making it a quick and convenient dinner with very little clean up.*

**Yield:** 4 servings

**Prep Time:** 10 minutes

**Cook Time:** 25 minutes

**Total Time:** 35 minutes

**Ingredients:**
2 cups diced, Yukon gold potatoes
1 tsp. olive oil
1 and 1/2 tsp. salt, divided
1 tsp. pepper, divided
1 lb. boneless skinless chicken breasts
1/2 lb. green beans

1. Toss the potatoes with the olive oil, 1 teaspoon of the salt, and 1 teaspoon of the pepper.

2. Place the potatoes in the bottom of the air fryer tray and arrange a metal rack on top of them.

3. Sprinkle both sides of the chicken with the remaining salt and pepper and place them on top of the metal rack over the potatoes.

4. Bake in the air fryer at 380°F for 15 minutes.

5. After the 15 minutes is up, slide the tray out and stir the potatoes. Arrange the green beans over top of the chicken.

6. Slide the tray back into the air fryer and cook for an additional 5-7 minutes, or until the green beans are just tender and the chicken is cooked through to 165°F. Remove the green beans and chicken from the air fryer.

7. If desired, place the potatoes back in for 3-5 minutes if you like a crispier potato.

# Air Fryer Chicken Fajita Dinner

*By Allie Doran*

*The beauty of these fajitas is that everything is cooked in the air fryer so you aren't standing over the stove stirring and fussing. You just put the chicken, peppers, onions, and seasonings into the air fryer until they're cooked through. Then you can put that mixture in tacos or onto a salad, or onto a rice bowl. Top with your favorite fajita fixings for a simple but delicious meal.*

**Yield:** 4 servings

**Prep Time:** 10 minutes

**Cook Time:** 18 minutes

**Total Time:** 28 minutes

**Ingredients:**
1 lb. boneless skinless chicken breast, sliced
2 bell peppers, sliced
1 onion, sliced
2 tsp. olive oil
2 tsp. chili powder
1 tsp. salt
1 tsp. cumin
1/2 tsp. pepper
a pinch cayenne

1. Combine the sliced chicken and vegetables in a bowl.
2. Add the olive oil, chili powder, salt, cumin, pepper, and cayenne.
3. Toss to combine and pour the contents out into the tray of an air fryer.
4. Slide the tray into the air fryer and cook at 360°F for 16–20 minutes, checking and stirring halfway through.

Photo: Emily Dingmann

# Air Fryer Chicken Fajita Kebabs

*By Emily Dingmann*

Here's another way to make fajitas in the air fryer, this time as kebabs. These are great as appetizers or as the filling for tacos.

# Air Fryer Chicken Fajita Kebabs

*Continued from previous page*

**Yield:** 4 servings

**Prep Time:** 10 minutes

**Cook Time:** 8 minutes

**Total Time:** 18 minutes

**Ingredients:**

*Kebabs*
- 15–20 small wooden skewers
- 2 Tbsp. lime juice
- 1 Tbsp. olive oil
- 1 tsp. dried oregano
- 1/2 tsp. garlic powder
- 1/2 tsp. salt
- 1/8 tsp. pepper
- 1 lb. boneless skinless chicken thighs, cut into 2-inch pieces
- 1 medium onion, cut into wedges
- 1 red pepper, cut into wedges
- 1 green pepper, cut into wedges
- Cooking spray

1. Soak wooden skewers in water for about 20 minutes.

2. In a medium bowl, mix together lime juice, olive oil, oregano, garlic powder, salt, and pepper. Add chicken and toss to coat. Set aside.

3. Grease air fryer basket with oil and preheat air fryer to 400°F for a few minutes to get it hot.

4. Thread chicken, peppers and onion onto skewers. Start with chicken then add onion and peppers. Repeat with remaining ingredients and skewers.

5. Spray finished skewers with cooking spray or brush with some cooking oil.

6. Working in batches so you don't crowd the air fryer, cook skewers at 400°F for 8 minutes, or until cooked through.

7. Repeat with remaining skewers.

# Air Fryer Chinese Chicken

*By Ilona Orzechowska*

*You'll need to cook the chicken in more than one batch for this recipe. After a batch is done cooking. Set it aside while cooking the subsequent batches. Then add all the chicken to the simmering sauce and let it heat through before serving.*

**Yield:** 4 servings

**Prep Time:** 25 minutes

**Cook Time:** 15 minutes

**Total Time:** 40 minutes

**Ingredients:**

*Chicken*
1 egg
1/2 cup cornstarch
1 tsp. salt
8 boneless chicken thighs, cut into 1/2-inch pieces
Cooking spray

*Sauce*
1/2 cup water
3 Tbsp. less-sodium soy sauce
2 and 1/2 Tbsp. hoisin sauce
2 Tbsp. rice vinegar
1/2 tsp. sesame oil
4 Tbsp. brown sugar
1 and 1/2 Tbsp. cornstarch
1 Tbsp. canola oil
1/4 tsp. minced fresh ginger
1 garlic clove minced
1 Tbsp. green onions

1. In a small bowl whisk the egg.
2. In another bowl mix cornstarch with salt.
3. Dip each piece of chicken into egg and then cornstarch.
4. Lightly oil the air fryer basket.
5. Add chicken chunks, leaving some space between the pieces. You will need to cook the chicken in several batches. Depending on the size of your air fryer it will take about 2 – 3 batches.
6. Spray chicken with cooking spray or brush with oil.
7. Set the air fryer to cook at 400°F for 15 minutes. After 5 minutes of cooking, shake the basket. Cook for the remaining 10 minutes. If the chicken has not reached 165°F on an instant read thermometer after 15 minutes, add 2 – 3 minutes more.
8. Meanwhile, make the sauce by combining water, soy sauce, hoisin sauce, rice vinegar, sesame oil, brown sugar, and cornstarch in a medium bowl. Set aside.
9. Heat the canola oil in a large frying pan.
10. Add ginger and garlic. Cook on low heat for about 30 seconds, being careful not to burn it.
11. Add the sauce mixture. Cook on medium-low heat for about 5 – 8 minutes until the sauce thickens, whisking often.
12. Add cooked chicken to the sauce, toss it and cook for about 1 – 2 minutes until the chicken is heated through and nicely coated with the sauce.

Photo: Ilona Orzechowska

# Air Fryer Cheesy Chicken Quesadillas

*By Ilona Orzechowska*

Quesadillas are fine to make on the stove top but making them in the air fryer means that you don't have to stand over them while they cook. You can walk away and they'll be ready when your timer beeps.

**Yield:** 1 serving

**Prep Time:** 10 minutes

**Cook Time:** 10 minutes

**Total Time:** 20 minutes

**Ingredients:**
1/3 cup cooked chicken
1/8 tsp. chili powder
1/8 tsp. cumin
2 (6-inch) tortillas
1/3 cup shredded cheddar cheese
1/2 cup shredded mozzarella cheese
1 Tbsp. chopped green onions
5 fresh spinach leaves
Cooking oil spray
2 Tbsp. sour cream

1. In a small bowl combine chicken with chili powder and cumin.
2. Spray the bottom of one tortilla and place in the air fryer.
3. Add cheddar cheese, chicken, chopped green onions, spinach leaves, and mozzarella cheese.
4. Top with another tortilla. Press down firmly. Spray with cooking oil.
5. Set temperature to 370°F and cook for 2 minutes. Open air fryer and make sure the top tortilla hasn't moved off of the toppings. Set it back in place and then press down again.
6. Cook until gold brown on the outside and cheese and chicken are heated through, about 7-9 more minutes.
7. Cut into wedges and serve with sour cream.

# Air Fryer Chicken Egg Rolls

*By Emily Dingmann*

Here are our three best egg roll tips:

1) Don't overfill them. You don't want them so big that you can't roll them tightly. (You've seen a massive burrito at Chipotle, right? It never ends well.) When you roll them, roll them as tightly as you can so they're compact. We found that with a standard size wrapper, about 1/3 cup of filling is a good amount.

2) Seal the edges with water so they stay shut. This is as simple as dipping your fingers in a dish of water and making sure all the seams are sealed.

3) Rub the outsides of the egg rolls with some vegetable oil before cooking. This last step ensures the crispy, golden brown crunch you know and love. You can also spray them with cooking spray (liberally!) but we prefer using oil.

**Yield:** 16 servings

**Prep Time:** 10 minutes

**Cook Time:** 16 minutes

**Total Time:** 26 minutes

**Ingredients:**
1 tsp. vegetable oil
1 Tbsp. minced ginger
3 green onions, chopped
1 lb. ground chicken
1/4 tsp. salt
3 cups coleslaw mix
1 Tbsp. oyster sauce
1 package egg roll wrappers

1. Heat large skillet over medium-high heat. Add oil to pan and when it shimmers, add ginger and onions. Cook for one minute.

2. Add chicken and season with salt. Break up with a spoon and cook until browned, about 4-5 minutes.

3. Add coleslaw mix and season with a sprinkle of salt. Cook until cabbage is soft, about 3-4 minutes. Stir in oyster sauce and remove from heat.

4. Put a little dish of water on the counter and lay 2-3 egg roll wrappers out on counter or cutting board diagonally so a point is facing you. Place about 1/3 cup egg roll mixture in the bottom of the wrapper and roll up, folding sides in to create an envelope. Dip fingers in water and wet the top corner and seal egg roll.

5. Set air fryer to 390°F and preheat for a few minutes. Rub the egg rolls with a bit of vegetable oil (or spray with cooking spray) and cook for 4 minutes. Flip and cook until browned all over, about another 4-5 minutes.

# Air Fryer Chicken Burgers

*By Emily Dingmann*

*Burgers are a great thing to cook in the air fryer. It takes about the same amount of time as cooking them in a frying pan or on a grill, but you don't have to stand there supervising the task. Simply put the burger patties into the air fryer, set the timer and then walk away.*

**Yield:** 4 servings

**Prep Time:** 5 minutes

**Cook Time:** 8 minutes

**Total Time:** 13 minutes

**Ingredients:**
1 lb. ground chicken
1 tsp. olive oil
1 tsp. Worcestershire sauce
3/4 tsp. salt
1/4 tsp. pepper
4 hamburger buns

*Toppings*
Lettuce leaves
Tomato slices
Onion slices
Pickles
Ketchup
Mayonnaise
Mustard

1. Gently mix together chicken, olive oil, Worcestershire sauce, salt, and pepper until just combined.

2. Divide into 4 sections and lightly form into burger patties. Make an indent in the center of each burger. This indent will stop the burgers from bulging as much in the center as they cook so that the finished burger has a more flat and even surface.

3. Grease the air fryer basket with oil and preheat air fryer to 360°F.

4. Put burgers in a single layer in the air fryer basket. If they don't all fit, you will have to do two batches. If this is necessary, set your oven to 250°F and put cooked burgers on a tray in the oven to stay warm while second batch cooks.

5. Cook at 360°F for 4 minutes. Flip burger over and cook for 4 more minutes at 400°F, until it reaches an internal temperature of 165°F on an instant read thermometer.

6. Serve on buns with desired toppings.

# Air Fryer Chicken Sandwich

*By Lauren Keating*

*The chicken breasts are brined in pickle juice for an hour before breading them. This makes them extra juicy and flavorful, just like the fried chicken in the sandwiches from your favorite fast food chain. But, here we're cooking them in the air fryer so we use way less oil making them a lot healthier.*

**Yield:** 4 sandwiches

**Prep Time:** 1 hour, 10 minutes

**Cook Time:** 10 minutes

**Total Time:** 1 hour, 20 minutes

**Ingredients:**
2 boneless skinless chicken breasts
1 (24 oz.) jar dill pickle slices
1 cup milk
2 eggs
1 and 1/2 cups all-purpose flour
2 Tbsp. pepper
2 tsp. paprika
1 tsp. salt
1 tsp. baking powder
1/4 tsp. cayenne pepper
4 hamburger buns
Cooking spray
2 tsp. unsalted butter

1. Split each chicken breast horizontally into 2 cutlets. Place the chicken in a zip top bag and add 1 cup of liquid from the jar of pickles. Close bag and refrigerate at least 1 hour.

2. Set air fryer to 400°F to preheat.

3. In a shallow dish, whisk together the milk and eggs.

4. In a second dish, combine the flour, pepper, paprika, salt, baking powder, and cayenne pepper.

5. Reserve 2 tablespoons of the dry flour mixture, then add 3 tablespoons of the milk mixture to the dish and mix until it resembles wet sand.

6. Remove the chicken from the brine and pat dry with a paper towel.

7. Lightly coat the chicken with the dry flour.

8. Working one piece at a time, dredge the chicken in the milk mixture, covering both sides.

9. Add the chicken to the flour mixture, turning to coat. Press as much of the flour mixture as you can onto the chicken breasts. Spritz the chicken with cooking spray or oil using an oil sprayer.

10. Add the chicken to the basket of your air fryer, working in batches if needed. Cook at 400°F for 8-10 minutes, or until golden brown and cooked though.

11. Meanwhile, butter the buns and cook, buttered-side-down, in a hot, dry pan for 1-2 minutes, or until lightly toasted.

12. To assemble the sandwiches, arrange pickle slices on the bottom buns. Top with a cooked chicken breast, then cover with the top buns.

# CHAPTER 4
# PRESSURE COOKER CHICKEN

Pressure Cooker Chicken Breasts
Pressure Cooker Chicken Thighs
Pressure Cooker Whole Chicken
Pressure Cooker Chicken Noodle Soup
Pressure Cooker Chicken Vegetable Soup
Pressure Cooker Chicken Wings
Pressure Cooker White Chicken Chili
Pressure Cooker Buffalo Chicken Dip
Pressure Cooker Pulled Chicken
Pressure Cooker Shawarma Chicken
Pressure Cooker Chicken from Frozen with Rice and Carrots
Pressure Cooker Chicken with Potatoes and Mushrooms
Pressure Cooker Orange Ginger Glazed Chicken Breast with Coconut Rice
Pressure Cooker Southwestern Chicken Rice Bowls
Pressure Cooker Chicken Alfredo
Pressure Cooker Southwest Chicken Pasta
Pressure Cooker Chicken Cacciatore
Pressure Cooker Honey Bourbon Chicken
Pressure Cooker Orange Chicken
Pressure Cooker Chicken Mac n Cheese

*All recipes in this chapter were developed using an Instant Pot.*

# Pressure Cooker Chicken Breasts

*By Kelly Nardo*

*The liquid that you end up with after cooking these chicken breasts is really delicious, especially if you start with stock. You can use it in sauces or soups but since there isn't very much of it, my favorite thing to do with it is to cook rice in it because the rice will absorb all of that flavor.*

**Yield:** 8-10 servings

**Prep Time:** 1 minute

**Cook Time:** 22 minutes

**Total Time:** 23 minutes

**Ingredients:**
1 cup low-sodium chicken stock or water
2 to 2 and 1/2 lbs. boneless skinless chicken breasts, fresh or frozen
1/4 tsp. salt
1/8 tsp. pepper

1. Pour stock or water into the insert of your electric pressure cooker.
2. If fresh chicken breasts are particularly large, cut them in half.
3. Add chicken breasts to the liquid and sprinkle with salt and pepper.
4. Close the lid and make sure it is locked and the valve is set to sealed.
5. Set to pressure cook on high for 6 minutes for fresh chicken breast or 10 minutes for medium-sized frozen chicken breasts or 12 minutes for extra large frozen chicken breasts.
6. Once the chicken has completed the cook cycle, let the pressure release naturally for 10 minutes. Then turn the valve to venting.
7. When the pressure button is lowered, open the lid and remove chicken breasts. Save liquid to use as stock, if desired.

# Pressure Cooker Chicken Thighs

*This recipe has instructions for fresh bone-in and boneless thighs, with and without the skin, as well as for frozen thighs. Whenever I cook chicken thighs in the electric pressure cooker, I include extra liquid (either water or low-sodium chicken stock) because the liquid turns into a delicious broth. What you can do is cook the thighs with the addition of onion and garlic as listed (celery, carrots, and bay leaves are good additions too!) and 3-4 cups of water. Remove the chicken after it's cooked and then chop two of the thighs up and add them to the liquid. Set the pressure cooker to sauté and add some fine egg noodles. Cook until desired doneness. You get a pot of homemade chicken noodle soup, plus 4-6 chicken thighs to use however else you'd like.*

**Yield:** 6 servings

**Prep Time:** 2 minutes

**Cook Time:** 22 minutes

**Total Time:** 24 minutes

**Ingredients:**
- 6–8 chicken thighs, fresh thighs or individually frozen thighs, with or without bone, with or without skin
- Salt
- Pepper
- Water
- 1/2 small onion (optional)
- 2 cloves peeled garlic (optional)

1. Season thighs liberally with salt and pepper.
2. Measure 1 cup of water into the bottom of your electric pressure cooker insert. Use up to 3 cups additional water if you want this to become a soup as described above.
3. Add onion and garlic to pressure cooker, if using.
4. Put the trivet or a steamer basket on top of the water/veggies. Put the thighs on top of the trivet.
5. Seal the pressure cooker and set the valve to sealed. Set the it to pressure cook on high for the following times:
   - Bone-in skin-on thighs: 10 minutes
   - Bone-in skinless thighs: 10 minutes
   - Boneless skinless thighs: 8 minutes
   - Frozen thighs of any kind: 12 minutes
6. Once the pressure cooker has counted down, let it do a natural release for 5 minutes before turning the valve to vent.
7. Once the pressure button drops, remove lid. Remove chicken thighs. Strain liquid if desired for use as a stock. Add some diced chicken and noodles to turn it into a soup.

# Pressure Cooker Whole Chicken

*A whole chicken in the pressure cooker is very versatile. You can brown it under the broiler (as in the optional step at the end of the recipe) and then serve it like a roasted chicken. Or you can treat it as poached chicken and use it in other recipes. Much like with the chicken thigh recipe previously, you can add extra liquid and other aromatic ingredients so that you end up with broth or soup as well.*

**Yield:** 4 servings

**Prep Time:** 5 minutes

**Cook Time:** 30 minutes

**Total Time:** 35 minutes

**Ingredients:**
1 cup water or low-sodium chicken stock
1 whole chicken (giblets removed)
1 small onion, cut in half
1 lemon, halved (optional)
2 tsp. garlic powder
1 tsp. salt
1/2 tsp. pepper

1. Put the trivet in the bottom of your electric pressure cooker insert and pour the water or stock into the pot. Stuff the cut onion and lemon (if using) in the cavity of the chicken.

2. In a small bowl combine the garlic powder, salt, and pepper. Sprinkle seasoning all over outside of chicken. Put chicken on trivet in pressure cooker.

3. Place the lid on and be sure the valve is on sealed. Cook on high pressure for 6 minutes per pound of chicken.

4. Once it has cooked, let the pressure naturally release for 15 minutes. Then, turn the valve to venting. Once the pressure button drops, remove lid.

5. Using an instant read thermometer, check that the chicken meat is at 165°F in the thigh. Reserve cooking liquid for another purpose.

6. Optional step to brown the chicken: Preheat broiler. Put chicken on pan and arrange so that the top of the chicken is 8 inches from the broiler elements. Broil, watching carefully, until top of chicken is golden brown.

*Photo: Lauren Keating*

# Pressure Cooker Chicken Noodle Soup

*By Lauren Keating*

*If you want to speed up this chicken noodle soup, use low-sodium chicken stock instead of water (or half stock and half water) and then set the pressure cooker for 15 minutes instead of 30.*

**Yield:** 6 servings

**Prep Time:** 5 minutes

**Cook Time:** 30 minutes

**Total Time:** 35 minutes

**Ingredients:**
1 Tbsp. olive oil
4 carrots, cut into rounds
4 celery stalks, chopped
1 medium onion, chopped
4 garlic cloves, minced
2 lbs. bone-in chicken thighs or drumsticks
8 cups water
2 bay leaves
1 Tbsp. dried parsley
1 tsp. salt
1/4 tsp. pepper
6 oz. egg noodles

1. Turn your electric pressure cooker on to the sauté setting. Add the oil. When the oil is hot, add the carrots, celery, onion and garlic. Cook 4-5 minutes, stirring frequently, until the vegetables begin to soften but do not turn brown.

2. Add the chicken, water, bay leaves, dried parsley, salt, and pepper. Close the lid tightly and make sure the vent is sealed.

3. Set it to pressure cook on high for 30 minutes.

4. When the cycle has completed, let the pressure release naturally and then remove the lid.

5. Remove the chicken from the pot and discard the skin and bones. Return the chicken to the pot. Taste broth. Add more salt if desired.

6. Switch the pot back to the sauté setting and bring the soup to a boil. Add the noodles and cook stirring occasionally until softened, 6-8 minutes.

# Pressure Cooker Chicken Vegetable Soup

*It's amazing how quickly vegetables cook in the pressure cooker. This recipe, packed with veggies, really highlights how great this is.*

**Yield:** 6 servings

**Prep Time:** 15 minutes

**Cook Time:** 15 minutes

**Total Time:** 30 minutes

**Ingredients:**

1 Tbsp. olive oil
1 medium onion, chopped
3 boneless skinless chicken breasts, cut into 1/2-inch pieces
1 tsp. salt
1/2 tsp. black pepper
2 cloves garlic, minced
1 Tbsp. tomato paste
2 cups chopped or shredded green cabbage
1 cup fresh green beans, cut into 1-inch pieces
3 large carrots, peeled and chopped
2 stalks celery, chopped
4 cups low-sodium vegetable stock or broth
1 (15 oz.) can diced tomatoes
2 tsp. Italian seasoning
2 cups chopped kale, ribs removed
1 (15 oz.) can cannellini beans, drained and rinsed

1. Add oil to the electric pressure cooker and select sauté to preheat.
2. Add the onion. Cook, stirring until the onion softens, about 3-5 minutes.
3. Add the chicken, salt, and pepper. Cook until chicken is white on the outside, 2-4 minutes.
4. Add the garlic and tomato paste. Stir and cook for 30 seconds.
5. Add the cabbage, green beans, carrots, and celery. Stir and cook for 2 minutes.
6. Add the stock, tomatoes, and Italian seasoning. Stir to combine.
7. Close and lock the lid. Make sure the steam release handle is in the sealed position.
8. Set to pressure cook on high for 2 minutes.
9. When the time is up, turn the steam release handle to the venting position and allow steam to escape. When the valve has dropped, unlock the lid and open carefully.
10. Switch the pressure cooker back to sauté. Stir in the kale and cannellini beans and heat until kale is wilted.

# Pressure Cooker Chicken Wings

*By Tawnie Kroll*

*Cooking wings in the pressure cooker is glorious. They cook up really quickly and have tender meat that is infused with sauce. We've used teriyaki on these ones but any sauce will work. Once they're done cooking in the pressure cooker, you pop them under the broiler for a short time to crisp up, and you're done!*

**Yield:** 6 servings

**Prep Time:** 5 minutes

**Cook Time:** 25 minutes

**Total Time:** 30 minutes

**Ingredients:**
2 lbs. chicken wings, patted dry
21 oz. teriyaki sauce
2 cloves garlic, chopped
1 tsp. red pepper flakes
1/2 tsp. pepper
2 tsp. corn starch

1. Add the wings to your electric pressure cooker. Pour the teriyaki sauce over the wings and add the garlic, pepper flakes, and pepper to the pot.

2. Seal the lid on top and make sure the valve is turned to sealed.

3. Set to cook on high pressure for 5 minutes. When the time is up, let the pressure naturally release for 10 minutes.

4. During that time, turn your oven on to broil and line a baking sheet with aluminum foil.

5. Using tongs, place the wings on the baking sheet and broil 6-8 inches from heat element until starting to brown, about 3-5 minutes. Flip and cook on the other side until brown, 3-5 minutes.

6. While wings are broiling, turn pressure cooker to saute mode. Mix the corn starch in a small bowl with a splash of water. Whisk into the teriyaki sauce in the pressure cooker. Stir occasionally until it comes to a simmer and thickens.

7. Toss broiled wings with sauce.

Photo: Kelly Nardo

# Pressure Cooker White Chicken Chili

*By Kelly Nardo*

For a thicker chili, after adding the shredded chicken back to the pressure cooker, stir together 2 tablespoons of cornstarch with 1/4 cup cold water until smooth. Add it to the chili and set the pressure cooker to sauté until it reaches a simmer. The broth will then have a bit more body. You can repeat this cornstarch step a second time if you want it even thicker (or double the amounts initially).

# Pressure Cooker White Chicken Chili

*Continued from previous page*

**Yield:** 6 servings

**Prep Time:** 5 minutes

**Cook Time:** 30 minutes

**Total Time:** 35 minutes

**Ingredients:**
1 Tbsp. cooking oil
1 large onion, chopped
3 cloves garlic, minced
2 (14 oz.) cans white northern beans, drained and rinsed
1 (4 oz.) can green chilis
4 cups low-sodium chicken stock
1 Tbsp. chili powder
1 Tbsp. cumin
1 tsp. salt
1/4 tsp. pepper
1 lb. boneless skinless chicken breasts
Optional toppings: sliced jalapeños, green onions, lime wedges, etc.

1. Set electric pressure cooker to sauté mode and add oil to heat. Add onion and garlic and sauté until softened, 3-5 minutes, stirring occasionally.

2. Turn off heat and add beans, chilis, stock, chili powder, cumin, salt, and pepper. Mix well to combine. Add chicken, making sure it is somewhat covered by the liquid.

3. Close lid, set vent to seal, and set it to manual high pressure cook for 12 minutes. Once done, either release pressure manually or let it naturally release.

4. Remove chicken and shred with two forks. Stir it back into the pot.

5. Serve with optional toppings if using.

# Pressure Cooker Buffalo Chicken Dip

*For this dip, the chicken is cooked in the pressure cooker with some Buffalo sauce and seasonings. Then at the end you add in some cheese and dressing to make it creamy.*

**Yield:** 6 servings

**Prep Time:** 5 minutes

**Cook Time:** 15 minutes

**Total Time:** 20 minutes

**Ingredients:**
2 boneless skinless chicken breasts
1 cup Buffalo wing sauce
1/4 cup water
1/2 tsp. garlic powder
1/2 tsp. onion powder
2 cups shredded cheddar cheese
8 oz. cream cheese
1/4 cup ranch or blue cheese dressing
Celery, carrots, chips for dipping

1. Place chicken, Buffalo sauce, water, garlic powder, and onion powder in the electric pressure cooker. Stir.

2. Set to cook on high pressure for 10 minutes.

3. Allow pressure to release naturally for 2 minutes and then switch valve to venting for a quick release.

4. Remove chicken from pot and shred. Return to pot along with cheddar, cream cheese, and dressing.

5. Switch pressure cooker to sauté function and cook, stirring continuously, until cheese is melted and mixture is smooth.

6. Serve with chips or veggies.

# Pressure Cooker Pulled Chicken

*Boneless, skinless chicken thighs are my go-to choice for pulled chicken. They're much moister than breast meat and they shred up nicer.*

**Yield:** 4 servings

**Prep Time:** 5 minutes

**Cook Time:** 20 minutes

**Total Time:** 25 minutes

**Ingredients:**
1 and 1/2 lbs. boneless skinless chicken thighs
1 tsp. salt
1 tsp. garlic powder
1/2 tsp. pepper
1 cup water

1. Season the thighs with salt, garlic powder, and pepper.
2. Put the trivet in the inner pot of the electric pressure cooker and pour in the water.
3. Place the thighs on the trivet.
4. Close and lock the lid. Make sure the steam release handle is in the sealed position.
5. Set to cook on high pressure for 13 minutes.
6. When time is up, turn the steam release handle to the venting position and allow steam to escape. When the button has dropped, unlock the lid and open carefully.
7. Remove the thighs to a plate and shred with two forks. Discard liquid or save to use as stock.

# Pressure Cooker Shawarma Chicken

*Chicken Shawarma is a warm spiced, spit or rotisserie roasted dish from the Middle East. Here we're using the same flavors but cooking it in the pressure cooker instead of on a spit.*

# Pressure Cooker Shawarma Chicken

*Continued from previous page*

**Yield:** 4 servings

**Prep Time:** 5 minutes

**Cook Time:** 20 minutes

**Total Time:** 25 minutes

**Ingredients:**
1 Tbsp. ground cumin
1/2 tsp. cinnamon
1/2 tsp. salt
a pinch of cayenne pepper
a pinch of cloves
4 bone-in, skinless chicken thighs
3/4 cup water or chicken stock
1/4 cup lemon juice
2 Tbsp. olive oil
1 English cucumber, sliced
1/2 red onion, sliced
4 pita breads
1/2 cup hummus, tzatziki, or Greek yogurt

1. In a small bowl combine the cumin, cinnamon, salt, cayenne, and cloves.

2. Rub all over the outside of the chicken thighs.

3. Into the electric pressure cooker measure the water, lemon juice, and olive oil. Stir.

4. Add the chicken thighs in a single layer. The liquid will not cover the thighs fully.

5. Set the pressure cooker to pressure cook on high for 13 minutes.

6. Once it has heated up and then run for 13 minutes, allow pressure to release naturally for 2 minutes and then turn valve to vent.

7. Once the pressure botton has dropped, remove lid carefully. Remove chicken from pressure cooker. Use two forks to shred meat. Discard any skin or bones.

8. Serve chicken with sliced cucumber, red onion, pita bread, and sauce of your choice.

# Pressure Cooker Chicken from Frozen with Rice and Carrots

*This dinner recipe is super convenient when you're in a hurry. Note that you can make this recipe with fresh chicken breasts instead of frozen. Set the pressure cooking time to 7 minutes instead of 9 minutes.*

**Yield:** 4 servings

**Prep Time:** 10 minutes

**Cook Time:** 14 minutes

**Total Time:** 24 minutes

**Ingredients:**
- 1 and 1/4 cups long grain white rice
- 2 and 1/2 cups low-sodium chicken stock
- 1 tsp. salt
- 1/2 tsp. pepper
- 4 (6-8 ounces each) individually-frozen, boneless skinless chicken breasts
- 2 tsp. Italian herb blend, or your favorite dried herb blend
- 5 −6 large carrots, peeled and cut into 1" pieces

1. Measure rice into bottom of an 8 quart electric pressure cooker.
2. Add chicken stock, salt, and pepper. Stir to combine.
3. Lay the frozen chicken breasts in a single layer on top of the rice and liquid. Season the chicken breasts with the herb blend.
4. Arrange carrots around chicken.
5. Cover pot, lock on the lid, and set the steam release valve to sealing.
6. Select Pressure Cook and make sure it's set to high. Set the time to 9 minutes.
7. When the cooking cycle has finished, allow the pot to sit for 5 minutes, and then do a quick release by moving the valve to venting.
8. Once the pressure button has dropped, remove lid carefully. Check that the chicken is 165°F in the center using an instant read thermometer.

# Pressure Cooker Chicken with Potatoes and Mushrooms

*To make this meal all cook in the same amount of time, the chicken is cut into pieces.*

**Yield:** 4 servings

**Prep Time:** 10 minutes

**Cook Time:** 30 minutes

**Total Time:** 40 minutes

**Ingredients:**
1 and 1/2 tsp. salt
1 tsp. dried thyme
1/2 tsp. pepper
1/2 tsp. dried oregano
3 large boneless skinless chicken breasts, cut into 1-inch pieces
2 Tbsp. olive oil
2 cloves garlic, minced
16 oz. cremini mushrooms, quartered
1/2 cup chopped onion
2 Tbsp. unsalted butter
1 cup low-sodium chicken stock
2 Tbsp. lemon juice
1 and 1/2 lbs. red potatoes, quartered
1/2 cup frozen peas

1. In a small bowl combine salt, thyme, pepper, and oregano.

2. Season the chicken pieces with the herb mixture. Set aside.

3. Add oil to the electric pressure cooker and select sauté to pre-heat. Add the chicken to the pot and cook, stirring occasionally, until the chicken starts to brown, about 3 – 4 minutes. Add the garlic and cook for another minute. Transfer chicken and garlic to a clean plate.

4. Add the mushrooms, onion, and butter to the pot and cook for 3 – 4 minutes.

5. Add the chicken stock and deglaze the pot, scraping the bottom to loosen all of the bits. Stir in the lemon juice.

6. Add the potatoes to the pot and stir to distribute all of the vegetables.

7. Place the chicken pieces on top of the potatoes along with any juices that may have accumulated on the dish.

8. Close and lock the lid. Make sure the steam release handle is in the sealed position. Set to pressure cook on high for 6 minutes.

9. When time is up, allow a natural pressure release of 5 minutes and then turn the steam release handle to the venting position and allow remaining steam to escape. When the button has dropped, unlock the lid and open carefully.

10. Add the frozen peas, replace the lid and allow the residual heat to warm the peas, about 3 minutes.

11. Scoop chicken and vegetables into a bowl and spoon some of the broth over the top.

*Photo: Leigh Olson*

# Pressure Cooker Orange Ginger Glazed Chicken Breast with Coconut Rice

*This is a great recipe for learning how to cook multiple things separately in the pressure cooker. The chicken is placed at the bottom of the pot with something over it (in this case a steamer basket or trivet). Then a pan of rice is put on top of that. The chicken and rice then cook at the same time but aren't affected by the liquid or flavorings from each other. In this way, you can get two components of a meal that have different flavorings.*

**Yield:** 4 servings

**Prep Time:** 10 minutes

**Cook Time:** 10 minutes

**Total Time:** 20 minutes

**Ingredients:**
4 boneless skinless chicken breasts
1/2 tsp. salt
1/4 tsp. pepper
3 Tbsp. olive oil
4 cloves garlic, minced
1 Tbsp. grated ginger
1 cup orange juice
1/4 cup soy sauce
1/4 cup water
1/4 cup brown sugar
2 Tbsp. tomato paste
1 tsp. Sriracha (optional)
2 Tbsp. cornstarch
2 Tbsp. water

*Rice*
1 and 1/2 cups long grain rice
1 and 1/2 cups water
1/2 cup match stick carrots
1/2 cup shredded coconut

1. Add oil to the electric pressure cooker and select sauté to pre-heat. When the indicator says hot, add the chicken to the pot and brown both sides, about 3 – 4 minutes per side. Transfer the chicken to a clean plate.

2. Add the garlic and ginger to pressure cooker and cook, stirring until they just start to brown, about 1 minute.

3. Add the orange juice and deglaze the pot, scraping the bottom to loosen all of the bits.

4. Stir in the soy sauce, water, brown sugar, tomato paste, and Sriracha (if using).

5. Place the chicken and any juices that have accumulated on the plate back into the pot.

6. Insert a steaming rack or tall trivet in the pot over the chicken and sauce. Place an 8" heatproof pan on the trivet, I use my 8" cake pan.

7. Add the rice, water, carrots, and coconut to the pan and stir to combine.

8. Close and lock the lid. Make sure the steam release handle is in the sealed position. Set it to cook on high pressure for 6 minutes.

9. Meanwhile, in a small mason jar or small bowl combine the water and the cornstarch. Shake the mason jar to combine or whisk with a fork if you're not using a mason jar. Set aside.

10. When time is up, allow a natural pressure release of 5 minutes and then turn the steam release handle to the venting position and allow remaining steam to escape. When the valve has dropped, unlock the lid and open carefully.

11. Wear oven mitts to remove the cake pan from the pressure cooker and set aside. Remove the trivet and transfer the chicken to a clean plate.

12. Make sure the cornstarch mixture hasn't settled. If it has either shake the mason jar or whisk again.

# Pressure Cooker Orange Ginger Glazed Chicken Breast with Coconut Rice

*Continued from previous page*

13. Select sauté on the pressure cooker. Pour in the cornstarch mixture and cook until the sauce has thickened, about 4 minutes.

14. Serve the chicken breasts over the rice and spoon some of the sauce over the top.

# Pressure Cooker Southwestern Chicken Rice Bowls

*By Kelly Nardo*

*Rice bowls can come together quickly for dinner if you use your pressure cooker. While the rice and chicken cook, prep your fresh toppings and take them to the table so that everything is ready to eat as soon as the pressure is released.*

**Yield:** 6 servings

**Prep Time:** 5 minutes

**Cook Time:** 25 minutes

**Total Time:** 30 minutes

**Ingredients:**
1 cup white jasmine rice
1 cup frozen corn
3/4 cup chopped onion
1 (14 oz.) can kidney beans, rinsed and drained
1 (10 oz.) can diced tomatoes with green chilis
2 cups water
1 Tbsp. taco seasoning
1 tsp. garlic powder
1/8 tsp. salt
1/8 tsp. pepper
1 pound boneless skinless chicken breast
Optional toppings: sliced jalapeños, cherry tomatoes, salsa, green onions, cilantro, lime wedges

1. Add rice, corn, onion, beans, tomatoes, and water to electric pressure cooker and stir to combine. Place chicken in mixture, making sure to cover some with the liquid. Sprinkle seasonings over chicken, rice, and bean mixture.

2. Close lid, set vent to seal. Set to pressure cook on high 12 minutes.

3. Allow pressure to release naturally for 5 minutes and then turn the vent to venting.

4. Once the pressure button has dropped, remove chicken and shred with two forks. Place it back in the pot, stir to incorporate and serve with optional toppings if using.

Photo: Leigh Olson

# Pressure Cooker Chicken Alfredo

*This creamy, garlicky Chicken Alfredo is a no-brainer one pot meal. All of the cooking, including the noodles, is done in the pressure cooker making getting dinner on the table and clean up a breeze.*

**Yield:** 4 servings

**Prep Time:** 15 minutes

**Cook Time:** 25 minutes

**Total Time:** 40 minutes

**Ingredients:**

3 large boneless skinless chicken breasts, cut into 1-inch pieces
1 tsp. salt
1/2 tsp. pepper
2 Tbsp. olive oil
2 Tbsp. unsalted butter
3 cloves garlic, minced
2 cups low-sodium chicken stock, divided
1 and 1/2 cups heavy cream
8 oz. dry fettuccine
1 cup grated Parmesan
a pinch of nutmeg
1/4 cup chopped flat leaf parsley

1. Season chicken with salt and pepper. Set aside

2. Add oil to the electric pressure cooker and select sauté to pre-heat. When the indicator says hot, add the chicken to the pot and cook stirring occasionally, until the chicken starts to brown, about 2–3 minutes.

3. Add the butter and the garlic and cook for another 4 minutes.

4. Add 1 cup of the chicken stock and deglaze the pot, scraping the bottom to loosen all of the bits.

5. Press cancel and add the cream. Stir to combine well. Do not stir after this point.

6. Break the fettuccine in half and place on top of the cream and chicken mixture. Do not stir.

7. Pour the remaining chicken stock over the noodles—remember, no stirring.

8. Close and lock the lid. Make sure the steam release handle is in the sealed position.

9. Set to pressure cook on high for 5 minutes.

10. When time is up, allow a natural pressure release of 5 minutes and then turn the steam release handle to the venting position and allow remaining steam to escape. When the button has dropped, unlock the lid and open carefully.

11. Press cancel and add the Parmesan and nutmeg stirring to combine.

12. Replace the lid and allow the residual heat to melt the Parmesan, about 3 minutes. Sprinkle with the parsley.

*Photo: Leigh Olson*

# Pressure Cooker Southwest Chicken Pasta

The list of ingredients in this recipe is a tad longer than I usually use, but it's still a super-quick breeze to make. You add ingredients and stir a bit near the beginning, and add more and stir a bit at the end. But, in the middle you get to sit back and relax.

**Yield:** 6 servings

**Prep Time:** 10 minutes

**Cook Time:** 20 minutes

**Total Time:** 30 minutes

**Ingredients:**
1 lb. boneless skinless chicken thighs, cut into 1-inch cubes
1/2 tsp. salt
1/4 tsp. pepper
2 Tbsp. olive oil
1/2 cup chopped onion
2 cloves garlic, chopped
1 Tbsp. chili powder
1 Tbsp. ground cumin
2 tsp. dried oregano
1 and 1/2 cups low-sodium chicken stock, divided
1 (15 oz.) can fire-roasted diced tomatoes
1 (4 oz.) can chopped green chilis
3/4 cup heavy cream
12 oz. fettuccine
1/2 cup shredded cheddar cheese
1/2 cup shredded pepper Jack cheese
1/4 cup chopped cilantro

1. Season chicken with salt and pepper. Set aside.
2. Set electric pressure cooker to sauté. Add oil and heat. Add the chicken to the pot and cook stirring occasionally, until the chicken starts to brown, about 2 – 3 minutes. Add the onion and the garlic and cook for another 4 minutes.
3. Stir in the chili powder, cumin, and oregano and cook for 2 minutes.
4. Add 1/2 cup of the chicken stock and deglaze the pot, scraping the bottom to loosen all of the bits.
5. Add the tomatoes and green chilis and stir to combine.
6. Press cancel and add the cream, stirring to combine well. Do not stir after this point.
7. Break the fettuccine in half and place on top of the cream and chicken mixture. Do not stir.
8. Pour the remaining chicken stock over the noodles – remember, no stirring.
9. Close and lock the lid. Make sure the steam release handle is in the sealed position. Set it to pressure cook on high for 5 minutes.
10. When time is up, allow a natural pressure release of 5 minutes and then turn the steam release handle to the venting position and allow remaining steam to escape. When the button has dropped, unlock the lid and open carefully.
11. Press cancel and add the cheddar and pepper jack cheeses, stirring to combine.
12. Replace the lid and allow the residual heat to melt the cheese, about 3 minutes. Stir in the cilantro.

# Pressure Cooker Chicken Cacciatore

*By Brittany Poulson*

*If you'd like your cacciatore to be thicker, combine 2 tablespoons of cornstarch with 1/4 cup of water. Add it to the pot after the pressure has been released. Then set the pot to sauté to heat it back to a simmer. You can repeat this step if you want it even thicker on top of that.*

**Yield:** 6 servings

**Prep Time:** 10 minutes

**Cook Time:** 25 minutes

**Total Time:** 35 minutes

**Ingredients:**
2 Tbsp. olive oil
1 and 1/2 lbs. boneless skinless chicken thighs
1 small onion, thinly sliced
1/2 green bell pepper, sliced
1/2 red bell pepper, sliced
4 oz. sliced mushrooms
3 cloves garlic, minced
1/4 cup red wine vinegar
3/4 cup low-sodium chicken stock
1 (15 oz.) can crushed tomatoes
1 tsp. minced fresh basil (or 1/2 tsp. dried)
1 tsp. minced fresh oregano (or 1/2 tsp. dried)
1/2 tsp. salt
1/4 tsp. pepper

1. Pour the olive oil into the electric pressure cooker and turn on sauté mode. When the oil is hot add the chicken and brown on both sides, about 3-4 minutes total. Remove from the pot and set aside.

2. Add the onion, bell pepper, and mushrooms and sauté for 2-3 minutes. Add in the minced garlic and continue sautéing an additional 30-60 seconds. Turn off the sauté function.

3. Return the chicken to the pot along with the red wine vinegar, chicken stock, crushed tomatoes, basil, oregano, salt, and pepper. Stir well to combine.

4. Secure the lid. Make sure it's set to sealing. Set to pressure cook on high for 8 minutes. When the timer is done, allow for a natural release of pressure.

5. Once pressure is completely released and pressure button has dropped, remove the lid and stir the cacciatore. Let it sit for 10 minutes to allow the sauce to thicken.

Photo: Lauren Keating

# Pressure Cooker Honey Bourbon Chicken

*By Lauren Keating*

You might wonder why bourbon is an optional ingredient in Bourbon Chicken. It's because the dish is named for the famous New Orleans street, and not for the famous beverage. But if you put some bourbon in there, as we have, then you can say that it's named for both! This is delicious served on fluffy white rice to catch all the tasty sauce.

# Pressure Cooker Honey Bourbon Chicken

*Continued from previous page*

**Yield:** 6 servings

**Prep Time:** 10 minutes

**Cook Time:** 1 hour

**Total Time:** 1 hour, 10 minutes

**Ingredients:**
2 lb. boneless skinless chicken thighs, cut into 1-inch pieces
1/2 tsp. salt
1/4 tsp. pepper
1 small onion, chopped
1/2 cup soy sauce
1/2 cup honey
1/4 cup ketchup
2 garlic cloves, minced
1 tsp. ginger, minced
1/2 tsp. crushed red pepper flakes
2 Tbsp. bourbon (optional)
2 Tbsp. cornstarch
1 Tbsp. water
2 scallions, sliced
1 Tbsp. sesame seeds

1. Season the chicken with salt and pepper. Add the chicken, onion, soy sauce, honey, ketchup, garlic, ginger, red pepper flakes, and bourbon to your electric pressure cooker. Close the lid and set the vent to sealing. Set for high pressure for 10 minutes.

2. When the cycle is completed, allow pressure to naturally release for 5 minutes, then quick release the remaining pressure by switching the valve to venting.

3. Once the pressure is fully released, remove the lid and set the pot to the sauté function. In a small bowl, mix together the cornstarch and water until smooth. Stir into pot.

4. Simmer the bourbon chicken until sauce thickens, about 5 minutes. Top with scallions and sesame seeds.

# Pressure Cooker Orange Chicken

*By Brittany Poulson*

*Don't skip the orange zest in this recipe. It brings so much freshness and extra orange flavor to the dish.*

**Yield:** 6 servings

**Prep Time:** 5 minutes

**Cook Time:** 25 minutes

**Total Time:** 30 minutes

**Ingredients:**
2 Tbsp. olive oil
2 lbs. boneless skinless chicken breasts, cut into 1 and 1/2" pieces
1 cup + 3 Tbsp. orange juice, divided
1/3 cup brown sugar
1/4 cup low-sodium soy sauce
1/4 cup tomato sauce
1 Tbsp. rice wine vinegar
2 cloves garlic, minced
2 Tbsp. fresh orange zest
1 Tbsp. fresh grated ginger
1/4 tsp. crushed red pepper flakes (optional)
2 Tbsp. cornstarch
2 green onions, chopped
1 Tbsp. sesame seeds

1. Turn the electric pressure cooker on the sauté function and add the olive oil. Once hot, add the chicken and cook until browned, about 4-5 minutes, stirring occasionally so it doesn't stick to the bottom. Turn off sauté mode.

2. In a medium bowl, whisk 1 cup of the orange juice, the brown sugar, soy sauce, tomato sauce, rice wine vinegar, garlic, orange zest, ginger, and red pepper flakes (if using). Add the sauce mixture to the pot and stir together with the chicken.

3. Secure the lid on the pressure cooker and set it to manual high for 5 minutes. When the timer is done, allow a natural release for 5 minutes.

4. Meanwhile, in a small bowl whisk together the remaining 3 tablespoons of orange juice and the cornstarch until there are no lumps.

5. When the 5 minutes is up, turn the steam valve to open to release any extra pressure. Once the pressure has fully released, remove the lid and turn the pressure cooker back to sauté mode.

6. Add the orange juice/cornstarch mixture and stir until the sauce is thickened. When sauce reaches desired thickness, turn off the Instant Pot and allow to sit for 5-6 minutes before serving.

7. Add garnish of green onions and sesame seeds.

# Pressure Cooker Chicken Mac n Cheese

*By Emily Dingmann*

*For this twist on the classic mac n cheese, the pasta and chicken are cooked in the pressure cooker with some flavorful ingredients. After they're done, you add the cheese and cream. The heat from the hot noodles and residual heat of the pot melts the cheese and heats the cream into a quick sauce.*

**Yield:** 6 servings

**Prep Time:** 5 minutes

**Cook Time:** 20 minutes

**Total Time:** 25 minutes

**Ingredients:**
16 oz. elbow macaroni
4 cups low-sodium chicken stock
2 Tbsp. unsalted butter
1/2 tsp. garlic powder
1/2 tsp. mustard powder
1/2 tsp. salt
2 chicken breasts, cut into 1/2" pieces
1/2 cup half & half
3 cups shredded sharp cheddar cheese

1. Add ingredients to the electric pressure cooker in this order — pasta, stock, butter, garlic powder, mustard powder, salt, chicken. Do not stir.
2. Lock pressure cooker lid and close pressure release valve.
3. Set it to pressure cook on high for 5 minutes.
4. Once all pressure has released, remove lid. Stir in half & half and cheese until heated through.

# CHAPTER 5
# SLOW COOKER CHICKEN

Slow Cooker Whole Chicken
Slow Cooker Buffalo Chicken Dip
Slow Cooker Chicken Burger Dip
Slow Cooker Shredded Chicken
Slow Cooker BBQ Pulled Chicken
Slow Cooker Pulled Chicken Sandwiches
Slow Cooker Chicken Carnitas
Slow Cooker Chicken Fajitas
Slow Cooker Chicken Burrito Bowl
Slow Cooker Chicken and Sausage Meatballs
Slow Cooker White Chicken Chili
Slow Cooker Chicken and Dumplings
Slow Cooker Coq au Vin
Slow Cooker Chicken Parmesan
Slow Cooker Chicken Stroganoff
Slow Cooker Chicken Stuffed Peppers
Slow Cooker Chicken Teriyaki
Slow Cooker Orange Chicken
Slow Cooker Chicken with 40 Cloves of Garlic
Slow Cooker Lemon Chicken
Slow Cooker Chicken Wings

Photo: Meghan Bassett

# Slow Cooker Whole Chicken

*By Meghan Bassett*

*The slow cooker cooks a whole chicken slowly then the broiler gives it a final blast of high heat. What you get is tender and juicy slow-cooked chicken, and wonderfully browned skin.*

**Yield:** 4 servings

**Prep Time:** 10 minutes

**Cook Time:** 6 hours, 5 minutes

**Total Time:** 6 hours, 15 minutes

**Ingredients:**
1/2 medium onion, chopped
2 russet potatoes, cubed
4 carrots, peeled and cut in half
4 ribs celery, cut in thirds
4 tsp. salt
1 and 1/2 tsp. paprika
1 and 1/2 tsp. chili powder
1 tsp. onion powder
1/2 tsp. garlic powder
1 (4–5 lbs.) whole chicken, giblets removed
5 garlic cloves, peeled and smashed
1 lemon, quartered

1. In the bottom of a slow cooker, place onions, potatoes, carrots, and celery.

2. In a small bowl, stir together salt, paprika, chili powder, onion powder, and garlic powder.

3. Rub the chicken inside and out with the spice mixture. Stuff the chicken with garlic cloves and lemon wedges. Tie together the chicken legs with twine.

4. Place the chicken on top of the vegetables. Cover and cook on low for 4 to 6 hours, until it reaches an internal temperature of 160°F on an instant read thermometer.

5. Turn on the broiler.

6. Carefully remove the chicken from the slow cooker to a cutting board. Strain the juices from the bottom of the slow cooker and add the vegetables to a large casserole dish.

7. Put the whole chicken on top of the vegetables. Broil the chicken with the vegetables until the skin is brown and crispy, approximately 4-6 minutes. The internal temperature of the chicken should be 165°F as read on an instant read thermometer.

8. Remove from oven and let rest for 10 minutes before carving.

# Slow Cooker Buffalo Chicken Dip

*By Lauren Sharifi*

*Buffalo Chicken Dip is always a crowd-pleaser. This version is made in the slow cooker making it very hands free, and you can leave it in there to stay warm all throughout your game day party.*

**Yield:** 8 servings

**Prep Time:** 10 minutes

**Cook Time:** 2 hours

**Total Time:** 2 hours, 10 minutes

**Ingredients:**
3 cups cooked shredded chicken
1 (8 oz.) package cream cheese
1 cup shredded cheddar cheese
1 cup shredded part-skim mozzarella cheese
3/4 cup Buffalo wing sauce
1/2 cup blue cheese or ranch dressing
1/2 tsp. garlic powder
1/2 tsp. onion powder

1. Add all ingredients to the slow cooker and mix to combine. It's okay if the cream cheese doesn't mix well.

2. Cook on low for 1-2 hour, or until cheeses are melted. Stir.

3. Switch slow cooker to warm to keep it melted while serving.

# Slow Cooker Chicken Burger Dip

*By Sam Ellis*

*When it's time to serve this dip, turn the slow cooker to low or warm. Then serve the dip directly from the slow cooker so it stays warm and melty.*

**Yield:** 4-5 servings

**Prep Time:** 25 minutes

**Cook Time:** 2 hours

**Total Time:** 2 hours, 25 minutes

**Ingredients:**
6 slices bacon
1 small onion, chopped
1 lb. ground chicken
1/2 tsp. pepper
1 tsp. chili powder
1 tsp. salt
1 (10 oz.) can of diced tomatoes & green chilies (like Rotel, not drained)
8 oz. cream cheese
1 cup shredded cheddar cheese
2 Tbsp. ketchup
1 Tbsp. Worcestershire sauce
1 Tbsp. yellow mustard

1. In a large skillet over medium heat, cook bacon until crispy, about 5-8 minutes. Remove with a slotted spoon and place on a plate lined with paper towel.

2. Add the onion to the bacon fat in the pan and cook until translucent, about 4-5 minutes.

3. Add ground chicken and cook until no longer pink, 8-10 minutes.

4. Stir in the pepper, chili powder, and salt. Crumble bacon into chicken mixture.

5. To a slow cooker, add chicken and bacon mixture, diced tomatoes & green chilies (not drained), cream cheese, shredded cheddar cheese, ketchup, Worcestershire sauce and yellow mustard. Mix together and cook 2 hours on high stirring occasionally.

*Photo: Sam Ellis*

# Slow Cooker Shredded Chicken

*By Sam Ellis*

*If you have a batch of shredded chicken in your fridge, you have so many dinner possibilities. It's great in sandwiches, wraps, and tacos, on salads, in a pasta sauce, on a rice bowl, pretty much anywhere that you can use chicken, you can use it. Note: If you use chicken thighs the meat will be juicier even for reheating.*

**Yield:** 6 servings

**Prep Time:** 5 minutes

**Cook Time:** 4-6 hours

**Total Time:** 4-6 hours, 5 minutes

**Ingredients:**
1 cup water
1 cube chicken bouillon
1/2 tsp. pepper
1 and 1/2 lbs. boneless skinless chicken breast or thighs or a mixture

1. In a small pot, bring water to a simmer. Dissolve chicken bouillon in the water. Add the salt and pepper.
2. In a slow cooker, place chicken breasts and pour in the chicken bouillon mixture. Cover and set on high for 4 hours or low for 6 hours.
3. Remove chicken from the slow cooker once done and shred with two forks.
4. Pour liquid out of slow cooker. Put 1/2 cup of it back in. Reserve the rest.
5. Place the shredded chicken back into the liquid in the slow cooker and stir.
6. Serve immediately or, if saving for later use, drizzle with a few tablespoons of the reserved liquid to keep it moist in the fridge. Refrigerate the rest of the liquid separately. Drizzle chicken with more liquid if necessary for moistness when reheating.

# Slow Cooker BBQ Pulled Chicken

*By Sara Blackburn*

*If you use chicken thighs for this recipe, it will be juicier. If you use breasts, you have a leaner and healthier meal. A mixture of both gets you the best of both worlds!*

**Yield:** 4-6 servings

**Prep Time:** 10 minutes

**Cook Time:** 4 hours, 20 minutes

**Total Time:** 4 hours, 30 minutes

**Ingredients:**
3 (6 oz.) cans no-salt-added tomato paste
2 cups water
1/2 cup apple cider vinegar
1/3 cup brown sugar
2 Tbsp. brown mustard
2 Tbsp. instant espresso
2 Tbsp. Worcestershire sauce
2 tsp. hickory flavored liquid smoke
1 Tbsp. coarse salt
2 tsp. red pepper flakes
3 lbs. boneless, skinless chicken breast or thighs or a mixture

1. Add tomato paste, water, apple cider vinegar, brown sugar, mustard, instant espresso, red pepper flakes, Worcestershire sauce, liquid smoke, and salt to slow cooker insert and stir until well combined.

2. Add chicken in a single layer.

3. Cover and cook on high for 4 hours, until internal temperature of chicken is at least 165°F.

4. Once cooked, use tongs to move chicken from slow cooker to a plate. Shred chicken using two forks. Return shredded chicken to slow cooker. Stir. Cover and cook for 20 minutes to allow chicken to soak up barbecue sauce.

# Slow Cooker Pulled Chicken Sandwiches

*Here's a less saucy version of pulled chicken that is great for piling onto sandwiches. For this recipe, I've added some cheese and put the sandwiches under the broiler for a moment so that everything is gooey and delicious.*

**Yield:** 8 servings

**Prep Time:** 25 minutes

**Cook Time:** 4-6 hours

**Total Time:** 4-6 hours, 25 minutes

**Ingredients:**
1 cup ketchup
1/2 cup brown sugar
1 Tbsp. Worcestershire sauce
1 tsp. tabasco
2 Tbsp. vinegar (white or cider)
1/2 tsp. salt
5 pounds boneless skinless chicken breasts or thighs or a mixture
2 Tbsp. dijon mustard
1 cup shredded cheddar cheese
8 burger buns

1. Put the ketchup, brown sugar, Worcestershire, tabasco, vinegar, and salt in the slow cooker. Stir well.

2. Add the chicken. Stir until well coated.

3. Cook for 4 hours on high or 6-8 on low. Check that the internal temperature is at least 165°F on an instant read thermometer.

4. Preheat broiler.

5. Remove chicken pieces from the sauce. Whisk the dijon mustard into the sauce. Use 2 forks to shred the chicken. Return chicken to sauce.

6. Split open the burger buns. Put them cut side up on a large pan and broil until toasted, 2-4 minutes. Remove bun tops from pan and set aside. Pile chicken onto bun bottoms. Top each with 2 tablespoons shredded cheese and return to broiler until cheese is melted, 2-3 minutes. Put the bun tops on top.

# Slow Cooker Chicken Carnitas

*By Sam Ellis*

*Here we put slow-cooked shredded chicken under the broiler to get it satisfyingly crunchy in places. The key is to alternate between broiling and adding liquid so that the chicken doesn't dry out as it gets crunchy.*

**Yield:** 6 servings

**Prep Time:** 5 minutes

**Cook Time:** 4-6 hours

**Total Time:** 4-6 hours, 5 minutes

**Ingredients:**
1 and 1/2 lbs. boneless skinless chicken breasts or thighs or a mixture of both
1 small onion, chopped
1 cup chicken stock
2 limes, juiced
1/4 cup orange juice
1 and 1/2 tsp. chili powder
1 tsp. cumin
1 tsp. garlic powder
1 tsp. oregano
2 bay leaves
1 tsp. salt
1 tsp. pepper

1. Combine all ingredients in a slow cooker. Cook on high for 4 hours or low for 6-7 hours.

2. With 30 minutes left, remove the chicken and shred with forks. Remove the bay leaves. Place chicken back in the slow cooker for the remaining 30 minutes.

3. Move an oven rack to 6 inches below the broiler. Set broiler to high. Using a slotted spoon, remove the chicken and place it on a cookie sheet.

4. Place chicken under broiler for 5 minutes. Remove from under broiler, spoon 1/4 cup of broth from slow cooker onto chicken and toss. Place back under broiler for 2 minutes. Spoon 2 tablespoons of broth onto the chicken and toss. Place back under broiler for 2 minutes. Spoon 2 tablespoons of broth onto the chicken and toss. Repeat until chicken has a nice crunch in many places. If it burns in small spots, break off the burnt bits and discard.

# Slow Cooker Chicken Fajitas

*By Jamie Silva*

*This dinner comes together so quickly. After you shred the chicken and put it back into the slow cooker, warm the tortillas and prep your other toppings. Then eat!*

**Yield:** 8 servings

**Prep Time:** 10 minutes

**Cook Time:** 4 hours

**Total Time:** 4 hours, 10 minutes

**Ingredients:**
1 red bell pepper, sliced
1 yellow bell pepper, sliced
1 green bell pepper, sliced
1 onion, sliced
2 lbs. of boneless skinless chicken breasts or thighs or a mixture
2 Tbsp. taco seasoning
4 cloves of garlic, minced
1 (10 oz.) can diced tomatoes, drained
2 Tbsp. lime juice
Flour tortillas

*Optional*
Shredded cheese
Sour cream
Guacamole
Limes

1. Put the sliced peppers, onions, and chicken in the slow cooker. Top chicken with taco seasoning then add in garlic, tomatoes and lime juice. Cook on high for 4 hours.

2. Remove chicken and shred with two forks. Turn the slow cooker down to low. Place the shredded chicken back into the slow cooker and cook for a few minutes until ready to serve.

3. Serve chicken fajitas on flour tortillas then top with sour cream, guacamole, shredded cheese, and a squeeze of lime, if desired.

Photo: Meghan Bassett

# Slow Cooker Chicken Burrito Bowl

*By Meghan Bassett*

*I don't really like how rice combined with other ingredients turns out in the slow cooker. I therefore either use leftover rice, or even store-bought pre-cooked rice. Heating it up and adding flavorings to it really spruces it up and makes it a wonderful base for burrito bowls. Alternatively, skip the rice and use lettuce for a delicious taco salad.*

**Yield:** 4-6 servings

**Prep Time:** 10 minutes

**Cook Time:** 4 hours

**Total Time:** 4 hours, 10 minutes

**Ingredients:**

*Slow Cooker Chicken:*
- 3 lbs. boneless skinless chicken breasts or thighs or a mixture
- 1/2 cup chicken stock
- 1 (14.5 oz.) can diced tomatoes with juice
- 1 tsp. garlic powder
- 1 tsp. chili powder
- 1/2 tsp. onion powder
- 1/2 tsp. cumin
- 1/2 tsp. cayenne pepper
- 1/2 tsp. salt
- 1/2 tsp. pepper

*Cilantro Rice:*
- 2 cups cooked rice
- 1 and 1/2 tsp. lime juice
- 1 tsp. freshly chopped cilantro

*Burrito Bowls:*
- 1 cup black beans, drained
- 1 avocado, peeled, pitted and sliced
- 1 cup pico de gallo
- 2/3 cup shredded Mexican style cheese
- Optional toppings: salsa, sour cream, freshly chopped cilantro

1. In the insert of a slow cooker, add chicken, chicken stock, diced tomatoes, garlic powder, chili powder, onion powder, cumin, cayenne pepper, salt, and pepper. Stir to combine.

2. Cook on high for 3 to 4 hours. Transfer chicken from the slow cooker to a bowl. Shred the meat using two forks. Set aside.

3. To make the rice, stir together warmed up cooked rice with lime juice and cilantro. Set aside.

4. To assemble the bowls, start with a base of cilantro lime rice. Top with shredded chicken, black beans, pico de gallo, Mexican style cheese, and avocado. Serve with salsa, sour cream, and additional freshly chopped cilantro.

# Slow Cooker Chicken and Sausage Meatballs

*By Tawnie Kroll*

*These meatballs are started in the oven so that they get a bit of a crust and to firm them up. If you put them straight into the slow cooker uncooked, they can more easily smoosh together and not hold their meatball shape. You can skip the oven step, just know that your meatballs might turn into a chunky meat sauce, which is also delicious, right?*

**Yield:** 22-28 meatballs

**Prep Time:** 20 minutes

**Cook Time:** 4 hours

**Total Time:** 4 hours, 20 minutes

**Ingredients:**
1 lb. ground chicken
1 lb. ground Italian sausage meat
36 oz. marinara sauce
1/2 cup Italian breadcrumbs
1/3 cup finely chopped onion
2 large eggs
2 Tbsp. whole milk
2 Tbsp. ketchup
1 Tbsp. Dijon mustard
2 tsp. Worcestershire sauce
1 tsp. Italian seasoning
1 tsp. salt
1/4 tsp. pepper
Cooking spray

1. Preheat oven to 450°F.

2. In a large bowl, mix breadcrumbs, milk, and eggs together. Add in ground chicken, sausage, and onion. Mix together using hands.

3. Make a well in the center of the meat mixture and add in ketchup, Dijon, Worcestershire, Italian seasoning, salt, and pepper. Incorporate ingredients together well using hands, but don't over-mix.

4. Spray a baking sheet with cooking spray.

5. Roll meat into balls (approximately 2 tablespoon sized balls).

6. Bake in the oven for 5 minutes on one side, flip and bake for another 5 minutes.

7. Pour enough sauce on the bottom of slow cooker to coat the bottom, then place meatballs in. Pour remaining marinara sauce over meatballs, cover with lid, and cook on low for 4 hours.

*Photo: Photostock*

# Slow Cooker White Chicken Chili

*By Sam Ellis*

*My favorite part of this chili is the smoked paprika. It gives it an earthy and smoky (obviously!) flavor that ties everything together.*

# Slow Cooker White Chicken Chili

*Continued from previous page*

**Yield:** 6-8 servings

**Prep Time:** 5 minutes

**Cook Time:** 4-6 hours

**Total Time:** 4-6 hours, 5 minutes

**Ingredients:**
1 and 1/2 lbs. boneless skinless chicken breasts, thighs, or ground chicken
1 small onion, chopped
2 cloves garlic, minced
4 cups low-sodium chicken stock
2 poblano peppers, seeded and finely chopped
1 (4.5 oz.) can chopped green chiles
1 tsp. cumin
1 tsp. oregano
1/2 tsp. coriander
1/2 tsp. smoked paprika
2 Tbsp. lime juice
1/2 tsp. salt
1/4 tsp. pepper
2 (15.5 oz.) cans cannellini beans, drained and rinsed
1 (15.25 oz.) can whole kernel corn, drained

1. Combine all ingredients except cannellini beans and corn in a slow cooker.

2. Cook on high for 4 hours or low for 6-7 hours.

3. With 30 minutes left, remove chicken breasts or thighs (if using) and shred with a fork. Return chicken to slow cooker.

4. Stir in cannellini beans and corn.

5. Stir. Cover for remaining 30 minutes.

# Slow Cooker Chicken and Dumplings

*By Jamie Silva*

*This one-pot dinner relies on some store-bought convenience foods to make cooking it a breeze. If you want to make it more from scratch, head to the Basics chapter for our homemade condensed soup recipe. You can also use fresh veggies instead of frozen. You'll just need to add them in sooner. Finally, you can absolutely make your own biscuit dough. But really, I'm exhausted thinking about this recipe now. I think I'll stick with the canned dough!*

**Yield:** 8 servings

**Prep Time:** 10 minutes

**Cook Time:** 6 hours

**Total Time:** 6 hours, 10 minutes

**Ingredients:**
4 boneless skinless chicken breast halves
2 Tbsp. unsalted butter
1 (10.75 oz.) can condensed cream of chicken soup
1 cup low-sodium chicken stock
1 medium onion, chopped
1/2 tsp. salt
1/4 tsp. pepper
1 (10 oz.) package refrigerated biscuit dough
2 cups frozen mixed vegetables (optional)

1. Place the chicken, butter, soup, chicken stock, onion, salt, and pepper in a slow cooker.

2. Cover and cook for 4 hours on high.

3. After 4 hours, tear biscuit dough into 2-inch pieces and place in a single layer in the liquid in the slow cooker. Cook until the dough is no longer raw in the center, approximately 1 to 1.5 hours, flipping biscuits over halfway through.

4. Stir in frozen vegetables (if using). Continue to cook for 30 more minutes before serving.

# Slow Cooker Coq au Vin

*By Tawnie Kroll*

Here is one of those slow cooker recipes that has you pre-cook a few ingredients before adding them to the slow cooker. If you're short on time (or just feeling beautifully lazy, you're allowed!) you can skip most of that. Here's what you do. Cook the bacon in the microwave on a plate topped with paper towel 30 seconds at a time until it's firm. Add that to the slow cooker and top with the completely raw chicken thighs. Add the butter to the slow cooker, along with the mushrooms, carrots, celery, and garlic. Skip the pearl onions and use a large onion cut into eighths instead. If you don't want to have to make a rice or potato side dish later, you can also add 2 large potatoes (diced) to the mix. Continue with step #4 of the recipe. Now, if you want to know if it will be the same, the answer is no. Precooking chicken and vegetables adds caramelization which adds flavor. Precooking vegetables also takes out some of their more astringent flavors. However, it will be barely noticeable and you will have saved so much time.

**Yield:** 4-6 servings

**Prep Time:** 30 minutes

**Cook Time:** 3-6 hours

**Total Time:** 3-6 hours, 30 minutes

**Ingredients:**
6 slices bacon, thick cut, chopped into 1/2-inch pieces
6 boneless skinless chicken thighs
2 Tbsp. unsalted butter
12 oz. button mushrooms, quartered
2 large carrots, chopped
2 celery ribs, chopped
5 oz. pearl onions, blanched & peeled
2 cloves garlic, minced
1 and 1/4 cups low-sodium chicken stock
1 and 1/2 cups red wine (ideally, a pinot noir)
1 tsp. ground thyme
2 fresh bay leaves
1 sprig rosemary, finely chopped
Salt and pepper to taste
Parsley for garnish

1. Heat a medium-sized heavy-duty skillet over medium heat and add the chopped bacon. Cook for about 6-7 minutes, removing from heat before bacon gets too crispy. Place bacon and drippings in bottom of slow cooker.

2. In a separate nonstick skillet over medium-high heat, melt 2 tablespoons butter and add the skinless chicken thighs. Cook until chicken is lightly browned on each side, about 3 minutes. Place chicken in slow cooker right on top of bacon.

3. Then, add mushrooms to skillet and cook for 3 minutes over medium heat. Then add in carrots, celery, pearl onions, and garlic. Cook these vegetables for another 5 minutes and transfer to the slow cooker.

4. In the slow cooker add in stock, red wine, thyme, bay leaves, rosemary, salt, and pepper. Cover and cook on high for 3 hours or on low for 6-7. Garnish with fresh parsley.

# Slow Cooker Chicken Parmesan

*Chicken Parmesan done in the slow cooker has all the flavors of a traditional version with much less work. The secret is a crunchy panko breadcrumb topping that you add before serving.*

**Yield:** 6 servings

**Prep Time:** 10 minutes

**Cook Time:** 4-6 hours

**Total Time:** 4-6 hours, 10 minutes

**Ingredients:**
3 Tbsp. cornstarch
3 Tbsp. water
1 (24 oz.) jar tomato sauce
6 boneless skinless chicken thighs
Salt and pepper
6 oz. mozzarella cheese, shredded, divided
2 oz. Parmesan cheese, grated, divided
1/2 cup panko breadcrumbs
1 Tbsp. olive oil

1. In a medium bowl combine cornstarch and water until smooth. Add tomato sauce and stir to combine.

2. Add enough of the sauce to just cover the bottom of the slow cooker. Keeping the chicken rolled up just as it is in its package, arrange it in the slow cooker over the tomato sauce in a single layer. Sprinkle lightly with salt and pepper. Top with half of the mozzarella cheese and half of the parmesan cheese.

3. Drizzle with remaining tomato sauce and cook until chicken is cook through, 3-4 hours on high, 6-8 hours on low.

4. Once the chicken is cooked, preheat the broiler (you're going to use it to quickly toast breadcrumbs to make a crunchy topping for your slow cooker chicken). Remove the lid from the slow cooker. Spoon off any fat that has accumulated at the top of the sauce. Discard. Sprinkle contents of slow cooker with remaining mozzarella. Put lid back on and cook just until cheese has melted.

5. On a baking sheet combine the panko breadcrumbs, olive oil, and a pinch each of salt and pepper. Put under the broiler just until browned a bit, 2-3 minutes.

6. Serve the chicken and sauce topped with the breadcrumbs and with the remaining Parmesan cheese.

# Slow Cooker Chicken Stroganoff

*There's nothing tastier than stroganoff made in the slow cooker. Everything goes in, and deliciousness comes out! Serve over boiled egg noodles, rice, mashed potatoes, or thick slices of bread.*

**Yield:** 6 servings

**Prep Time:** 10 minutes

**Cook Time:** 5-8 hours

**Total Time:** 5-8 hours, 10 minutes

**Ingredients:**
1 medium onion, chopped
16 oz. sliced mushrooms
2 lbs. boneless skinless chicken thighs, cut into 2-inch chunks
2 cloves garlic, minced
1/2 tsp. salt
1/4 tsp. pepper
1 cup plus 6 Tbsp. low-sodium chicken stock, divided
3 Tbsp. cornstarch
1/2 cup sour cream
1 Tbsp. Dijon mustard (optional)

1. Put the onions, mushrooms, and chicken into a slow cooker.

2. Scatter garlic over top and sprinkle with salt and pepper.

3. Pour over 1 cup of the chicken stock.

4. Cook until meat is cooked through to 165°F, on high for 4-5 hours or on low for 6-8 hours. Skim off the fat, if desired.

5. Mix together corn starch with remaining 6 tablespoons of stock. Stir until smooth.

6. Pour the cornstarch mixture into the slow cooker. Stir. Cook for 30 more minutes to thicken the sauce.

7. Turn off slow cooker and stir in sour cream. Taste, add more salt and pepper, if desired. Stir in mustard for some tang, if desired.

Photo: Jamie Silva

# Slow Cooker Chicken Stuffed Peppers

*By Jamie Silva*

*These stuffed peppers call for cooked rice. You can use leftover rice or store-bought pre-cooked rice. If neither of those options appeals to you, you can use raw riced cauliflower. Add extra though because it's going to shrink down as it cooks.*

# Slow Cooker Chicken Stuffed Peppers

*Continued from previous page*

**Yield:** 6 servings

**Prep Time:** 10 minutes

**Cook Time:** 2 hours, 40 minutes

**Total Time:** 2 hours, 50 minutes

**Ingredients:**

6 large bell peppers, tops sliced off, stemmed and seeded
1 lb. ground chicken
1 and 1/2 cups cooked rice
1 (15 oz.) can corn kernels, drained
1 (15 oz.) can black beans, drained and rinsed
1 cup salsa
1 tsp. cumin
1 tsp. chili powder
1 tsp. salt
1/4 tsp. pepper
3/4 cup shredded cheese

1. In a large bowl, combine ground chicken, rice, corn, black beans, salsa, cumin, chili powder, salt, and pepper.

2. Divide filling between the bell peppers.

3. Place bell peppers in the slow cooker in a single layer.

4. Cover and cook on high for 2.5 hours, or until the peppers are tender and the chicken is cooked through to 165°F in the middle on an instant read thermometer.

5. Top each pepper with 2 tablespoons of shredded cheese. Cover slow cooker. Cook until cheese has melted, about 10 minutes.

# Slow Cooker Chicken Teriyaki

*By Ellie O'Brien*

*The key to this dish is the teriyaki sauce, a savory teriyaki made with honey, soy sauce, rice wine vinegar, and ginger. The sauce comes together in two parts. First it's cooked with the chicken in the slow cooker. This keeps the chicken moist and gives it a ton of flavor. Then it's thickened with cornstarch over the stove before being added back to the chicken.*

**Yield:** 4-6 servings

**Prep Time:** 10 minutes

**Cook Time:** 4 hours

**Total Time:** 4 hours, 10 minutes

**Ingredients:**
- 2 lbs. boneless skinless chicken breasts or thighs or a mixture
- 1/2 cup honey
- 1/2 cup soy sauce
- 1/4 cup rice wine vinegar
- 1/2 tsp. ground ginger
- 1/4 tsp. pepper
- 3 cloves garlic, minced
- 1 small onion, chopped
- 1/4 cup cold water
- 3 Tbsp. cornstarch
- 1 and 1/2 cups cooked white rice
- 2 green onions, chopped

1. Add chicken to the bottom of the slow cooker in a single layer.
2. In a small bowl, whisk together honey, soy sauce, rice wine vinegar, ginger, pepper, garlic, and onion. Pour over the chicken and place cover on slow cooker.
3. Set slow cooker to low for 4 hours, and cook until internal temperature of the chicken reaches 165°F. Begin checking at 3 hours.
4. Once cooked, transfer chicken to a large bowl and shred using two forks.
5. Transfer the sauce from the slow cooker into a medium pot.
6. In a small bowl, whisk water and cornstarch together until the cornstarch is dissolved. Add the cornstarch mixture to the sauce, whisking to combine.
7. Bring to a boil over medium-high heat and let it boil until thickened, 1-2 minutes. Remove from heat and pour over the shredded chicken. Toss to combine.
8. Serve with white rice and top with sliced green onions.

Photo: Meghan Bassett

# Slow Cooker Orange Chicken

*By Meghan Bassett*

*I like to serve this chicken dish over white rice. If you want something even quicker though, try serving it with fine rice noodles (also called rice sticks or rice vermicelli), which cooks really quickly. To cook fine rice noodles, put them in a large bowl with a tablespoon of vegetable oil. Cover them completely with boiling water and then let sit for a minute or two. Once they're softened, drain off the water. Drizzle with another teaspoon of vegetable oil to stop them from sticking to each other. You can serve them cold, at room temperature, or cover with boiling water again just for 30 seconds to reheat.*

**Yield:** 4 servings

**Prep Time:** 10 minutes

**Cook Time:** 2 hours

**Total Time:** 2 hours, 10 minutes

**Ingredients:**
2 Tbsp. olive oil
2 lbs. boneless skinless chicken breasts or thighs, cut into 1-inch cubes
1/3 cup cornstarch
1/2 tsp. salt
1/2 tsp. pepper
1 cup orange marmalade
1 Tbsp. brown sugar
1/3 cup soy sauce
1 Tbsp. rice wine vinegar
1 and 1/2 tsp. sesame oil
1 tsp. ground ginger
1 tsp. garlic powder
1/2 tsp. cumin powder
1/2 tsp. cayenne pepper
1/2 tsp. sesame seeds (optional)
1 green onion, chopped (optional)

1. Add 1 tablespoon olive oil to the bottom of a slow cooker.
2. In a ziptop bag, combine chicken, cornstarch, salt, and pepper. Shake to coat the chicken pieces.
3. Add chicken to the slow cooker.
4. In a medium bowl, whisk together orange marmalade, brown sugar, soy sauce, rice wine vinegar, sesame oil, ground ginger, garlic powder, cumin powder, and cayenne pepper until well combined.
5. Pour sauce over chicken and stir to coat.
6. Cook on high for 2 hours.
7. Garnish with sesame seeds and sliced green onion, if desired.

# Slow Cooker Chicken with 40 Cloves of Garlic

*By Ellie O'Brien*

*This recipe is traditionally made in the oven and cooked for 1-2 hours. We're doing it more slowly in the slow cooker. We've opted for chicken thighs here instead of a whole chicken so you don't have to cut it into pieces after it's done cooking.*

**Yield:** 4-6 servings

**Prep Time:** 10 minutes

**Cook Time:** 8 hours

**Total Time:** 8 hours, 10 minutes

**Ingredients:**
Cooking spray
1 lemon, divided
2 cups low-sodium chicken stock
3 Tbsp. all-purpose flour
2 Tbsp. unsalted butter, melted and cooled
1 and 1/2 lbs. boneless and skinless chicken thighs
2 tsp. salt, divided
1/2 tsp. pepper, divided
1 and 1/2 lbs. medium red potatoes, quartered
40 garlic cloves, peeled
15 fresh thyme sprigs

1. Spray the slow cooker with cooking spray.

2. Cut the lemon in half. Juice half of it into a small bowl. Cut the other half into wedges. Set wedges aside for serving.

3. To the lemon juice add the stock, flour, and butter. Whisk to combine. Pour mixture into the slow cooker.

4. Use 1 teaspoon of the salt and 1/2 teaspoon of pepper to season the chicken thighs. Place them into the slow cooker.

5. Add potatoes, garlic, and thyme over the chicken. Cook on low for 6-8 hours or high for 3-4 hours.

6. Discard thyme and arrange potatoes and garlic on a platter. Top with chicken and season with remaining salt and pepper. Serve with the lemon wedges on the side.

# Slow Cooker Lemon Chicken

*By Ellie O'Brien*

*Browning the chicken in a frying pan before putting it into the slow cooker adds an extra level of flavor (from the caramelization of the meat) and color. If you have an electric multicooker, you can brown the chicken in there and then set it to the slow cooker function, thus dirtying one less pan. Or, if you're in a hurry, you can skip the browning step. The recipe will still work it will just be ever so slightly less good.*

**Yield:** 4 servings

**Prep Time:** 15 minutes

**Cook Time:** 4 hours

**Total Time:** 4 hours, 15 minutes

**Ingredients:**
4 boneless skinless chicken breasts or thighs
1 tsp. dried oregano
3/4 tsp. salt
1/2 tsp. pepper
2 Tbsp. olive oil
1 cup low-sodium chicken stock
2 Tbsp. lemon juice
2 garlic cloves, minced

1. Spray the slow cooker with cooking spray.

2. In a small bowl mix together oregano, salt, and pepper. Rub mixture over the chicken.

3. Heat skillet to medium heat and add 1 tablespoon olive oil. Sear 2 chicken pieces until brown — 2 minutes per side. Repeat with the remaining olive oil and chicken. Add chicken to slow cooker.

4. Mix together chicken stock, lemon juice, and garlic. Pour over chicken.

5. Cook on low for 3.5 hours. Baste chicken with juices and continue cooking for an additional 30 minutes.

# Slow Cooker Chicken Wings

*By Brittany Poulson*

*Cooking wings in the slow cookers makes the meat juicy and tender. Since the sauce is in there while they cook, it really infuses into the wings as well. Once they're done cooking, transfer them to a pan under the broiler to crisp them up. This recipe is great for game day because you're cooking 4 pounds of wings all at once.*

**Yield:** 8 servings

**Prep Time:** 15 minutes

**Cook Time:** 1 hour, 30 minutes

**Total Time:** 1 hour, 45 minutes

**Ingredients:**
4 lbs. fresh whole chicken wings, cut into wingettes and drumettes. Discard tips or use for a stock.
3/4 cup hot sauce
1/2 cup unsalted butter
1 Tbsp. distilled white vinegar
1/2 tsp. Worcestershire sauce
1/4 tsp. garlic powder
1/8 tsp. salt

1. Spray slow cooker with cooking spray. Add wings.

2. Add the remaining ingredients to a small pot. Cook over medium heat, stirring occasionally, until all the ingredients are blended together and the sauce is bubbling, about 5 minutes. Remove from heat and pour over the wings in the slow cooker.

3. Place the lid on the slow cooker, turn on high and cook for 2 hours (or on low for about 3-4 hours) or until wings are fully cooked to an internal temp of 165°F.

4. Prepare baking sheet by placing an oven-safe rack on top. When the wings are fully cooked transfer wings to rack. Brush sauce from the slow cooker onto the wing pieces. Place the baking sheet in the oven and broil on high until the wings are nice and crispy, about 3-4 minutes. Turn wings over and broil an additional 2 minutes on the opposite side. Watch them carefully so they don't burn. Remove from oven, brush with additional sauce if desired.

# CHAPTER 6
# ONE-POT OR PAN DINNERS

Baked Chicken with Tomatoes, Basil, and Chilis
Chicken with Butternut Squash and Sage
Spatchcock Chicken with Potatoes, Asparagus, and Lemon
One Pan Chicken with Broccoli and Cheese
BLT Chicken
Unstuffed Chicken Cordon Bleu
Cheesy Chicken and Rice Casserole
One Pot Cheesy Chicken Pasta Dinner
One Pot Chicken, Broccoli, and Cheese Pasta Dinner
No-Boil Pasta Bake with Chicken Sausage
One Pot Cheesy Chicken and Rice
One Pot Mexican Chicken and Rice Bowls
One Pot Chicken Gallo Pinto (Costa Rican Rice and Beans)
One Pan Chickpea and Sausage Dinner
One Pot Cozy Barley Chicken Dinner
Chicken Parm One Skillet Dinner
Chicken Fried Cauliflower Rice
One Pot Chicken Alfredo
Chicken Porcupine Meatballs
One Pot Pasta with Chicken, Brussels Sprouts, and Parm
Chicken and Riced Cauliflower Bowls with Hummus Dressing
Quick Chicken and Cheese Stuffed Peppers
Greek Chicken Stuffed Peppers

Buffalo Chicken Stuffed Peppers
Tater Tot Casserole with Chicken
Quickest Chicken Chili
Cream of Chicken Soup
Hearty Chicken and Farro Soup
Chicken Stew
Breakfast Sliders with Chicken Sausage for a Crowd
Sweet Potato and Sausage Hash
Cranberry Chicken Meatballs
Grape Jelly Chicken Meatballs

# Baked Chicken with Tomatoes, Basil, and Chilis

*This is one of my all-time favorite recipes. The chicken ends up juicy, the tomatoes break down into a bit of a sauce, and the flavors from the basil and red chili peppers are intense and wonderful.*

**Yield:** 4-6 servings

**Prep Time:** 6 minutes

**Cook Time:** 45 minutes

**Total Time:** 51 minutes

**Ingredients:**
6 to 8 bone-in chicken thighs
1 pint grape tomatoes
1–2 red chilis, sliced
15 large basil leaves (torn up a bit) plus 10-12 smaller ones for garnish
1 Tbsp. olive oil
1 tsp. salt
1/2 tsp. pepper

1. Preheat oven to 425°F.
2. Arrange chicken pieces in a single layer in a large rimmed pan or baking dish. Topple in the tomatoes. Scatter everything with the chili slices and the 15 large basil leaves. Drizzle with the olive oil and sprinkle with salt and pepper.
3. Bake until chicken is cooked through, about 40-45 minutes. The chilis and basil leaves will be blackened. But they taste good, don't worry. Scatter the remaining 10-12 basil leaves over top before serving.

# Chicken with Butternut Squash and Sage

*I have an oversized cast iron skillet that I love for baking this kind of recipe. It's so large that it fits eveything easily and gives it all room to brown a bit, and the black of the iron really sets off the colors in the dish.*

**Yield:** 4 servings

**Prep Time:** 15 minutes

**Cook Time:** 45 minutes

**Total Time:** 1 hour

**Ingredients:**
1 (2 lb.) butternut squash
14 medium-sized fresh sage leaves, divided
2 Tbsp. unsalted butter, melted
8 chicken drumsticks, with or without skin
1 tsp. vegetable oil
1/2 tsp. salt
1/4 tsp. pepper

1. Preheat oven to 425°F.

2. Peel the squash and trim 1/4-inch off of the top and bottom. Discard. Cut squash in half lengthwise. Scoop out seeds and discard (or you can set them aside to wash and roast separately as you would pumpkin seeds). Cut into cubes (roughly 1/2 to 3/4 inches each).

3. Transfer squash cubes to a large bowl. Tear 10 sage leaves in half and add them along with the butter. Toss to coat.

4. Put the chicken in a single layer in a large pan. Drizzle it with the oil and rub it around to coat.

5. Arrange squash and sage around the chicken pieces (not over the chicken) trying to keep the sage up on top so that it will toast nicely. Sprinkle everything with the salt and pepper.

6. Bake until chicken is cooked through to 165°F on an instant read thermometer and squash is soft, about 45 minutes.

7. Garnish with remaining 4 sage leaves.

# Spatchcock Chicken with Potatoes, Asparagus, and Lemon

*Spatchcocking a chicken is a technique where you remove the back bone so that you can make the chicken flat instead of rounded. This reduces the cooking time and results in more even cooking for all parts of the chicken.*

# Spatchcock Chicken with Potatoes, Asparagus, and Lemon

*Continued from previous page*

**Yield:** 4 servings

**Prep Time:** 15 minutes

**Cook Time:** 50 minutes

**Total Time:** 1 hour, 5 minutes

**Ingredients:**
Olive oil
2 lemons, sliced 1/4-inch thick
Salt
Pepper
1 (4lb.) chicken
28 oz. small red potatoes (if any are larger than 1 and 1/2-inches, cut those ones in half)
1/2 tsp. dried thyme leaves
1 lb. asparagus, trimmed

1. Preheat oven to 425°F.

2. Rub a large (18"x 13") rimmed pan with 1 teaspoon olive oil. Add the lemon slices in a single non-overlapping layer. Sprinkle with 1/4 teaspoon salt and 1/4 teaspoon pepper.

3. Take your chicken and flip it so that it's breast-side-down. Locate the backbone. Using sharp kitchen shears, cut all along one side of the backbone (you'll be going through some little ribs so press hard to cut). Then cut along the other side of the backbone, thus removing the backbone completely. Discard the backbone or save it for making stock.

4. Open the chicken up so that it is one wide piece. Flip it breast-side-up. Push down on it all over with the palms of your hands to flatten it to a more even thickness.

5. Transfer the chicken to the middle of the pan, lying it over some of the lemon slices.

6. In a medium bowl toss together the potatoes with 2 teaspoons of olive oil, the thyme, 1/2 teaspoon of salt, and 1/4 teaspoon of pepper. Scatter the potatoes on the pan around the chicken. Put the pan into the preheated oven for 30 minutes.

7. Meanwhile, put the asparagus into the bowl that the potatoes were in. Add 1/2 teaspoon olive oil, 1/4 teaspoon salt, and 1/4 teaspoon pepper. Once the chicken and potatoes have roasted for 30 minutes remove the pan from the oven and tuck the asparagus in around the potatoes and chicken. You want everything to still be in a single layer over the lemon slices. Put the pan back into the oven until an instant read thermometer placed into the middle of a breast and into the middle of a thigh reads 165°F, 20-30 minutes more. Let rest for 10 minutes before serving.

# One Pan Chicken with Broccoli and Cheese

*I love broccoli and cheese together. In this recipe, the cheese is mixed with bread crumbs and they crisp up together on the broccoli florets.*

**Yield:** 4 servings

**Prep Time:** 10 minutes

**Cook Time:** 40 minutes

**Total Time:** 50 minutes

**Ingredients:**
- 6 to 8 bone-in skinless chicken thighs
- Salt
- Pepper
- 4 sprigs of fresh thyme (or 1/2 tsp. dried thyme leaves)
- 1 (1 and 1/2 lb.) head of broccoli
- 1/2 cup panko breadcrumbs
- 1 cup shredded cheddar cheese
- 2 Tbsp. olive oil

1. Preheat oven to 350°F.
2. Lightly oil a large skillet or rimmed baking dish. Arrange the chicken thighs in the skillet in a single layer.
3. Sprinkle lightly with salt and pepper. Put 1/2 of a sprig of thyme on each chicken piece (or use a pinch of dried thyme leaves per piece).
4. Break the florets off of the broccoli. If you'd like, peel and chop the stalks to include them also. Arrange broccoli florets and chopped peeled stalks around chicken pieces.
5. In a medium bowl toss together the bread crumbs, cheddar, olive oil, 1/4 teaspoon salt, and 1/4 teaspoon coarse pepper.
6. Arrange bread crumb mixture over the broccoli in the pan. It's okay if some gets on the chicken but concentrate on the broccoli. Bake until chicken is cooked through to 165°F on an instant read thermometer, 40-50 minutes.

# BLT Chicken

*This recipe has all the flavors of a BLT sandwich but as a chicken dinner. The bonus is that the bacon cooks on top of the chicken and tomatoes which gives everything a delicious, salty, bacony flavor. The iceburg lettuce counters that richness with some fresh crunch.*

**Yield:** 4-5 servings

**Prep Time:** 5 minutes

**Cook Time:** 40 minutes

**Total Time:** 45 minutes

**Ingredients:**
8–10 skinless bone-in chicken thighs
Salt
Pepper
8–10 tomato slices, sliced 1/4-inch thick (about 2 tomatoes)
4–5 bacon slices, cut in half
1 head of iceberg lettuce, shredded
1/4 cup mayonnaise

1. Preheat oven to 425°F.
2. Lightly oil a rimmed baking sheet. Put in chicken thighs. Season lightly with salt and pepper. Top each with a tomato slice and half slice of bacon.
3. Bake for 40–45 minutes, until bacon is crisp and chicken is cooked through.
4. Meanwhile, divide lettuce between dinner plates.
5. Put mayonnaise in a ziptop bag. Cut a tiny corner off of the bag. Drizzle over lettuce. Top with the cooked chicken.

# Unstuffed Chicken Cordon Bleu

*This version of Chicken Cordon Bleu comes together more quickly than the traditional way. Instead of stuffing the chicken pieces, you lay everything on top of the chicken, which really saves time. The ham is the bottom layer though, which is brilliant because it then catches any of the melted cheese that drips off of the chicken. Note that this recipe calls for boneless, skinless chicken thighs. You can use breasts instead but if they're too big to fit on the ham, cut them in half.*

**Yield:** 4 servings

**Prep Time:** 10 minutes

**Cook Time:** 20 minutes

**Total Time:** 30 minutes

**Ingredients:**
2 tsp. olive oil, divided
1/2 cup panko bread crumbs
1/8 tsp. salt
1/8 tsp. pepper
1/4 tsp. garlic powder
4 (1 oz.) slices baked or honey ham
4 boneless skinless chicken thighs
4 (1 oz.) slices Swiss cheese
1 large tomato, sliced

1. Preheat the oven to 400°F. Rub a medium-sized baking sheet with 1 teaspoon of the olive oil.

2. In a medium bowl combine the bread crumbs, salt, pepper, garlic powder, and the remaining teaspoon of olive oil. Set aside.

3. Lay the 4 slices of ham out on the baking sheet in a non-overlapping layer. Take a chicken thigh and unroll it so that it is a flat single-layered piece. Put it on top of one of the slices of ham. Repeat with the remaining chicken thighs.

4. Top each chicken thigh with a slice of cheese. Top cheese with tomato and then with bread crumb mixture.

5. Bake until chicken is cooked through to 165°F on an instant read thermometer, and bread crumbs are browned, about 20 minutes.

6. In case any cheese has browned and stuck to the pan, use a metal spatula to really get under it. You want all that gooey, chewy, browned cheese for sure!

# Cheesy Chicken and Rice Casserole

*By Allie Doran*

This casserole is perfect for when you have leftover chicken and rice. If you don't, you can use any cooked chicken and you can use store-bought cooked rice. Note that the recipe calls for canned condensed cream of chicken soup but if you want to make this recipe less processed, you'll find a recipe for homemade condensed soup in Chapter 1.

**Yield:** 6 servings

**Prep Time:** 10 minutes

**Cook Time:** 25 minutes

**Total Time:** 35 minutes

**Ingredients:**

1 small onion, chopped
12 oz. frozen, mixed vegetables, defrosted
2 cups chopped cooked chicken
2 cups cooked brown rice
2 (10.5 oz.) cans condensed cream of chicken soup
2 cups shredded cheddar cheese, divided
2 Tbsp. unsalted butter, melted

1. Preheat the oven to 375°F.
2. To a large bowl add the onion, vegetables, chicken, brown rice, cream of chicken soup, 1 cup of the cheese, and the butter. Mix well.
3. Spoon the mixture into a greased 9"×13" casserole dish and top with the remaining 1 cup of cheese.
4. Pop the dish into the oven for 25 minutes, or until heated through and the cheese is bubbling and browned.

# One Pot Cheesy Chicken Pasta Dinner

*The pasta for this recipe is cooked in cream and tomatoes so the pasta itself is rich and tasty. Then you add some cheese, which melts into the remaining cream and tomatoes to become the sauce. So much flavor and only one pot to wash afterwords!*

**Yield:** 4 servings

**Prep Time:** 5 minutes

**Cook Time:** 25 minutes

**Total Time:** 30 minutes

**Ingredients:**
2 Tbsp. olive oil, divided
1 pound chicken breasts or thighs or a mixture, cut into 1/2-inch pieces
1 tsp. salt, divided
1/4 tsp. black pepper
1 small onion, chopped
2 cloves garlic, minced
1 tsp. Italian seasoning
1 (14.5 oz.) can diced tomatoes, drained
3 and 1/2 cups low-sodium chicken stock, divided
1 cup heavy cream
12 oz. penne pasta
1 cup mozzarella cheese
1/2 cup shredded Parmesan, divided

1. In a large pot heat 1 tablespoon of the olive oil over medium heat.

2. Sprinkle chicken with salt and pepper. Add chicken to pot. Cook stirring occasionally until cooked through, 5-7 minutes. Transfer chicken to a plate. Cover with aluminum foil. Set aside.

3. Return pot to the heat. Add the remaining 1 tablespoon of oil and the onion. Cook stirring occasionally until onion is softened, 2-3 minutes.

4. Add Italian seasoning and garlic. Stir and cook for 30 seconds.

5. Add 3 cups of the stock, diced tomatoes, cream, and 1/2 teaspoon salt. Increase heat to high and bring to a boil while stirring often.

6. Add penne. Return to a boil. Reduce heat to a simmer and cook stirring occasionally until pasta is to your desired tenderness, 13-15 minutes. If the pasta becomes dry, add the remaining 1/2 cup of stock.

7. Add the chicken back to skillet along with the mozzarella and 1/4 cup of the Parmesan. Stir to melt cheese.

8. Serve with more Parmesan to garnish.

# One Pot Chicken, Broccoli, and Cheese Pasta Dinner

*Broccoli, cheddar, chicken, and crunchy panko breadcrumbs all go together so well that they just had to be put into a pasta dish together.*

**Yield:** 4 servings

**Prep Time:** 5 minutes

**Cook Time:** 25 minutes

**Total Time:** 30 minutes

**Ingredients:**
2 Tbsp. olive oil, divided
1 small onion, chopped
2 cloves garlic, minced
1 pound ground chicken
1 tsp. salt, divided
1/4 tsp. pepper
3 and 1/2 cups low-sodium chicken stock
1 cup heavy cream
12 oz. rotini pasta
2 cups broccoli florets
1 cup shredded cheddar cheese
1/2 cup panko breadcrumbs

1. In a large oven-safe pot, heat 1 tablespoon of the olive oil over medium heat.

2. Add onion and cook until softened, 2-3 minutes. Stir in garlic and cook while stirring for 30 seconds.

3. Add ground chicken, salt, and pepper. Cook stirring occasionally until cooked through, 5-6 minutes. Transfer chicken and onion mixture to a plate. Cover with aluminum foil. Set aside.

4. Return pot to the heat.

5. Add the stock, cream, and 1/2 teaspoon salt. Increase heat to high and bring to a boil while stirring often.

6. Add rotini. Return to a boil. Reduce heat to a simmer and cook stirring occasionally for 8 minutes. Add the broccoli. Stir. Continue to cook until pasta and broccoli are tender, 5-7 minutes more.

7. Meanwhile, combine the panko with the remaining tablespoon of olive oil and turn on the broiler.

8. Once the pasta is cooked, add the chicken back to skillet along with the cheddar cheese. Stir to melt cheese.

9. Sprinkle top with the panko and put under the broiler until browned, 2-4 minutes.

# No-Boil Pasta Bake with Chicken Sausage

This pasta bake is done in one pan and doesn't require you to even boil the pasta first. It's amazing how delicious it is when you literally only need to spend 5 minutes prepping it. This one is going to save your weeknights for sure! Note: When you mix together milk with something acidic like tomatoes and heat it up, sometimes it can curdle. I've found that the higher content of whole milk makes this less likely here so don't use fat-free milk in its place in this recipe.

# No-Boil Pasta Bake with Chicken Sausage

*Continued from previous page*

**Yield:** 4 servings

**Prep Time:** 5 minutes

**Cook Time:** 1 hour, 10 minutes

**Total Time:** 1 hour, 15 minutes

**Ingredients:**

8 oz. uncooked dried pasta shells

12 oz. (4 links) fully cooked chicken sausage (Asiago flavored, if possible), sliced thinly

1 (28 oz.) can diced tomatoes with the juice

2 cups shredded mozzarella, divided

1/2 tsp. garlic powder

1/2 tsp. salt

1/4 tsp. pepper

2 cups whole milk

Heavy duty aluminum foil

1/2 cup shredded Parmesan cheese

1. Preheat oven to 400°F. Grease a 2 and 1/2 to 3 quart shallow casserole dish with olive oil.

2. To the casserole dish add the uncooked pasta, sausage, diced tomatoes with juice, 1 cup of the mozzarella cheese, garlic powder, salt, and pepper. Stir.

3. Pour the milk over top and make sure that all of the pasta is submerged.

4. Cover with two layers of aluminum foil and make sure it is very well sealed.

5. Bake until the pasta is tender, 50-60 minutes.

6. Remove from oven and sprinkle with remaining mozzarella and the Parmesan. Return to oven uncovered just until cheese has melted, 5 minutes.

7. Remove from oven. Let the pasta bake rest for 15 minutes uncovered before serving. This is important because the sauce really thickens up in this time.

# One Pot Cheesy Chicken and Rice

*The heat from the the rice melts the cheese in this deliciously quick one pot chicken and rice dinner.*

**Yield:** 4-6 servings

**Prep Time:** 5 minutes

**Cook Time:** 25 minutes

**Total Time:** 30 minutes

**Ingredients:**
3 Tbsp. olive oil, divided
1 pound ground chicken
1 tsp. salt, divided
1 small onion, chopped
1 green bell pepper, chopped
2 cloves of garlic, minced
1 tsp. Italian seasoning or dry oregano
2 cups long grain white rice
3 and 1/2 cups water
1 cup shredded mozzarella
1/4 cup Parmesan cheese
1 pint grape or cherry tomatoes, halved

1. In a medium pot that has a lid warm 1 tablespoon of the olive oil over medium-high heat.

2. Add the ground chicken and 1/2 teaspoon of the salt. Cook stirring occasionally until cooked through, 5-7 minutes. Transfer to a plate, cover with aluminum foil, and set aside.

3. Warm another tablespoon of the olive oil in the same pot over medium-high heat.

4. Add the onion and bell pepper. Cook stirring occasionally for a few minutes until everything is nice and soft.

5. Add the garlic and the Italian seasoning and stir and cook for 30 seconds.

6. Stir in the rice, 1/2 teaspoon of the salt, and the water.

7. Increase heat to high and let it come to a boil. Reduce the heat to low, cover the pot and simmer it until the rice is tender, 16-20 minutes.

8. Stir in the cooked chicken, mozzarella, and Parmesan. Heat through for a minute.

9. Remove from heat and stir in the grape tomatoes.

# One Pot Mexican Chicken and Rice Bowls

*In this recipe you make a pico de gallo of tomatoes, green onion, avocado, and other ingredients. You can instead, however, keep all the ingredients separate and then allow everyone to choose which toppings they'd like to add.*

**Yield:** 6 servings

**Prep Time:** 5 minutes

**Cook Time:** 25 minutes

**Total Time:** 30 minutes

**Ingredients:**
1 Tbsp. olive oil
1 medium onion, sliced thinly
1 green bell pepper, sliced thinly
1 tsp. salt, divided
1/2 tsp. smoked paprika
1/4 tsp. cayenne pepper
1 lb. boneless skinless breasts or thighs, cut into 1/2-inch pieces
2 cups long grain white rice
1 Tbsp. chili powder
3 and 1/2 cups water
1 (14.5 oz) can black beans, drained and rinsed
1/2 cup frozen corn, defrosted
2 tomatoes, chopped
1 avocado, chopped
1 green onion, chopped
1/4 cup cilantro leaves, chopped
1 lime, cut into 8 wedges
3/4 cup shredded cheddar
1/2 cup sour cream

1. In a medium pot that has a lid warm 1 tablespoon of the olive oil over medium-high heat. Add the onions and peppers and cook stirring occasionally until starting to soften, 2-3 minutes.

2. Meanwhile, mix together 1/2 teaspoon of the salt, smoked paprika, and cayenne. Sprinkle it on the cut up chicken.

3. Add the chicken to the onions and peppers. Cook stirring occasionally until cooked through, 6-8 minutes. Transfer chicken and onion mixture to a plate. Cover with aluminum foil. Set aside.

4. Measure the rice, chili powder, and water into the pot. Add the remaining 1/2 teaspoon of salt. Stir.

5. Increase heat to high and let it come to a boil. Reduce the heat to low, cover the pot and simmer it until the rice is tender, 16-20 minutes.

6. Meanwhile, in a medium bowl combine the corn, tomatoes, avocado, green onions, and cilantro. Squeeze two of the lime wedges into the bowl. Stir. Taste and add salt if desired.

7. When the rice is cooked, remove from the heat and stir in the cooked chicken, onions, and peppers, and the black beans. Divide among 6 soup bowls.

8. Top each portion with some of the tomato mixture, cheddar, and sour cream. Serve with lime wedges on the side.

*Photo: Leigh Olson*

# One Pot Chicken Gallo Pinto (Costa Rican Rice and Beans)

This Costa Rican-inspired rice and beans dish has tons of flavor. It's sometimes served with a fried egg on top. Please put the fried egg on top even though you technically need to dirty an extra skillet. It's truly the best part!

# One Pot Chicken Gallo Pinto (Costa Rican Rice and Beans)

*Continued from previous page*

**Yield:** 4-6 servings

**Prep Time:** 5 minutes

**Cook Time:** 25 minutes

**Total Time:** 30 minutes

**Ingredients:**
3 Tbsp. olive oil, divided
1 lb. ground chicken
1 tsp. salt, divided
1/2 tsp. cumin
1 cup shredded carrots
1 small onion, chopped
1 red bell pepper, chopped
3 cloves of garlic, finely chopped
1 Tbsp. chili powder
2 cups long grain white rice
3 and 1/2 cups water
1 (14 oz.) can of chickpeas, drained and rinsed
4–6 eggs (optional)

1. In a medium pot that has a lid warm 1 tablespoon of the olive oil over medium-high heat.

2. Add the ground chicken, 1/2 teaspoon of the salt, and the cumin. Cook stirring occasionally until cooked through, 5-7 minutes. Transfer to a plate, cover with aluminum foil, and set aside.

3. Warm another tablespoon of the olive oil in the same pot over medium-high heat.

4. Add the carrots, onion, and bell pepper. Cook stirring occasionally for a few minutes until everything is nice and soft.

5. Add the garlic and the chili powder and stir and cook for 30 seconds.

6. Stir in the rice, 1/2 teaspoon of the salt, and the water.

7. Increase heat to high and let it come to a boil. Reduce the heat to low, cover the pot and simmer it until the rice is tender, 16-20 minutes.

8. Stir in the chickpeas and the cooked chicken. Heat through for a minute.

9. Remove the pot from the heat and replace the lid so that everything stays warm.

10. Optional: Heat the remaining 1 tablespoon of olive oil in a non-stick skillet over medium heat. Crack in the eggs. Cook to desired doneness (sunny side up and still runny is how I do it here).

11. Taste the rice mixture and add more salt if needed. Serve rice topped with fried eggs, if using.

# One Pan Chickpea and Sausage Dinner

*This is one of my favorite weeknight dinners. It's made in one pan and has very little prep to do before it goes in the oven just until heated through. All in under 30 minutes. And the combination of chicken sausage and chickpeas is so hearty and delicious.*

**Yield:** 4 servings

**Prep Time:** 5 minutes

**Cook Time:** 25 minutes

**Total Time:** 30 minutes

**Ingredients:**
- 2 (15 oz.) cans low-sodium chick peas, drained
- 1 (14 oz.) can diced tomatoes, drained
- 11 oz. (4 links) fully cooked flavored chicken sausages (like roasted pepper and asiago), sliced
- 1 small onion, chopped
- 1 red bell pepper, chopped
- 1 tsp. ground cumin
- 1/4 tsp. pepper
- 1/4 cup chopped fresh cilantro or chives (optional)

1. Preheat oven to 400°F.
2. In a 9"×13" baking dish combine chickpeas, tomatoes, sausage, onion, bell pepper, cumin, and pepper.
3. Cover with a tight-fitting lid or with foil and bake until heated through, 25 minutes.
4. Garnish with cilantro or chives (if using) before serving.

# One Pot Cozy Barley Chicken Dinner

*We usually think of barley as a soup ingredient but it's lovely as a pilaf or even as the main part of a dinner, just like we've used it here. Mushrooms and barley, especially with lots of garlic, are always a wonderful, and cozy, combination.*

**Yield:** 4 servings

**Prep Time:** 5 minutes

**Cook Time:** 40 minutes

**Total Time:** 45 minutes

**Ingredients:**
2 Tbsp. olive oil, divided
4 chicken thighs, cut into 1/2-inch pieces
1 tsp. salt, divided
1/4 tsp. pepper
1 small onion, chopped
2 ribs celery, chopped
2 carrots, peeled and sliced
8 oz. button mushrooms, sliced
3 cloves of garlic, finely chopped
1 and 1/2 cups pearl barley
3 and 1/2 cups low-sodium chicken stock

1. In a medium pot that has a lid warm 1 tablespoon of the olive oil over medium-high heat.

2. Season the chicken with 1/2 teaspoon of the salt and the pepper. Cook stirring occasionally until cooked through, 5-7 minutes. Transfer to a plate and refrigerate until later.

3. Warm another tablespoon of the olive oil in the same pot over medium-high heat.

4. Add the onion, celery, carrots, and mushrooms. Cook stirring occasionally for 5 minutes.

5. Add the garlic and cook for 30 seconds.

6. Stir in the barley, 1/2 teaspoon of the salt, and the stock.

7. Increase heat to high and let it come to a boil. Reduce the heat to low, cover the pot and simmer it until the barley has softened, 25-30 minutes. If there is unabsorbed stock left in the pot, drain it off.

8. Stir in the cooked chicken. Heat through for a minute.

Photo: Sam Ellis

# Chicken Parmesan One-Pot Skillet Dinner

*By Sam Ellis*

The spaghetti for this dish is cooked in the skillet while you prep the chicken. Then the spaghetti is drained and the chicken is cooked in the same skillet. Once the chicken is ready, you can either heat the pasta by pouring boiling water over it and letting it sit for a minute, or add it to the skillet with the chicken and tomato sauce and heat it through in the oven. However you do it, you're only dirtying one pan for this dinner, and that's always a good thing!

# Chicken Parmesan One-Pot Skillet Dinner

*Continued from previous page*

**Yield:** 4 servings

**Prep Time:** 15 minutes

**Cook Time:** 50 minutes

**Total Time:** 1 hour, 5 minutes

**Ingredients:**

12 oz. dry spaghetti
3 tsp. salt, divided
2 large boneless skinless chicken breasts
1/4 cup all-purpose flour
1 tsp. pepper, divided
1 egg, beaten
1/2 cup Italian breadcrumbs
1/2 cup grated Parmesan cheese
1/4 cup olive oil
1 (28 oz.) jar tomato sauce
1/2 Tbsp. dried basil
1/2 Tbsp. dried parsley
1 tsp. dried oregano

1. Preheat oven to 350°F.

2. In an oven-proof skillet, add 6 cups of water and 1 teaspoon of the salt and bring to a boil. Add spaghetti and cook 10-11 minutes. Drain when done and set aside.

3. While spaghetti is cooking, cut a chicken breast in half horizontally creating 2 thin chicken cutlets. Repeat with second chicken breast. Mix together flour, 1 teaspoon of salt, and 1/2 teaspoon of pepper on a plate. Add beaten egg to a bowl. Mix together breadcrumbs and Parmesan on a plate. Dredge chicken breasts through flour, covering entirely. Add to the egg ensuring all of it has been covered. Dredge through breadcrumb mixture and set aside. Repeat for remaining chicken cutlets.

4. Once spaghetti has been drained, wipe out skillet, turn heat to low, and add olive oil to skillet. Add chicken cutlets to skillet and cook 2-3 minutes until golden brown and repeat for the other sides. Remove chicken and set aside.

5. Add tomato sauce, basil, parsley, oregano, and remaining 1 teaspoon of salt, and 1/2 teaspoon of pepper to skillet. Mix together and place chicken breasts back into skillet. Use a spoon to cover chicken breasts with tomato sauce and top each with a slice of mozzarella. Bake for 30 minutes or until chicken is cooked through to 165°F on an instant read thermometer.

6. Shortly before chicken is ready, put a kettle of water on to boil. Pour boiling water over spaghetti to warm it back up. Drain. Alternatively, mix spaghetti with tomato sauce in skillet, spreading it around the chicken and put the skillet back into the oven for 5 minutes to heat through.

# Chicken Fried Cauliflower Rice

*I think the reason that riced cauliflower has become so popular recently is that companies have started pre-chopping it for us, their grateful customers. We no longer have to get a big head of cauliflower and break it down into little pieces ourselves, covering our counters in cauliflower bits. Now we can buy these little crumbles of cauliflower at the grocery store, both in the produce section and in the freezer. If you're not a fan of cauliflower rice, go ahead and use regular rice. Simply add cooked white rice to the recipe instead of cauliflower. It won't need to be cooked as long now since you only need to heat it through.*

**Yield:** 4 servings

**Prep Time:** 10 minutes

**Cook Time:** 20 minutes

**Total Time:** 30 minutes

**Ingredients:**
Cooking spray
2 large eggs, beaten
1 Tbsp. olive oil
1 small onion, chopped
1 cup frozen mixed vegetables
2 cloves garlic, minced
1 lb. ground chicken
16 oz. riced cauliflower
1/4 cup low-sodium soy sauce
4 green onions, chopped

1. Heat large skillet or wok over medium heat and spray with cooking spray. Add eggs and cook 2 minutes, or until cooked through. Remove from pan and set aside.

2. Return skillet to heat and add oil, onions, mixed vegetables, and garlic, and cook 4-5 minutes, or until softened.

3. Add chicken and stir to break up. Cook stirring occasionally until browned a bit, about 3-5 minutes.

4. Increase heat to medium-high. Add cauliflower and soy sauce. Mix well, cover and cook 7-10 minutes, stirring frequently, or until the cauliflower is tender and chicken is cooked through.

5. Remove from heat, mix in scrambled egg and top with green onions.

# One Pot Chicken Alfredo

*By Allie Doran*

*Cooking the pasta right in the sauce is a great trick for making a quick dinner that doesn't involve much washing up after. Win-win!*

**Yield:** 4-6 servings

**Prep Time:** 5 minutes

**Cook Time:** 20 minutes

**Total Time:** 25 minutes

**Ingredients:**
1 Tbsp. olive oil
1 lb. boneless skinless chicken breast, cut into 1-inch pieces
4 Tbsp. unsalted butter
1 small onion, finely chopped
2 garlic cloves, minced
1 tsp. salt
1/2 tsp. pepper
3 cups water
1 and 1/2 cups heavy cream
12 oz. linguini
1/2 cup grated Parmesan cheese

1. Heat the olive oil in a large pot over medium heat.

2. Add the chicken breast and cook, stirring occasionally, until browned and no longer pink inside, about 10 minutes. Remove the chicken and set it aside on a plate.

3. Add the butter directly into the pot, scraping the bits of cooked chicken off the bottom of the pot.

4. Add the onion and garlic and sauté until soft, about 5 minutes. Add the salt and pepper and stir.

5. Add the water and heavy cream. Increase heat to high and bring to a boil.

6. Stir in pasta and reduce heat to a simmer. Allow this to cook, stirring frequently for 9 minutes, or until the pasta is al dente.

7. Stir in the cooked chicken and Parmesan and allow it to heat.

Photo: Brittany Poulson

# Chicken Porcupine Meatballs

*By Brittany Poulson*

Porcupine meatballs are a fun dish that my mom used to make when I was a kid. Uncooked rice is mixed with ground meat. That's then formed into meatballs that you cook in a tomato sauce. The result is a delicious one-pan meal of rice-studded meatballs in tomato sauce.

# Chicken Porcupine Meatballs
*Continued from previous page*

**Yield:** 20 meatballs

**Prep Time:** 15 minutes

**Cook Time:** 1 hour

**Total Time:** 1 hour, 15 minutes

**Ingredients:**
Cooking spray
1 and 1/4 lb. ground chicken
1/2 cup uncooked rice
1 small onion, finely chopped
1 clove garlic, minced
1 tsp. salt
1 tsp. Italian seasoning
1/4 tsp. pepper
1/4 cup milk
2 cans (10.75 oz.) condensed tomato soup
2 tsp. Worcestershire sauce
1 cup water
Optional: Parmesan or mozzarella cheese
Optional: Chopped parsley

1. Preheat oven to 350°F. Spray an 8"×8" baking dish with cooking spray and set aside.

2. To a large bowl add the chicken, rice, onion, garlic, salt, Italian seasoning, pepper, and milk.

3. Use your hands to mix it together until well-combined, but don't over mix as it will make the meatballs tough.

4. Form into 20 meatballs and place in prepared baking dish.

5. In the same bowl, whisk together the tomato soup, Worcestershire sauce, and water.

6. Pour over the meatballs in the baking dish.

7. Cover baking dish with tin foil and place in the oven. Bake for 45 minutes. Remove the tin foil and continue baking an additional 15 minutes or until the meatballs are fully cooked (reach an internal temperature of 165°F as read on an instant read thermometer) and the rice inside is tender. Remove from oven.

8. If desired, sprinkle with cheese and garnish with chopped parsley.

# One Pot Pasta with Chicken, Brussels Sprouts, and Parmesan

*For this recipe, you cook the pasta in a pot and then add the Brussels sprouts in to cook for the last few minutes. Then you quickly sauté some chicken breast in the same pot, add in pesto and Parmesan cheese, return the pasta and sprouts to the pot, stir then serve. You only have to monitor one thing on the stove at a time, and you only dirty one pot. How great is that? Oh, and it's a new delicious way to enjoy Brussels sprouts too. Bonus!*

**Yield:** 6 servings

**Prep Time:** 5 minutes

**Cook Time:** 16 minutes

**Total Time:** 21 minutes

**Ingredients:**
1 lb. fettuccine pasta
1 lb. Brussels sprouts, trimmed and halved (quartered if large)
3 Tbsp. olive oil, divided
3 boneless skinless chicken breasts, sliced into 1/4-inch slices
6 Tbsp. pesto sauce
1/2 cup shredded Parmesan, plus more for serving
1/2 tsp. coarse salt
1/4 tsp. pepper

1. Cook fettuccine according to package directions but add Brussels sprouts for the last 5 minutes of cooking.

2. Drain pasta and Brussels sprouts. Set aside.

3. Set the cooking pot over medium-high heat. Add 1 tablespoon of the olive oil. Let heat then add the chicken. Stir until cooked through, 4-5 minutes.

4. Add pesto, remaining 2 tablespoons of olive oil, Parmesan, salt, and pepper, and the pasta with Brussels sprouts.

5. Toss ingredients together. Serve topped with additional Parmesan cheese, if desired.

# Chicken and Riced Cauliflower Bowls with Hummus Dressing

*This recipe is a rice bowl (the kind of thing you might order at Chipotle) that uses riced cauliflower (very finely chopped cauliflower) instead of rice. You can make your own riced cauliflower or find it in the produce section and freezer sections of your grocery store.*

**Yield:** 4 servings

**Prep Time:** 15 minutes

**Cook Time:** 12 minutes

**Total Time:** 27 minutes

**Ingredients:**
2 Tbsp. plus 1/4 cup mild-flavored olive oil, divided
2 chicken breasts, cut into 1/2-inch pieces
Salt
Pepper
16 oz. cauliflower rice (4–5 cups uncooked)
1/4 cup hummus
2 tsp. lemon juice
1 (14 oz.) can low-sodium chickpeas, drained
2 avocados, chopped
1/2 English cucumber, sliced
8 radishes, sliced
4 Tbsp. toasted sunflower seeds
1/4 cup fresh dill fronds

1. Warm a large skillet over medium-high heat. Add 1 tablespoon of the olive oil and heat.

2. Add the chicken and season with 1/4 teaspoon salt and 1/8 teaspoon pepper. Cook stirring occasionally until cooked through, 4-5 minutes. Transfer to a plate.

3. Heat another tablespoon of the olive oil over medium heat. Add the cauliflower, stir, cover, and reduce heat to low. Cook until soft, about 5 minutes. Remove from heat.

4. In a small bowl, whisk together the hummus, remaining 1/4 cup olive oil, lemon juice, 1/8 teaspoon salt, and 1/8 teaspoon pepper until smooth. This may take a minute of whisking to achieve.

5. Divide cauliflower among 4 deep bowls.

6. Top with chicken, chickpeas, avocado, cucumber, and radishes.

7. Divide hummus dressing among the bowls. Top with sunflower seeds and dill.

# Quick Chicken and Cheese Stuffed Peppers

*These stuffed peppers are super-quick to make because the filling isn't cooked before the peppers are stuffed. You mix up the raw chicken and the cheese, scoop it into bell pepper halves and then bake. The filling will cook through in the time it takes the peppers to soften. Yes, really. It's amazing and delicious all at once!*

**Yield:** 4 servings

**Prep Time:** 10 minutes

**Cook Time:** 22 minutes

**Total Time:** 32 minutes

**Ingredients:**
1/3 cup panko bread crumbs
1/4 tsp. garlic powder
1/2 tsp. salt, divided
1/8 tsp. pepper
1 tsp. olive oil
1 cup shredded cheddar cheese, divided
3/4 lb. chicken breasts, cut into 1/4-inch cubes
1 Tbsp. chopped fresh thyme leaves (1 tsp. dried leaves)
2 tsp. all-purpose flour
4 red bell peppers, halved from stem to base and de-seeded

1. Preheat oven to 400°F.

2. In a small bowl combine the panko, garlic powder, 1/4 teaspoon of salt, pepper, olive oil, and 1/3 cup of the shredded cheese. Use your fingers to rub the crumbs and cheese together until the bits of cheese are about the size of the larger crumbs. Set aside.

3. In a second bowl combine the chicken, thyme, 1/4 teaspoon of salt, the remaining 2/3 cup cheese, and the flour.

4. Arrange peppers on a baking sheet cut-side-up. Fill each half of pepper with approximately 1/4 cup of the chicken filling and then top each with about 1 tablespoon of the crumbs.

5. Bake until the chicken is cooked through and the crumbs on top are golden brown, 22-25 minutes.

# Greek Chicken Stuffed Peppers

*For these stuffed Greek peppers you also use uncooked chicken, just like the last recipe. And like the last recipe, the peppers are cut in half from stem to base before stuffing. The halved peppers hold less filling so it cooks through quicker than if you use a whole pepper.*

**Yield:** 4 servings

**Prep Time:** 10 minutes

**Cook Time:** 35 minutes

**Total Time:** 45 minutes

**Ingredients:**

1 pound boneless skinless chicken thighs or breasts, in 1/4-inch cubes
1 pint grape tomatoes, halved
2 cups cooked rice
2 Tbsp. all-purpose flour
2 Tbsp. red wine vinegar
2 Tbsp. olive oil
2 tsp. lemon juice
2 tsp. dried oregano
1 tsp. salt
1/2 tsp. garlic powder
1/4 tsp. pepper
1/8 tsp. sugar
4 red bell peppers, halved from stem to base and deseeded
1 cup crumbled feta cheese, divided

1. In a large bowl mix the chicken, tomatoes, cooked rice, and flour.

2. In a medium bowl whisk together red wine vinegar, olive oil, lemon juice, oregano, salt, garlic powder, black pepper, and sugar.

3. Add vinegar mixture and 1/2 cup of the feta to the chicken and stir.

4. Arrange peppers cut-side-up in baking dish. Fill with chicken mixture.

5. Bake until chicken is cooked through to at least 165°F (use an instant-read thermometer to check), 35-40 minutes.

6. Top with remaining feta.

# Buffalo Chicken Stuffed Peppers

*Here's one last stuffed pepper variation for you. With this technique of using pieces of raw chicken stuffed loosely into halved peppers, you'll be able to try all kinds of flavor combinations. In this version, the flour is mixed with the chicken to catch juices from the chicken so that the peppers don't end up wet.*

**Yield:** 4 servings

**Prep Time:** 10 minutes

**Cook Time:** 30 minutes

**Total Time:** 40 minutes

**Ingredients:**

- 1 lb. boneless skinless chicken breast, chopped into 1/2-inch pieces
- 3 tsp. all-purpose flour
- 1/2 tsp. salt
- 2 medium carrots, shredded
- 2 medium ribs celery, thinly sliced
- 1 cup shredded cheddar cheese, divided
- 3 Tbsp. Buffalo wing sauce
- 2 Tbsp. ranch dressing
- 4 bell peppers, each cut in half from stem to base, seeds removed

1. Preheat oven to 400°F.

2. In a medium bowl toss the chicken with the flour and salt. Add the carrots, celery, 1/2 cup of the cheese, the wing sauce, and the ranch dressing.

3. Place the pepper halves on a large rimmed baking sheet. Divide the chicken mixture among the peppers. Top each pepper with 1 tablespoon of the remaining cheese.

4. Bake until chicken is cooked through and peppers have achieved desired softness, 30-40 minutes.

# Tater Tot Casserole with Chicken

*Often Tater Tot Casserole (which I believe some people call "Hot Dish") is made with canned condensed soup. For this recipe, we've instead made a quick pan sauce. It's a great techniquie that you'll be able to use for all kinds of meals when you want things to get a bit saucy in a jiffy.*

**Yield:** 6 servings

**Prep Time:** 30 minutes

**Cook Time:** 30 minutes

**Total Time:** 1 hour

**Ingredients:**
2 Tbsp. olive oil, divided
1 lb. ground chicken
Salt
Pepper
1 medium onion, chopped
12 oz. button mushrooms, finely chopped
1 Tbsp. chopped fresh rosemary or 1 tsp. dried rosemary
1 Tbsp. chopped fresh thyme or 1 tsp. dried thyme
3 cloves garlic, minced
3 Tbsp. all-purpose flour
1 and 1/2 cups whole milk
1 cup frozen corn, defrosted
1 cup frozen peas, defrosted
2 cups shredded white cheddar
1 lb. frozen tater tots (about 50-60)

1. Preheat the oven to 425°F. Heat a medium (10-inch), oven-safe skillet over medium-high heat. Add olive oil.

2. Add the chicken. 1/4 teaspoon salt, and 1/4 teaspoon pepper. Brown, using a wooden spoon to break it up as it cooks. Cook for 5 to 7 minutes, until cooked through. Transfer to a plate. Set aside.

3. Add another tablespoon of oil to the skillet to heat up. Then add the onion and mushrooms. Season with 1/4 teaspoon salt and 1/8 teaspoon pepper. Cook, stirring occasionally, for 5 to 7 minutes, until the onions are translucent.

4. Add in the rosemary, thyme, and garlic. Stir to combine. Cook for another 1 to 2 minutes, then return the chicken to the skillet, stirring to combine.

5. Sprinkle the flour over the chicken, onions, and mushrooms, stirring to combine. Cook for 2 minutes.

6. While stirring, slowly add in the milk.

7. Reduce the heat to low and cook, stirring occasionally, for 5 minutes, until the sauce is bubbling and thickened.

8. Add the corn and peas, stirring to combine. Taste and season with additional salt and pepper as desired.

9. Turn the heat under the skillet off and top the chicken and mushroom sauce with the shredded cheddar. Add the tater tots, one at a time, arranging them in a single layer that covers the top of the casserole completely.

10. Bake the tater tot casserole for 30 minutes, until the tater tots are golden brown. Cool for a few minutes before serving.

# Quickest Chicken Chili

*This chili is so quick because of a special secret ingredient: Salsa! You're not going to believe how delicious it gets in only 18 minutes.*

**Yield:** 6 servings

**Prep Time:** 6 minutes

**Cook Time:** 12 minutes

**Total Time:** 18 minutes

**Ingredients:**
1 tsp. olive oil
2 lbs. ground chicken
1 Tbsp. garlic powder
2 Tbsp. chili powder, divided
1 tsp. salt
2 cups salsa (or one 16 oz. jar)
1 (28 oz.) can diced tomatoes
2 (15 oz.) cans reduced-sodium kidney beans, drained and rinsed

1. Warm the olive oil in a large skillet over medium heat.
2. Add the ground chicken, garlic powder, 1 tablespoon of the chili powder, and the salt.
3. Stir often to crumble up the chicken until cooked through, 5-7 minutes.
4. Stir in the remaining 1 tablespoon of chili powder, the salsa, diced tomatoes, and kidney beans.
5. Cover. Cook, stirring occasionally, until heated through and bubbling, 6-8 minutes.

# Cream of Chicken Soup

*By Allie Doran*

*Once you get the hang of making this creamed soup, you'll be able to make all kinds of different variations. Note that this is not condensed soup and should not be used in recipes calling for canned condensed soup. However, head to Chapter 1 for the condensed soup version.*

**Yield:** About 8 cups

**Prep Time:** 5 minutes

**Cook Time:** 20 minutes

**Total Time:** 25 minutes

**Ingredients:**
4 Tbsp. unsalted butter
1 small onion, very finely chopped
2 garlic cloves, very finely chopped
1/3 cup all-purpose flour
1 tsp. salt
a pinch of pepper
6 cups chicken stock
1 cup heavy cream
3/4 cup finely chopped cooked chicken

1. Add the butter to a large pot and heat over medium heat until melted and bubbly.
2. Add the onion and garlic and sauté for 3 minutes, stirring occasionally.
3. Then, add the flour, salt, and pepper and cook for an additional 3 minutes, stirring occasionally.
4. Pour in the chicken stock and whisk it into the flour.
5. Bring to a boil, reduce the heat to low, add the cream and chicken, and simmer for 10 minutes, stirring frequently.
6. Remove from the heat.

# Hearty Chicken and Farro Soup

*I really love barley soups. However, I don't like it when the barley soaks up all the liquid and turns it into more of a stew. This happens if I have leftovers and put them in the fridge overnight. Interestingly, that doesn't seem to happen as much with the grain farro. It's similar in texture and flavor to cooked barley but it retains that texture even if kept in liquid longer. I therefore started using farro in soups instead of barley. This recipe is a great example of that. Farro is available at some grocery stores near the quinoa and rice, or you can get it online. If you'd prefer to use barley though, go right ahead. It'll be just as delicious, even if the leftovers are stewier.*

**Yield:** 8 servings

**Prep Time:** 10 minutes

**Cook Time:** 35 minutes

**Total Time:** 45 minutes

**Ingredients:**

1 Tbsp. olive oil
3 carrots, peeled and chopped
2 ribs of celery, chopped
1 medium onion, chopped
1 lb. ground chicken
1/2 tsp. salt
1/4 tsp. pepper
1 cup cooked farro
4 cups low-sodium chicken stock
1 (28 oz.) can diced tomatoes

1. Heat the oil in a large pot over medium heat. Add the carrots, celery, and onion. Cook until softened, 4-5 minutes.

2. Add the chicken, salt, and pepper. Cook until browned, 4-5 minutes.

3. Add the farro, chicken stock, and diced tomatoes. Increase heat to high and heat until it reaches a boil.

4. Reduce to a simmer and cook until farro is tender, 25-30 minutes. Taste and season with more salt and pepper if desired.

Photo: Jill Silverman Hough

# Chicken Stew

*We usually think of stew being made with beef, but it can totally be made with chicken. It's delicious and it cooks up quicker since you don't need the long simmering time that stewing beef requires.*

**Yield:** 6 servings

**Prep Time:** 35 minutes

**Cook Time:** 40 minutes

**Total Time:** 1 hour, 15 minutes

**Ingredients:**

- 1 and 1/2 Tbsp. olive oil
- 1 and 1/2 lb. boneless skinless chicken breasts or thighs or a mixture, cut into 1-inch pieces
- 1 large onion, chopped
- 3 cloves garlic, minced
- 1 Tbsp. chopped fresh rosemary or 1 tsp. dried rosemary
- 1 Tbsp. chopped fresh thyme or 1 tsp. dried thyme
- 1/2 tsp. salt
- 1/2 tsp. pepper
- 5 and 1/2 cups low-sodium chicken stock, divided
- 1/4 cup all-purpose flour
- 1 lb. baby carrots or whole carrots cut into 3/4-inch pieces
- 12 oz. boiling potatoes, cut into 3/4-inch pieces
- 1 cup fresh or frozen peas

1. In a large pot over medium-high heat, warm the oil.
2. Add the chicken and cook, stirring occasionally, until lightly browned, 4 to 5 minutes. Transfer to a plate and set aside.
3. Add the onions to the pot. Cook, stirring occasionally, until starting to soften, 3 to 4 minutes.
4. Add the garlic, rosemary, thyme, salt, and pepper. Cook, stirring, until fragrant, about 30 seconds.
5. Add 5 cups of the stock, stirring to loosen any browned bits on the bottom of the pot, and bring to a boil.
6. Meanwhile, whisk the flour into the remaining 1/2 cup of stock and set aside.
7. Add the carrots. Adjust the heat to maintain a simmer and cook 5 minutes.
8. Add the potatoes and cook 10 minutes.
9. Return the chicken to the pot and simmer until the chicken is cooked through and the vegetables are tender, 2 to 3 minutes.
10. Rewhisk the stock-flour mixture and add it to the pot. Increase the heat to medium-high and cook, stirring occasionally, until the liquid comes to a boil and thickens, 1 to 2 minutes.
11. Add the peas and cook until warmed through, about 2 minutes.
12. And more salt and pepper to taste.

# Breakfast Sliders with Chicken Sausage for a Crowd

*The perfect brunch for a group, these chicken sausage and egg sliders come together really fast because they use pre-cooked chicken sausage. The other reason that they're so quick is that you use a bunch of little slider buns that are connected to each other. You add toppings while they're still connected, rather than making each sandwich separately. Then you bake them. When they're done, you slice them into individual sliders.*

**Yield:** 8 servings

**Prep Time:** 15 minutes

**Cook Time:** 13 minutes

**Total Time:** 28 minutes

**Ingredients:**

6 eggs
2 Tbsp. water
2 Tbsp. chopped chives
24 mini potato party rolls connected in two flats
8 fully-cooked chicken breakfast sausage, sliced
1 cup shredded cheddar cheese
1/2 cup unsalted butter, melted
2 Tbsp. maple syrup
1/2 tsp. Dijon mustard
1/2 tsp. garlic powder

1. Preheat the oven to 350°F.
2. Crack the eggs into a medium microwave-safe bowl. Add the water and whisk until well-mixed. Stir in the chives.
3. Microwave on high for one minute. Stir. Microwave for 30 seconds at a time until set, stirring well between each session. Stir really well, mashing with a fork so that the eggs pieces are quite small.
4. Meanwhile, use a long serrated knife to slice through a flat of rolls horizontally, such that you end up with a bottom flat and a top flat.
5. Repeat with the other flat of rolls.
6. Put the bottom flats side by side in a 9×13" pan.
7. Top each with the sausage slices, divided evenly into smooth layers.
8. Sprinkle with the cheese. Top with the scrambled egg.
9. Add the top flats, cut side down, lining each one up with its bottom.
10. Put the butter, maple syrup, Dijon, and garlic powder into a medium bowl. Whisk until the mustard is well-incorporated into the butter.
11. Drizzle it over the rolls making sure that the top of each bun gets a bit. Use a brush or your fingers to spread the butter mixture around so that all the buns are evenly coated.

12. Cover the pan with foil and bake until the sandwiches are heated through and the cheese is melted, about 10 minutes.

13. Uncover and bake until the tops of the buns are crisp when you tap on them, 2-3 minutes.

14. Use two large spatulas to get under a flat of rolls and transfer it to a cutting board. Use a big sharp knife to cut the rolls apart along their perforations, yielding 12 sliders.

15. Repeat with the second flat of rolls.

# Sweet Potato and Sausage Hash

*By Lyndsay Burginger*

This is a great dish to serve for Sunday breakfast or brunch and it's pretty quick to make too. The key is to use chicken sausage that is fully cooked at purchase. You can find this in the lunchmeat section of your grocery store. Also, make sure that your cubes of potato are nice and small since that helps them to cook more quickly.

**Yield:** 4 servings

**Prep Time:** 10 minutes

**Cook Time:** 30 minutes

**Total Time:** 40 minutes

**Ingredients:**
- 1 Tbsp. olive oil
- 3 sweet potatoes, peeled and chopped
- 1/2 onion, diced
- 8 oz. fully cooked apple maple chicken sausage, cut into 1/2-inch pieces

1. In skillet over medium heat, add olive oil. Add sweet potatoes and onion and stir occasionally. Cook until the onion and potato are starting to brown, about 10 minutes.

2. Cover the skillet and cook another ten minutes, stirring occasionally.

3. Add sausage and cook until sausage is heated through, about 5 minutes. Take off heat.

# Cranberry Chicken Meatballs

*These are basic chicken meatballs in a cranberry BBQ sauce. To save time, you can make our 1-ingredient meatballs from the Basics chapter, or even use store-bought frozen meatballs. These are great as an appetizer for a party or potluck.*

**Yield:** 55 meatballs

**Prep Time:** 15 minutes

**Cook Time:** 15 minutes

**Total Time:** 30 minutes

**Ingredients:**
1 lb. ground chicken
1/2 cup breadcrumbs
1 large egg
1 Tbsp. whole milk
2 tsp. salt, divided
1/2 tsp. garlic powder
1 and 1/2 tsp. pepper, divided
2 Tbsp. cooking oil
1 can (14 oz.) cranberry sauce
1 cup barbecue sauce
1 tsp. ground cumin
1 tsp. smoked paprika

1. To a large bowl add the chicken, breadcrumbs, egg, milk, 1 teaspoon of the salt, garlic powder, and 1/2 teaspoon of the pepper.

2. Use hands to mix until evenly combined, but don't overmix.

3. Use 1 tablespoon of the mixture at a time to roll into small balls. Place in a single layer on a plate.

4. In a large pot heat the cooking oil over medium-high.

5. Add the meatballs in a single layer with some space around them. You may need to do this in batches. Cook until browned on all sides, moving them around occasionally, about 6-8 minutes. Transfer to a clean plate.

6. Once all meatballs are browned and removed from the pot, add the cranberry sauce, barbecue sauce, cumin, paprika, 1 teaspoon of salt, and 1 teaspoon of pepper. Stir.

7. Bring to a boil, stirring occasionally. Add meatballs and lower heat to a simmer.

8. Simmer sauce and meatballs together until meatballs are cooked through, about 10-15 minutes.

# Grape Jelly Chicken Meatballs

*To make really quick meatballs, we've used seasoned chicken sausage meat. If your grocery store doesn't have this, you can use 2 pounds of regular ground chicken seasoned with 1 teaspoon salt, 1/2 teaspoon garlic powder, 1/2 teaspoon pepper, and 1/2 teaspoon Italian seasoning or oregano. 1/2 teaspoon of crushed fennel seends would be great in there too, if you have them. Fennel seeds are a frequent ingredient in Italian sausages and so that flavor really makes it all taste extra sausagey.*

**Yield:** 64 meatballs

**Prep Time:** 15 minutes

**Cook Time:** 20 minutes

**Total Time:** 35 minutes

**Ingredients:**

2 lbs. raw mild Italian chicken sausages or seasoned chicken sausage meat
1 (12 oz.) jar grape jelly
1 (12 oz.) bottle chili sauce
1/8 tsp. smoked paprika

1. If using sausages, remove casings from sausages. Take about 2 tablespoons of chicken meat and roll into a ball. Place on a plate. Repeat with remaining meat.

2. Heat oil in a large pot. Add meatballs in a single layer. You might have to cook them in more than one batch.

3. Cook, turning occasionally, until browned on all sides, about 6-8 minutes. Transfer to clean plate once cooked.

4. Once all meatballs are cooked and removed from pot, make the grape jelly sauce: To the pot add the grape jelly, chili sauce, and paprika. Heat over medium and stir until melted together.

5. Add the meatballs. Stir to coat. Cook at a low simmer until meatballs are cooked through, 10-15 minutes.

# CHAPTER 7
# GRILLING CHICKEN

Grilled Chicken Spice Blends
Perfect Grilled Chicken Breasts
Perfect Grilled Chicken Pieces for a Crowd
Whole Grilled Chicken
Grilled Chicken Thighs
Grilled Chicken Wings
Spiced Chicken Skewers with Yogurt Dipping Sauce
Chicken Sausage and Apple Kebabs
Grilled Spatchcock Chicken
Jerk Chicken
Grilled Chicken Parmesan
Margarita Chicken
Grilled Chicken Souvlaki Pitas with Homemade Tzatziki
Smoked Chicken Breasts

# Grilled Chicken Spice Blends

*Several of the recipes in this chapter show basic techniques and have minimal seasonings. Try one of these chicken seasoning blends to spice things up!*

## Jamaican Jerk Spice Seasoning

1 and 1/2 tsp. kosher salt
1 tsp. sweet paprika
1 tsp. garlic powder
1/2 tsp. pepper
1/4 tsp. allspice
1/8 tsp. ground nutmeg
a pinch of cayenne pepper

## Mexican Spice Seasoning

1 and 1/2 tsp. kosher salt
1 tsp. dried oregano
1/2 tsp. garlic powder
1/2 tsp. onion powder
1/2 tsp. ground cumin
1/2 tsp. chili powder
1/4 tsp. ground chipotle

## Lemon Herb Rub

1 and 1/2 tsp. kosher salt
1 tsp. lemon pepper
1 tsp. garlic powder
1 tsp. fresh thyme leaves
1 tsp. chopped fresh rosemary

# Perfect Grilled Chicken Breasts

*Have a look at the breaded chicken cutlets from Chapter 1 to see how to flatten the chicken breasts here. Note though that you don't need them as thin as for a cutlet. What you want to do is flatten the rounded, thicker end just enough so that it's the same thickness as the thinner pointed end. This is so that the chicken cooks evenly and doesn't dry out in one spot before being fully cooked in another.*

**Yield:** 4 servings

**Prep Time:** 10 minutes + 1 hour marinade time

**Cook Time:** 8 minutes

**Total Time:** 1 hour, 18 minutes

**Ingredients:**
4 boneless skinless chicken breasts
1/2 cup olive oil
1/4 cup lemon juice
1 tsp. dried thyme leaves
1/4 tsp. garlic powder
1/4 tsp. salt
1/4 tsp. pepper
2 Tbsp. oil with a high smoking point, like vegetable or grapeseed

1. Cover one chicken breast in plastic wrap to stop chicken juice from flying around as you pound chicken. Use the flat side of a meat tenderizer or a rolling pin to pound chicken to an even thickness. Repeat with all chicken.

2. Put chicken into a ziptop bag or a large bowl. In a medium bowl combine the olive oil, lemon juice, thyme, garlic powder, salt, and black pepper. Pour it over the chicken breasts. Refrigerate for an hour at most. You're just trying to get some flavor on there. (Alternatively, you can brine your chicken breasts. See Chapter 1 for how to brine chicken).

3. Oil your grill grates: When your grill is cold, dip paper towel into an oil that has a high smoking point, like vegetable oil or grapeseed oil. Then use tongs to rub the oiled towel onto the grates. Then preheat the grill for direct cooking over medium-high heat (around 400°F).

4. Once your grill is at the right temperature, remove the chicken breasts from the marinade, shaking off any excess. Discard the marinade. Put the chicken breasts onto the grill in a single layer, as spaced out as you can given your surface and the number of breasts you have. Cook until 165°F on an instant read thermometer, about 4-5 minutes per side.

5. Take them off of the grill and put them on a clean serving plate. Let them rest for 5 minutes before serving.

# Perfect Grilled Chicken Pieces for a Crowd

*This grilled chicken is pre-cooked in the oven (low and slow) before hitting the grill. That way, you know it's fully cooked and juicy so you can relax and enjoy your guests without worrying about feeding them under-cooked or dry chicken.*

**Yield:** 8 servings

**Prep Time:** 10 minutes

**Cook Time:** 1 hour, 10 minutes

**Total Time:** 1 hour, 20 minutes

**Ingredients:**
2 tsp. salt
1 tsp. pepper
1 tsp. garlic powder
2 Tbsp. brown sugar
6 lbs. bone-in drumsticks or thighs
BBQ sauce

1. Preheat oven to 300°F.
2. In bowl combine salt, pepper, garlic powder, and brown sugar. Rub on chicken and then arrange in a single layer on a large rimmed baking sheet or two if needed. Bake for 1 hour.
3. Let cool for 15 minutes. If your chicken is skin on, carefully remove the skin before grilling, if desired.
4. Brush each piece with about 2 tablespoons of BBQ sauce. Cover and refrigerate up to 24 hours.
5. 10 minutes before eating, prepare grill for direct cooking over medium-high heat.
6. Add chicken pieces and cook until grill marks appear on underside, 4-5 minutes. Flip and cook until heated through, another 4-5 minutes.

# Whole Grilled Chicken

*With this recipe for whole grilled chicken, you won't battle flare-ups or have burnt skin and undercooked meat because the chicken is cooked over indirect heat the whole time.*

**Yield:** 4-6 servings

**Prep Time:** 10 minutes

**Cook Time:** 1 hour to 1 hour, 30 minutes

**Total Time:** 1 hour, 10 minutes to 1 hour, 40 minutes

**Ingredients:**

1 (3 to 4 lb.) whole chicken, brined for at least 8 hours (brining is optional, but delicious)
3 Tbsp. olive oil
1 and 1/2 tsp. kosher salt
1 tsp. pepper

1. Preheat grill to 350°F according to instructions below. Remove chicken from packaging and remove giblets from the body cavity and/or neck.

2. Truss legs and tuck wings under the back of the chicken.

3. Massage olive oil over the breast, legs, wings, and back of the chicken.

4. Season with salt and pepper making sure that the legs and wings are seasoned.

5. Place chicken on the rack that has a drip pan beneath it and cook until thermometer inserted into thickest part of the thigh reads 165°F, about 1 to 1 and 1/2 hours.

6. Transfer to a cutting board and allow to rest for 10 minutes before carving.

**Prepping the Grill for Indirect Heat:**

**Three Burner Gas Grill** — turn the left and right burners to medium and ignite. Leave the center burner off. Place the drip pan over the non-lit burner under the grate. You'll place the chicken in the center over the non-lit burner

**Four Burner Gas Grill** — turn the two left burners to medium and ignite. Leave the two right burners off. Place the drip pan over the non-lit burners under the grate. You'll place the chicken in the center of the two burners that are off.

**Charcoal Grill** — light the charcoal using a chimney lighter. Pour the charcoal out of the chimney and push over to one side of the grill. Leave the other side free of coals. Place the drip pan on the non-charcoal side under the grate. You'll place the chicken on the side of the grill with no charcoal.

# Grilled Chicken Thighs

*Chicken thighs are wonderful on the grill because their juicy dark meat prevents them from getting dried out. The instructions here are for both boneless and bone-in chicken thighs, whether or not they have skin. I've kept the seasoning very simple so go ahead and try one of the seasoning blends from the beginning of this chapter, or an interesting sauce or marinade.*

**Yield:** 4 servings

**Prep Time:** 2 minutes

**Cook Time:** 20 minutes

**Total Time:** 22 minutes

**Ingredients:**
8 skinless chicken thighs, with or without bone
2 Tbsp. olive oil
1/2 tsp. salt
1/4 tsp. pepper

1. Preheat grill for direct cooking over medium heat, around 350°F.

2. If the thighs are boneless, unroll them to make cooking faster. Brush thighs with olive oil and sprinkle with salt and pepper.

3. Put thighs onto the prepared grill. Keep grill lid down except when you open it to flip the chicken. Cook the chicken on the grill flipping it every couple of minutes until cooked through to 165°F as read on an instant read thermometer. That will be a total time of 10-12 minutes for unrolled (and thus thinner) boneless thighs, 15-17 minutes for rolled up boneless thighs, and 25-30 minutes for bone-in thighs.

# Grilled Chicken Wings

*Grilled wings turn out less crispy than deep-fried, but they have tons of flavor and a good chew.*

**Yield:** 4 servings

**Prep Time:** 5 minutes

**Cook Time:** 15 minutes

**Total Time:** 20 minutes

**Ingredients:**
10 whole chicken wings, cut into drumettes and wingettes
1/2 cup to 3/4 cup BBQ sauce

1. Oil your grill racks and then prepare your grill for direct grilling over medium heat, about 350°F. Keep one burner off or on low in case some wings are cooked before others.

2. Put the wings in a single layer on the grill over the heat. Cook the wings for about 20-25 minutes total. Start by leaving them on there, lid closed, for a few minutes. Then use big tongs to have a look underneath them all. Some tend to get darker faster due to hot spots on the grill. If some are starting to char too much, flip those over. Keep monitoring and flipping as they all darken. If a few pieces seem to be dark before others, shift them to a cooler part of the grill. They'll keep cooking but not browning.

3. After about 18 minutes of flipping and moving them around as needed, use an instant read thermometer in the center of a few wings to make sure that they've all reached 165°F. If some aren't quite there, give them another 5 minutes. What you want are wings that are nicely charred on all sides and cooked through.

4. Use tongs to transfer fully-cooked wings to a bowl. Add BBQ sauce. Start with 1/2 cup. Toss. If it's a strong-tasting sauce, don't add more. If it's milder, add up to another 1/4 cup.

# Spiced Chicken Skewers with Yogurt Dipping Sauce

*For these skewers, you make a yogurt marinade but only use half of it as an actual marinade. The other half gets some extra ingredients added to it so that it becomes a flavorful dipping sauce.*

**Yield:** 6 servings

**Prep Time:** 25 minutes

**Cook Time:** 10 minutes

**Total Time:** 35 minutes

**Ingredients:**
12-6" skewers
1 and 1/2 cup Greek yogurt, divided
1 small onion, peeled and cut into 4 pieces
1 red chili, seeded and cut into a few pieces
2 cloves garlic
1 tsp. ground cumin
1/2 tsp. curry powder
6 boneless skinless chicken thighs
1 medium tomato, cut into a few pieces
1/3 cup cilantro leaves
Salt

1. Fill a large pot or sink with warm water. Add the skewers.

2. Into a food processor put 1 cup of the Greek yogurt and the onion pieces, red chili, garlic, cumin, and curry powder. Purée until smooth.

3. Poke each chicken thigh all over with a fork. Unroll a thigh on a cutting board. Cut it in half lengthwise so that you have two long strips of chicken meat. Thread each strip onto a wet skewer and put them into a 9"x11"pan. Repeat with the remaining chicken thighs.

4. Pour HALF of the yogurt and onion mixture from the food processor over the chicken skewers (set the remaining mixture in the food processor aside. It will be used to make a sauce). Turn the chicken skewers to coat them. Cover and refrigerate for at least an hour but up to 12 hours.

5. Meanwhile, squeeze some of the juice out of the tomato pieces (discard juice) and then add them to the yogurt and onion mixture in the food processor. Also add the cilantro and 1/2 teaspoon of salt. Purée until smooth. Gently stir in the remaining 1/2 cup of yogurt. Cover and refrigerate the sauce.

6. When ready to cook the chicken, preheat grill for medium direct heat grilling, about 350°F. Shake excess sauce off of chicken. Discard all the sauce that the raw chicken was sitting in.

7. Sprinkle the chicken skewers on all sides with salt. Put chicken skewers on the grill and let them sit until nice grill marks appear on the undersides, about 3-5 minutes. Flip. Continue to cook the chicken, flipping occasionally, until cooked through, about another 5-7 minutes.

8. Remove from grill and serve with the chilled yogurt sauce.

# Chicken Sausage and Apple Kebabs

*Apples and onions go really well together. Pairing them with a sweet, fully-cooked chicken sausage makes for a quick and tasty dinner.*

**Yield:** 4 servings

**Prep Time:** 20 minutes

**Cook Time:** 10 minutes

**Total Time:** 30 minutes

**Ingredients:**

8 – 6" skewers
1/3 cup grainy mustard
1/4 cup honey
1 Tbsp. lemon juice
1/4 tsp. salt
1 medium sweet onion, cut into 8 wedges
12 oz. fully-cooked sweet apple and chicken sausages, cut into 16 pieces
2 red apples, cut into 8 wedges each

1. Soak skewers in warm water. Preheat grill for direct cooking over medium heat.

2. In a small bowl combine the mustard, honey, lemon juice, and salt.

3. Divide the layers from each onion wedge such that you have two pieces.

4. Onto a skewer thread a piece of sausage, then an apple wedge, then an onion piece, then sausage, apple, and onion again. Put it into a 9"x11" pan. Repeat with remaining seven skewers and remaining ingredients.

5. Pour mustard sauce over sausage skewers.

6. Put skewers on grill. Grill on one side until undersides of sausages are blackened in spots and apples have some grill marks, 3-5 minutes. Flip and grill until undersides are browned as well, another 3-5 minutes.

# Grilled Spatchcock Chicken

*Spatchcocking or butterflying a chicken before grilling helps it to cook evenly creating a juicy, perfectly done chicken. The presentation is pretty impressive too.*

**Yield:** 4 servings

**Prep Time:** 10 minutes

**Cook Time:** 45 minutes

**Total Time:** 55 minutes

**Ingredients:**
1 (4 to 5 lb.) whole chicken
2 Tbsp. olive oil
1 tsp. salt
1 tsp. pepper

**Prepping the Grill for Indirect Heat:**

**Three Burner Gas Grill** – turn the left and right burners to medium and ignite. Leave the center burner off. Place the drip pan over the non-lit burner under the grate. You'll place the chicken in the center over the non-lit burner

**Four Burner Gas Grill** – turn the two left burners to medium and ignite. Leave the two right burners off. Place the drip pan over the non-lit burners under the grate. You'll place the chicken in the center of the two burners that are off.

**Charcoal Grill** – light the charcoal using a chimney lighter. Pour the charcoal out of the chimney and push over to one side of the grill. Leave the other side free of coals. Place the drip pan on the non-charcoal side under the grate. You'll place the chicken on the side of the grill with no charcoal.

1. Prepare the grill as instructed below and heat to medium, about 350°F.

2. Remove chicken from packaging and remove giblets from body cavity and/or neck.

3. Lay the chicken on working surface breast-side-down. Locate the backbone. Using a pair of kitchen shears, cut along one side of the backbone (you'll be going through some little ribs so press hard to cut). Repeat on the other side of the backbone. Discard the backbone or save it for making stock. Turn the chicken over and press on the center of the breast to flatten it. Tuck the wings under the body by grabbing the wing tip, pulling it toward the neck cavity, and tucking it under the body to secure.

4. Massage olive oil over the breast, legs, and wings of the chicken.

5. Season with salt and pepper making sure that the legs and wings are seasoned.

6. Place breast-side-up on prepared grill. Cook for 45 minutes or until a thermometer inserted into the thickest part of the thigh, without touching the bone, reads 165°F.

7. Transfer to a cutting board and allow to rest for 10 minutes before carving.

Photo: Jill Silverman Hough

# Jerk Chicken

It turns out that three ingredients are key to jerk chicken—allspice, Scotch bonnet (super spicy!) chiles, and thyme. Other ingredients that are relatively common include garlic, brown sugar, onions, scallions, soy sauce, citrus juice, rum, pepper, cinnamon, and nutmeg. Bottom line, the ingredients list is sometimes long, but most of the items are things you probably have already.

**Yield:** 4-6 servings

**Prep Time:** 25 minutes, plus time to marinate chicken

**Cook Time:** 45 minutes

**Total Time:** 1 hour, 10 minutes, plus time to marinate chicken

**Ingredients:**
6 green onions
1 medium onion, quartered
2 Scotch bonnet or habanero chilis, halved, stemmed, and seeded
4 garlic cloves
a 1-inch piece of ginger, sliced into quarters
3 Tbsp. fresh lime juice
3 Tbsp. cooking oil
3 Tbsp. soy sauce
3 Tbsp. packed brown sugar
4 tsp. ground allspice
1 Tbsp. fresh thyme leaves
1 and 1/2 tsp. salt
1 tsp. pepper
3/4 tsp. ground nutmeg
5-6 lbs. bone-in skin-on chicken thighs and/or drumsticks

1. Cut 4 green onions into rough 1-inch pieces and put them in a blender or food processor. Thinly slice the remaining 2 green onions and set aside.

2. Add the onion quarters, chilis, garlic, ginger, lime juice, oil, soy sauce, sugar, allspice, thyme, salt, pepper, and nutmeg to the blender or food processor and purée.

3. Set aside 3/4 cup of the sauce. Pour the rest of the sauce in a resealable bag and add the chicken. Refrigerate for at least an hour and as long as overnight.

4. One hour before you're ready to cook, remove the chicken from the fridge and set it aside at room temperature.

5. Prepare a grill to medium heat, with areas for direct and indirect cooking, and lightly oil the grate. Cook the chicken over direct heat, skin side down, until it has nice grill marks, about 5 minutes.

6. Move the chicken to indirect heat and close the lid on the grill. Cook to an internal temperature of 165°F, 35 to 40 minutes. While you're cooking, check the grill every 10 minutes or so and adjust the heat as needed to maintain an "oven" temperature of about 350°F. Move and flip chicken if it's getting too dark on one side.

7. Serve the chicken sprinkled with the sliced green onions, with the reserved sauce on the side.

# Grilled Chicken Parmesan

*Here's a summery new take on the classic Chicken Parmesan. The chicken is cooked on the grill and is topped with cheese, tomatoes, toasted breadcrumbs, and basil.*

**Yield:** 4 servings

**Prep Time:** 10 minutes

**Cook Time:** 10 minutes

**Total Time:** 20 minutes

**Ingredients:**
4 boneless skinless chicken breasts
Olive oil
2 Tbsp. lemon juice
1/2 cup panko bread crumbs
1/2 cup finely shredded (not grated) Parmesan cheese
Salt
1/4 tsp. garlic powder
Pepper
1 large tomato, sliced into 8 slices
1 cup shredded mozzarella cheese
8–12 fresh basil leaves

1. Flatten the chicken breasts: Put one breast into a large ziptop bag but keep it unzipped. Use a flat mallet or heavy rolling pin to hit the chicken breast at the thickest part. Continue to do so, moving around a bit, until the chicken is of an even thickness of approximately 3/4-inch. Remove chicken from bag and repeat one at a time with remaining breasts.

2. If the bag is in good shape (no holes) measure 1/4 cup of olive oil and the lemon juice into the bag (or use a new bag or a baking dish). Add the flattened chicken and turn to coat. Refrigerate while preparing the rest of the ingredients.

3. Into a small skillet measure the panko, Parmesan, 1 tablespoon of olive oil, 1/4 teaspoon of salt, and 1/4 teaspoon of garlic powder. Put over medium-low heat and stir frequently so that the Parmesan doesn't clump up as it melts. Stir and cook until toasted to a golden crunchy brown, about 3-4 minutes. Transfer immediately to a large plate so that the crumbs stop cooking and cool. Set aside.

4. Prepare the grill for direct cooking on medium-high heat.

5. Drain the liquid off of the chicken breasts and discard. Sprinkle chicken lightly with salt and pepper on both sides. Transfer to prepared grill. Cover and cook until there are nice dark grill marks, 3-4 minutes. Flip the breasts over. Top each one with 2 slightly overlapping slices of tomato, 1/4 cup of the shredded mozzarella and 1/4 of the toasted bread crumbs. Cover and cook just until breasts are cooked through and cheese is melted, 3-4 minutes longer. Transfer to serving plate and top each breast with 2-3 basil leaves.

# Margarita Chicken

These chicken drumsticks are pre-cooked in the oven, finished on the grill, and then topped with your favorite margarita flavors.

# Margarita Chicken

*Continued from previous page*

**Yield:** 6 servings

**Prep Time:** 10 minutes

**Cook Time:** 1 hour, 10 minutes

**Total Time:** 1 hour, 20 minutes

**Ingredients:**
Cooking spray
3 lbs. skinless bone-in chicken drumsticks (or thighs)
1/2 cup agave nectar, divided
2 Tbsp. tequila
1/4 tsp. table salt
1/8 tsp. pepper
2 Tbsp. olive oil
1 lime, juiced
1 tsp. coarse salt

1. Preheat oven to 300°F. Line a large pan with foil and spray it with cooking spray.

2. Put the chicken in a single layer on the pan.

3. In a small bowl combine 1/4 cup of the agave nectar, tequila, table salt, and pepper. Drizzle it all over the chicken pieces.

4. Bake for 1 hour. Test that it has reached 165°F using an instant-read thermometer.

5. Let cool for 15 minutes on the counter. Cover and refrigerate until ready to grill, up to 36 hours.

6. Brush chicken all over with the olive oil.

7. 15 minutes before eating, prepare grill for direct cooking over medium-high heat.

8. Add chicken pieces and cook until grill marks appear on underside, 4-5 minutes. Flip and cook until heated through, another 4-5 minutes.

9. Remove chicken from the grill and put in a single layer on a serving plate. Drizzle chicken with the remaining 1/4 cup agave nectar and with the lime juice. Sprinkle with the coarse sea salt.

# Grilled Chicken Souvlaki Pitas with Homemade Tzatziki

*Usually yogurt is strained before making tzatziki sauce. I typically skip this step and the result is still nice and thick and delicious. However, the next day there is sometimes some liquid accumulated on top of the sauce. Just drain that off and then stir the sauce. It keeps in the fridge for 3 days but is best on the first day.*

**Yield:** 8 servings

**Prep Time:** 10 minutes

**Cook Time:** 15 minutes

**Total Time:** 25 minutes

**Ingredients:**
2 Tbsp. olive oil
2 Tbsp. + 1 tsp. lemon juice, divided
1 tsp. dry oregano
1/2 tsp. garlic powder
Salt
1/4 tsp. pepper
4 boneless skinless chicken thighs
8 wooden skewers
3 inches of cucumber, peeled and minced
1 clove garlic, minced
1 cup Greek yogurt
2 Tbsp. chopped chives
1 tsp. lemon juice
8 soft pitas
1 large tomato, chopped
1/2 red onion, chopped
1/2 cup crumbled feta cheese

1. Into a ziptop bag measure the olive oil, 2 tablespoons of the lemon juice, oregano, garlic powder, 1/2 teaspoon of salt, and pepper. Swish it around to mix.

2. Slice each chicken thigh into two long strips. Thread each strip onto a skewer. Put chicken in bag of lemon juice mixture and seal bag. Put bag on a large plate in case it accidentally gets punctured. Refrigerate for one hour.

3. Meanwhile, begin making the tzatziki sauce by lining a plate with several layers of paper towel. Put the minced cucumber on it and sprinkle with a pinch of salt. Toss it around to mix it in.

4. Wrap the towel around the cucumber and press down gently. Leave it there, wrapped in the dampening towel for 15 minutes. Squeeze liquid out again. Discard towel. Transfer cucumber to a medium bowl.

5. To the cucumber add the garlic, yogurt, chives, the remaining 1 teaspoon of lemon juice, and 1/4 teaspoon of salt. Stir. Cover and refrigerate until needed.

6. After the chicken is finished marinating, drain off and discard the marinade.

7. Prepare grill for direct cooking over medium heat, about 350°F. Add chicken skewers and cook 3-5 minutes per side until cooked through to 165°F in the middle. Transfer chicken to a clean plate.

8. Warm the pita for 30 seconds in the microwave.

9. Smear each pita with tzatziki on one side. Add a skewer of chicken and some tomato, onion, and feta.

Photo: Leigh Olson

# Smoked Chicken Breasts

*I'm going to be honest here: There are no short cuts when making smoked chicken breasts that are worth eating. Okay, now that we've established that, the steps to making juicy, tender smoked chicken breasts are not difficult. They just take a little planning and time. But, I promise that you'll really love the results.*

**Yield:** 4 servings

**Prep Time:** 15 minutes + time to brine

**Cook Time:** 1 hour, 30 minutes

**Total Time:** 1 hour, 45 minutes + time to brine

**Ingredients:**
4 boneless skinless chicken breasts, brined for 4 hours as explained in Chapter 1
2 tsp. brown sugar
2 tsp. paprika
1 tsp. garlic powder
1/2 tsp. onion powder
1/3 cup BBQ sauce

1. In a small bowl, combine sugar, paprika, garlic powder, and onion powder.
2. Prepare your smoker according to manufacturer's specification and heat to 250°F.
3. Remove the chicken breasts from the brine and pat dry.
4. Sprinkle the chicken breasts with the spice mixture, making sure to cover all sides. Allow to rest for 15 minutes.
5. Place the chicken in the smoker and cook for 60 to 90 minutes or until an instant read thermometer registers 165°F.
6. Remove the chicken from the smoker and place on a platter. Allow to rest for 5 – 7 minutes before slicing.
7. Serve with BBQ sauce on the side for dipping.

# CHAPTER 8
# WINGS AND BUFFALO THINGS

Homemade Buffalo Wing Sauce
Classic Fried Wings
Crispy Oven Wings
Fancier Buffalo Wings
Grilled Thai Wings
Crispy Indian-Spiced Dry Wings with Yogurt Dipping Sauce
Quick Breaded Wings
Boneless Chicken Wings
BBQ Chicken Wings
Buffalo Chicken Salad
Flatbread Salad with Buffalo Chicken and Grilled Onions
Buffalo Chicken Tenders
Buffalo Chicken Dip
Buffalo Chicken Chili Dip
Buffalo Chicken Macaroni and Cheese
Buffalo Chicken Meatballs
Buffalo Chicken Parmesan
Buffalo Chicken Pasta
Buffalo Chicken Poutine

# Homemade Buffalo Wing Sauce

*Store-bought versions of Buffalo sauce tend to contain "butter flavor" and other oils. If you have time to make it yourself, give it a try. The flavor and texture of actual butter really is just so much better.*

**Yield:** 1 and 1/4 cup

**Prep Time:** 2 minutes

**Cook Time:** 5 minutes

**Total Time:** 7 minutes

**Ingredients:**
3/4 cup hot sauce
1/2 cup unsalted butter
1/4 tsp. garlic powder
1/8 tsp. salt

1. Combine all ingredients in a small pot. Heat, stirring occasionally, over medium high until bubbling. Remove from heat.

# Classic Fried Wings

To be honest, as delicious as deep fried wings are, I never make them at home. The reason is that you can't do very many at a time. If you're just making wings for one or two people, go for it. If you've got more people, try the baked crispy wings coming up next, or look at the Instant Pot, Slow Cooker, and Grilling chapters for the wing recipes there.

**Yield:** 1-2 servings

**Prep Time:** 10 minutes

**Cook Time:** 10 minutes

**Total Time:** 20 minutes

**Ingredients:**
Vegetable or canola oil, enough to fill a pot by 1 and 1/2 inches
4 chicken wings
1/4 cup Buffalo wing sauce

1. In a large pot, pour in 1 and 1/2 inches of vegetable or canola oil. Attach candy thermometer so it's in the oil, but not touching the pot. Heat on medium to 350°F.

2. Meanwhile, cut wings into two pieces each.

3. Use tongs to carefully lower the 8 wing pieces into the oil. The oil temperature may drop when the wings are added. Try to keep oil at 350-375°F. If it drops too low, increase heat. If temperature rises, reduce heat. If it keeps rising, take the pot off of heat and transfer to a cool element for 1 minute. Monitor.

4. Flip wings occasionally until well browned and the chicken's internal temperature reaches 165°F on an instant-read thermometer, 8-10 minutes. Place on a plate with a paper towel to remove excess oil.

5. Toss with sauce.

# Crispy Oven Wings

*This is legitimately my go-to recipe for when I have a group over to watch a movie or just hang out. You can make a huge batch of wings (depending on how many pans you have) that are all crispy and delicious and are all ready at the same time. You can alternatively space trays of wings out though if you want to stagger when they're ready. You can also do different sauces or flavors to the wings. Once they're cooked you can toss half a pan with Buffalo sauce and the other half can stay dry and just get a good sprinkling of salt and lemon pepper. There are three things to note about this recipe. First, the baking powder is not meant to create a real coating on the wings. Instead, it's there to change the ph of the chicken skin, which makes it crisp up better. That's why the recipe calls for so little baking powder. Second, the recipe calls for baking powder, not baking soda. Do not use baking soda. Third, baking powder does have a slightly strong flavor that some people are particularly sensitive to. Try buying an aluminum-free baking powder, which seems to help with this. Most people don't detect the baking powder flavor at all, no matter what type is used. But the odd person sometimes tastes it so it's best to go with the aluminum-free, and remember to not use more than is called for in the recipe.*

**Yield:** 20 wings

**Prep Time:** 5 mintues

**Cook Time:** 1 hour, 20 minutes

**Total Time:** 1 hour, 25 mintues

**Ingredients:**
10 whole chicken wings, cut into drumettes and wingettes
1 Tbsp. aluminum-free baking powder (NOT baking soda)
1/2 tsp. salt
1/2 cup wing sauce like Buffalo or teriyaki

1. Preheat oven to 250°F.
2. Line a cookie sheet with aluminum foil. Place a oven-safe rack on top of cookie sheet.
3. In a large bowl, use your hands to toss the wingettes and drumettes with the baking powder and salt until chicken is evenly coated. But do not add extra baking powder. Just mix them so they all have some.
4. Place wings on the rack in single layer. Transfer rack and cookie sheet to oven and cook for 30 minutes. This baking at a low temperature dries the wings out and allows the baking powder to penetrate.
5. After 30 minutes, leave the wings in the oven but raise the heat to 425°F. Continue to cook until brown and crispy, 40-50 minutes.
6. Put the sauce into a large bowl. Add wings and toss to coat.

# Fancier Buffalo Wings

Here we take Buffalo sauce to a new level by using olive oil instead of butter. It makes for a lighter sauce with a slightly different flavor. Then the lemon juice and fresh garic tie it all together.

**Yield:** 25 wings

**Prep Time:** 10 minutes

**Cook Time:** 40 minutes

**Total Time:** 50 minutes

**Ingredients:**
25 wing drumettes and wingettes
1/4 cup hot sauce
1/4 cup olive oil
2 Tbsp. lemon juice
2 cloves garlic, minced

1. Cook wings either by baking (see page 198), deep frying (see page 196), or grilling (see page 182).

2. Meanwhile, in large microwave-safe bowl, combine hot sauce, olive oil, lemon juice, and garlic.

3. When wings are nearly done, microwave sauce 30 seconds at a time, just until heated through.

4. When wings are done, add them to the bowl of sauce and use tongs to toss them.

5. Use tongs to transfer wings to a plate. Dot wings with any garlic remaining in the sauce.

# Grilled Thai Wings

*By Stephanie Manley*

*These wings are doused in a spicy, tangy Thai-style sauce before going on the grill. The delicious wings with the sauce and the slight charring flavor from the grill are out of this world!*

**Yield:** 6 servings

**Prep Time:** 30 minutes

**Cook Time:** 25 minutes

**Total Time:** 55 minutes

**Ingredients:**
2 pounds whole chicken wings
1/4 cup chili sauce
1/4 cup Sriracha or other hot sauce
1/4 cup soy sauce
2 Tbsp. fish sauce
2 Tbsp. lime juice
2 cloves garlic, minced
2 tsp. ginger paste or minced ginger
Cilantro
Lime wedges

1. Cut the wings into drumettes and wingettes. Save the wing tips for stock preparation or discard them.

2. In a large bowl combine chili sauce, Sriracha, soy sauce, fish sauce, lime juice, garlic, and ginger. Add the wings. Put in fridge to marinate for 30 minutes to 1 hour.

3. Preheat grill to 350°F. Shake excess marinade off of wings. This helps to prevent flareups.

4. Place chicken on the hot grill, cook for about 15 minutes, turn over chicken, and cook for another 10 minutes. Monitor it carefully after about the first 10 minutes to make sure it isn't burning underneath. Serve with cilantro and lime wedges.

# Crispy Indian-Spiced Dry Wings with Yogurt Dipping Sauce

*I am particularly partial to dry wings. They're less messy to eat than sauced wings. I sometimes just toss wings with salt, pepper, and garlic powder after cooking them. But if I'm in the mood for something more interesting, this Indian dry rub and yogurt dipping sauce are a great way to go.*

# Crispy Indian-Spiced Dry Wings with Yogurt Dipping Sauce

*Continued from previous page*

**Yield:** 3-4 servings

**Prep Time:** 5 minutes

**Cook Time:** 45 mintues

**Total Time:** 50 minutes

**Ingredients:**
20 chicken wing drumettes and wingettes
1 cup Greek yogurt
2 Tbsp. chopped cilantro
2 garlic cloves, minced
1/4 tsp. salt
1/8 tsp. pepper
2 tsp. curry powder
1 tsp. cumin
1/4 tsp ground ginger
1/2 tsp. cayenne
1/2 tsp. salt

1. Cook wings either by baking (see page 198) or deep frying (see page 196).

2. Meanwhile, make a yogurt dip by combining Greek yogurt, cilantro, garlic, salt, and pepper. Refrigerate.

3. Make a dry rub by mixing together curry powder, cumin, ginger, cayenne, and salt in a bowl.

4. Once wings are cooked, transfer to a large bowl.

5. Sprinkle wings with lime juice. Toss. Then sprinkle with dry rub. Toss.

6. Serve with yogurt sauce for dipping.

# Quick Breaded Wings

*This quick method for breading wings can be used on other kinds of chicken as well. You toss the chicken pieces with mustard and then arrange them on a baking sheet. Sprinkle the tops of the pieces with panko breadcrumbs (these are the crunchiest breadcrumbs!). Then spray with cooking spray and bake until golden brown and chicken is cooked through. The reason this is so quick is that you're not individually breading all sides of each piece of chicken. You're just doing the tops of the chicken, and in such a way that takes much less time.*

**Yield:** 4 servings

**Prep Time:** 10 minutes

**Cook Time:** 45 minutes

**Total Time:** 55 minutes

**Ingredients:**
Cooking spray
8 chicken wings, cut into wingettes and drumettes
2 Tbsp. mustard
Salt
Pepper
1/2 cup panko crumbs

1. Preheat oven to 375°F. Line a baking pan with foil and spray with cooking spray.

2. Put wings in a bowl and add mustard. Mix it all up.

3. Put the wings in a single layer on the pan. Season with salt and pepper. Sprinkle each wing with panko breadcrumbs. Press down on the breadcrumbs so they stick and are evenly distributed on each wing.

4. Spray each wing with cooking spray. Bake until chicken is cooked through (use an instant read thermometer and get it up to 165°F) and breadcrumbs are nice and brown 45-50 minutes.

# Boneless Chicken Wings

*Psst...these aren't really wings! I've used chicken thighs here instead. You get the same great dark meat taste as with wings but without the bones.*

**Yield:** 4 servings

**Prep Time:** 10 minutes

**Cook Time:** 25 mintues

**Total Time:** 35 minutes

**Ingredients:**
1 and 1/2 cups breadcrumbs
1 tsp. chili powder
1 tsp. salt
1 tsp. sugar
1/2 tsp. garlic powder
1/2 tsp. onion powder
1/4 tsp. cayenne powder
2 Tbsp. vegetable oil
8 boneless skinless chicken thighs

1. Preheat oven to 425°F. Combine breadcrumbs and seasonings in a large ziptop bag. Add oil. (The oil is going to help brown the breadcrumbs during baking. Don't skip it!). Massage the crumb mixture through the bag to make sure the oil is spread out well.

2. Put a boneless skinless chicken thigh on a cutting board. Unroll the thigh into a fillet shape. Cut the thigh into three pieces. It will essentially be along the folds from when the thigh was rolled up. Repeat with remaining chicken thighs and then put them all into the ziptop bag with the oiled breadcrumbs. Shake the bag all around to completely coat all of the chicken pieces.

3. Put the pieces of chicken thigh onto a foil-lined oiled baking sheet. Some of the pieces will already have a wing-type shape to them. Leave those alone. Others benefit from a squeeze at one end to give them a drumette shape. So give those a squeeze.

4. Bake until cooked through to 165°F and well-browned, about 25-30 minutes.

# BBQ Chicken Wings

*These wings are baked until crispy and then tossed in a sweet and tangy BBQ sauce. You can eat them right after tossing, or you can put them back into the oven to let the sauce sink in and dry on a bit. Note that if you put them back in, they lose some of their crispness, but get sticky in a good way instead.*

**Yield:** 4 servings

**Prep Time:** 10 minutes

**Cook Time:** 1 hour, 18 mintues

**Total Time:** 1 hour, 28 minutes

**Ingredients:**

- 10 whole chicken wings (or you can cut them each into wingettes and drumettes, discarding the wing tip or saving it for another purpose)
- 1 Tbsp. aluminum-free baking powder (NOT baking soda)
- 1/2 tsp. salt
- 1 and 1/2 cups ketchup
- 1/4 cup prepared yellow mustard
- 1/4 cup honey
- 2 tsp. hot sauce
- 1 tsp. chili powder
- 1 tsp. garlic powder
- 1/2 tsp. smoked paprika
- Salt
- Pepper

1. Preheat oven to 250°F.
2. Place a rack onto a cookie sheet.
3. In a large bowl, toss the wings with the baking powder and salt. Place wings on the rack in single layer and cook for 30 minutes.
4. After 30 minutes, leave them in there and raise the heat to 425°F until brown and crispy, 40-50 minutes.
5. Meanwhile, in a large bowl combine the ketchup, mustard, honey, hot sauce, chili powder, garlic powder, and smoked paprika. Taste and add salt and pepper if desired.
6. When wings are done, add to the bowl of sauce and coat well. Remove wings (discard remaining sauce) and serve, or put them back on the rack and back into the oven until the sauce is dry and sticky-looking, 8-10 minutes more.

# Buffalo Chicken Salad

*By Rebecca Clyde*

*When you have leftover cooked chicken, a common use for it is on a salad. Using ranch and hot sauce as the dressing for the salad makes it taste like Buffalo wings, which is a real treat. Note that some ranch dressings are thicker than others. If the one you have it really thick, instructions are given for thinning it down with a bit of milk.*

**Yield:** 4 servings

**Prep Time:** 5 minutes

**Cook Time:** 5 minutes

**Total Time:** 10 minutes

**Ingredients:**
3/4 cup ranch dressing
Hot sauce to taste
1/4 cup skim milk (optional)
1 large head romaine lettuce, chopped
1 lb. cooked chicken breasts, shredded
4 stalks celery, chopped finely
2 large carrots, chopped
1 whole English cucumber, sliced and quartered
1/4 cup roasted sunflower seeds

1. Measure ranch in a jar with a tight-fitting lid. Add a few drops (or more, to taste) of the hot sauce. Stir. If sauce is very thick, add some or all of the milk. Put lid on jar and shake to combine.

2. Lay lettuce in bowl, add the chicken, celery, carrots, cucumber, and sunflower seeds. Drizzle top with some of the ranch mixture. You likely will not need all of the dressing. Refrigerate for another use.

# Flatbread Salad with Buffalo Chicken and Grilled Onions

*A flatbread salad is a grilled flatbread with melted cheese that is topped with fresh crisp salad. This flatbread salad has grilled Buffalo chicken and grilled sweet onions. A perfect summer recipe!*

**Yield:** 2 servings

**Prep Time:** 10 minutes

**Cook Time:** 18 minutes

**Total Time:** 28 minutes

**Ingredients:**

1 medium sweet onion
5 Tbsp. Buffalo wing sauce, divided
2 boneless skinless chicken breasts
2 naan breads (9-inch) or pre-baked pizza crusts
1 tsp. olive oil
1/2 cup shredded cheddar cheese
4 cups salad greens
1 carrot, peeled and then shredded using a potato peeler
1 stalk celery, thinly sliced
4 Tbsp. ranch dressing

1. Preheat grill to medium-high heat.

2. Trim the ends off of the onion and peel it. Slice onion into three thick slices. Keep rings intact. Brush onion slices with 1 tablespoon of the wing sauce.

3. Brush each chicken breast with 1 tablespoon of wing sauce.

4. Grill the three onion slices and the chicken breasts over direct heat, flipping occasionally, until chicken is cooked through and onion slices are blackened, 12-15 minutes. Do not turn off grill.

5. Use the remaining 2 tablespoons of wing sauce to brush the chicken and onions again. Let rest off of the heat while preparing flatbreads.

6. Oil one side of each flatbread with 1/2 teaspoon of olive oil. Put flatbreads oil side down on the grill. Top each with 1/4 cup cheese. Grill just until bottom is starting to brown and cheese is melted, 3-4 minutes.

7. Cut each flatbread into 8 wedges and arrange each set of 8 on a plate.

8. Slice chicken into 1/2-inch slices. Separate onions into rings, discarding outer rings if they are very blackened. Top each plate of flatbread wedges with 2 cups of salad greens, half of the carrot, half of the celery, 2 tablespoons of ranch dressing and half of the chicken and onion rings.

*Photo: Amanda Dorich*

# Buffalo Chicken Tenders

*By Amanda Dorich*

*These are traditional breaded chicken tenders that are oven-baked until crunchy and then tossed in a quick homemade Buffalo wing sauce. The recipe can easily be doubled or tripled if you have a group over.*

**Yield:** 6 tenders

**Prep Time:** 10 minutes

**Cook Time:** 16 mintues

**Total Time:** 26 minutes

**Ingredients:**
Cooking spray
1/2 cup plain panko breadcrumbs
1/2 cup seasoned breadcrumbs
1/2 cup flour
1 egg
1 Tbsp. water
2 Tbsp. dry ranch seasoning
6 chicken tenderloins
4 Tbsp. unsalted butter
1 cup hot sauce
1 tsp. garlic powder
Ranch dressing

1. Preheat oven to 425°F. Spray a baking sheet with cooking spray.

2. In a shallow bowl or plate, stir together the two types of bread crumbs. In a separate container, whisk together the egg and water. In a third container, stir together the flour and ranch seasoning.

3. Dip each tender first into the flour mixture and then in the egg mixture and finally in the breadcrumbs. Place on baking sheet and bake for 8 minutes, then flip, and bake another 8 minutes, or until both sides are golden brown and internal temperature is 165°F.

4. While chicken is cooking, put butter in a large microwave-safe bowl. Put in microwave for 15 seconds at at time until melted.

5. To the butter add the hot sauce and the garlic powder.

6. When chicken is done cooking, remove from oven and let cool for 1 minute so the breadcrumbs can crisp up. Add chicken to the sauce and toss gently to coat. Serve immediately with ranch dressing on the side for dipping.

# Buffalo Chicken Dip

*By Tawnie Kroll*

*Buffalo Chicken Dip has become a staple at house parties in recent years. This one has some options for making it a little bit lighter, if you're interested in that. You can use low-fat cream cheese and you can swap out nonfat Greek yogurt for the sour cream. Either way, it's a cheesy, tasty dip that is always a party-pleaser.*

**Yield:** 8-10 servings

**Prep Time:** 15 minutes

**Cook Time:** 25 minutes

**Total Time:** 40 minutes

**Ingredients:**
- 2 cooked chicken breasts, shredded
- 2 cups shredded cheddar cheese, divided
- 8 oz. regular or low fat cream cheese, softened
- 1 cup sour cream or nonfat plain Greek yogurt
- 1 cup Buffalo wing sauce
- 1/2 tsp. garlic powder
- 1/2 tsp. onion powder
- 1/4 cup crumbled Gorgonzola
- 2 Tbsp. chopped green onion
- Celery, carrots, crackers for dipping

1. Preheat oven to 350°F.
2. In a large bowl mix together the chicken, 1 cup cheddar cheese, cream cheese, sour cream, Buffalo sauce, garlic powder, and onion powder. Stir until well combined. Pour into a cast iron skillet or an oven safe baking dish.
3. Top with remaining 1 cup cheddar cheese and bake until heated through, 25-30 minutes.
4. Top with Gorgonzola and green onions. Serve immediately with veggies and crackers.

# Buffalo Chicken Chili Dip

*This dip uses leftover chili as its base. So next time you have leftover chili, you know what you've got to do. If you don't have leftover chili, you can use canned chili instead, or mix together 1 pound of cooked ground chicken with a jar of salsa. It's going to be delicious no matter how you do it.*

**Yield:** 6 servings

**Prep Time:** 2 minutes

**Cook Time:** 15 minutes

**Total Time:** 17 minutes

**Ingredients:**
1 cup chicken chili (leftover or canned), strain a bit if it's liquidy
2 Tbsp. Buffalo wing sauce (or more to taste)
2 Tbsp. ranch dressing
1/4 cup shredded cheddar cheese (plus a bit more for garnish)

1. Preheat oven to 400°F.
2. Spoon the chili into a small baking dish. Use a fork to break up any big pieces, if any.
3. Stir in 2 tablespoons of Buffalo wing sauce, the ranch dressing, and the cheddar cheese.
4. Taste it. You may need more wing sauce depending on how spicy the original chili was and on how hot you like your dip. Add more wing sauce to taste.
5. Top with a sprinkle more of shredded cheese and then bake until heated through and cheese on top is just starting to brown at the edges, about 15-20 minutes.

Photo: Sam Ellis

# Buffalo Chicken Macaroni and Cheese

*By Sam Ellis*

*This recipe uses cheddar jack cheese. That's the orange and white marbled cheese that combines the sharp cheddar flavors with the milder jack cheese. It melts really well resulting in a smooth sauce. The cornstarch in the sauce makes it thicken more which helps coat and stick to the pasta and chicken.*

**Yield:** 6 servings

**Prep Time:** 5 minutes

**Cook Time:** 20 mintues

**Total Time:** 25 minutes

**Ingredients:**
1 cup milk
2 Tbsp. cornstarch
2 cups shredded cheddar jack cheese, divided
1/2 cup Buffalo wing sauce
1/4 cup ranch dressing
4 cups cooked shredded chicken
1/3 cup plain breadcrumbs
2 Tbsp. green onions, chopped

1. Preheat broiler on low.
2. In a large pot, cook elbow pasta according to box. Drain and set aside.
3. In the same pot over low heat, add milk and cornstarch together. Whisk together until smooth.
4. Stir in 1 and 3/4 cups of the cheese, Buffalo sauce, and ranch dressing and whisk until melted.
5. Add cooked pasta and shredded chicken and mix until everything is coated evenly.
6. In an oven-proof baking dish, spread out the Buffalo chicken mac and cheese. Top with remaining 1/4 cup of cheese and breadcrumbs evenly. Place under the broiler until breadcrumbs are toasted, about 5 minutes. Sprinkle with green onions.

Photo: Jamie Silva

# Buffalo Chicken Meatballs

*By Jamie Silva*

*To check if meatballs are seasoned enough to your liking, make a small meatball from your raw seasoned chicken mixture and microwave it on a plate 10 seconds at a time until cooked through. It won't take long. Let it cool a bit and then taste it. You'll then know if the amount of seasoning is right for you or if more is needed.*

**Yield:** 20-24 meatballs

**Prep Time:** 15 minutes

**Cook Time:** 20 mintues

**Total Time:** 35 minutes

**Ingredients:**
Cooking spray
2/3 cup Buffalo wing sauce
2 Tbsp. unsalted butter, melted
1 lb. ground chicken
3/4 cup panko bread crumbs
1 large egg
1/2 tsp. garlic powder
1/4 tsp. salt or more to taste
1/4 tsp. pepper or more to taste
Ranch dressing for drizzling (optional)

1. Preheat oven to 400°F. Line a baking sheet with parchment paper and spray with cooking spray. Set aside.

2. In a bowl, mix Buffalo sauce with butter. Set aside.

3. In another bowl, combine ground chicken, bread crumbs, egg, 1/3 cup of the now buttery Buffalo sauce, garlic powder, salt, and pepper. Don't overmix.

4. Shape the mixture into small 1" balls and place them on the baking sheet. Bake until no longer pink inside, about 20-25 minutes. Remove from oven.

5. Toss meatballs with remaining Buffalo-butter sauce. Drizzle with ranch dressing.

Photo: Allie Doran

# Buffalo Chicken Parmesan

*By Allie Doran*

*There are very few things better than a great mash-up recipe. Taco salad, spaghetti pie, pizza pasta...and perhaps the greatest of them all — Buffalo Chicken Parmesan. Is there really anything better than enjoying two of your favorite flavors all during one meal?*

**Yield:** 4 servings

**Prep Time:** 1 hour, 15 minutes

**Cook Time:** 15-18 mintues

**Total Time:** 1 hour, 30 minutes

**Ingredients:**
1 lb. chicken cutlets
1/2 cup hot sauce, divided
1/2 cup panko breadcrumbs
1 tsp. garlic powder
1 tsp. salt
1/2 tsp. pepper
1/2 tsp. onion powder
1/4 tsp. chili powder
2 Tbsp. unsalted butter
1 Tbsp. ranch dressing
4 slices mozzarella cheese

1. Begin by pulling your chicken from the refrigerator and placing it into a large plastic bag. Pour 1/4 cup of the hot sauce into the bag over the chicken, place back into the refrigerator, and let marinate for 1 hour.

2. Preheat the oven to 400°F.

3. Measure the panko breadcrumbs, garlic powder, salt, pepper, onion powder, and chili powder into a bowl and mix.

4. Take out a large cast iron or oven-safe skillet and place over medium heat. Remove chicken from the refrigerator. You're going to take each piece of marinated chicken and coat it in the seasoned breadcrumb mixture. When all of the chicken has been coasted in the crumb mix, add the butter to the pan and swirl it around until it's melted. Lay the cutlets in the hot pan and let them cook, about 6-8 minutes per side. You want the crust to be golden, and the insides to be cooked through.

5. While the chicken is cooking, take the remaining 1/4 cup of hot sauce and mix with the ranch dressing. When the chicken has finished cooking, remove the skillet from the heat, drizzle the hot ranch sauce evenly over each cutlet, and lay a piece of mozzarella over each piece of chicken.

6. Place into the oven for 3-4 minutes, or until the cheese melts and bubbles.

# Buffalo Chicken Pasta

*By Amy Getman*

*The spice level in this dish is fairly mild but if you're looking for more fire, add extra wing sauce or garnish with a generous sprinkling of red pepper flakes at the end.*

**Yield:** 8 servings

**Prep Time:** 5 minutes

**Cook Time:** 30 minutes

**Total Time:** 35 minutes

**Ingredients:**
1 lb. dry penne pasta
8 oz. cream cheese
3/4 cup milk
1 cup shredded cheddar cheese
1/3 cup Buffalo wing sauce
2 cups cooked shredded chicken
1/2 cup blue cheese crumbles
1/2 cup panko bread crumbs
Chopped green onion, cilantro, and red pepper flakes for garnish

1. Cook pasta according to package.
2. While pasta is cooking, combine cream cheese, milk, shredded cheese, and wing sauce in a pot over medium heat. Stir frequently and cook until cheese is melted and mixture is smooth.
3. Add shredded chicken and cooked pasta to cheese mixture and stir thoroughly.
4. Turn on broiler.
5. Place pasta mixture in a 9"x13" casserole dish and sprinkle blue cheese and panko bread crumbs over the top.
6. Place under broiler until breadcrumbs start to brown, about 5 minutes. Watch closely to avoid burning.
7. Serve topped with green onion, cilantro, and red pepper flakes, or extra wing sauce, if desired.

# Buffalo Chicken Poutine

*Poutine is a dish from Quebec, Canada that consists of french fries topped with cheese curds and gravy. In recent years I've been seeing variations of poutine all across North American, and beyond. This variation is one that I came up with that celebrates my Canadian roots and my love of all things Buffalo chicken.*

# Buffalo Chicken Poutine

*Continued from previous page*

**Yield:** 4 servings

**Cook Time:** 30 mintues

**Total Time:** 30 minutes

**Ingredients:**
3 medium russet potatoes
3 Tbsp. vegetable oil
1 (1 oz.) package of ranch salad dressing seasoning mix
4 Tbsp. unsalted butter
3 Tbsp. all-purpose flour
1/2 cup beer
1/2 cup Buffalo wing sauce
1 cup low-sodium chicken stock
1/4 tsp. salt
1/4 tsp. pepper
2 cups cooked shredded chicken
2 cups shredded mozzarella cheese

1. Preheat oven to 450°F.

2. Cut the potatoes into 1/4 to 1/2-inch strips. Put in a large bowl with the oil and 2 tablespoons of the ranch seasoning mix. Toss to coat. Transfer to a large baking sheet making sure no fries are overlapping. Put into the oven even if it has not yet finished preheating. Cook for 15 minutes. Use a metal spatula to scrape under fries and flip them. Cook for another 10 minutes. Sprinkle fries with remaining ranch seasoning.

3. While the fries cook, melt the butter in a medium pot over low heat. Whisk in the flour. While whisking constantly, slowly drizzle in the beer. Make sure it's smooth. Continue to whisk as you add the wing sauce and then the broth. Add the salt and pepper. Increase heat to medium and stir frequently until it reaches a simmer. Reduce heat to low and stir occasionally until the fries are ready. Taste and add more salt and pepper if desired.

4. Just before the fries are ready, put the chicken on a microwave-safe plate and heat in the microwave until very hot, 1-2 minutes.

5. Assemble the poutine by dividing the fries among 4 plates. Top each serving of fries with 1/2 cup cheese, 1/2 cup chicken, and 1/3 cup of the beer sauce. Let sit for 30 seconds to allow the hot fries and sauce to melt the cheese. (Note that you will have sauce leftover. Cover and refrigerate so that you have an excuse to make more poutine tomorrow!)

# CHAPTER 9
# WORLD FLAVORS

Chicken Tetrazzini
Chicken Parmesan from Frozen
Chicken Marsala
Chicken Piccata
Chicken Cacciatore
Chicken Goulash
Chicken Paprikash
Chicken Cordon Bleu from Frozen
Panko Crusted Chicken Kiev
Chicken Enchilada Casserole
Chinese Garlic Chicken
Leftover Chicken Faux Pho
Chicken Curry
Chicken Korma
Chicken Vindaloo
Chicken Tikka Masala
Quick Moroccan Stew with Chick Peas and Chicken
Colombian Crema de Aquacate (Cream of Avocado Soup) with Chicken
Chinese Chicken Meatballs
Italian Chicken Meatballs
Chicken Albóndigas
Swedish Chicken Meatbals

# Chicken Tetrazzini

*By Sam Ellis*

*Even though Chicken Tetrazzini has an Italian name, it's actually an American dish. It's believed to have been created in the early 1900s in San Francisco and named after a well-loved Italian opera singer, Luisa Tetrazzini. I've included it in the World Flavors section though because it has a lot of the flavors that we think of as Italian.*

**Yield:** 6 servings

**Prep Time:** 20 minutes

**Cook Time:** 40 minutes

**Total Time:** 1 hour

**Ingredients:**
2 Tbsp. unsalted butter
1 (8 oz.) package sliced mushrooms
2 Tbsp. all-purpose flour
1/4 cup white wine
1 and 1/2 cups low-sodium chicken stock
1 cup heavy cream
1/4 cup chopped fresh parsley, plus more to garnish
1/8 tsp. ground nutmeg
3 cups chopped cooked chicken
1 lb. cooked linguine
1/3 cup shredded Parmesan cheese

1. Preheat oven to 350°F.
2. In a medium sized saucepan over medium heat, add butter and let melt.
3. Add in sliced mushrooms and mix to coat with melted butter. Let cook, stirring occasionally, until softened, about 5 minutes.
4. Sprinkle in flour and stir to coat.
5. Drizzle in white wine, stir well, and let simmer making sure the flour incorporates into a thick sauce.
6. Add in chicken stock and bring to a boil to thicken.
7. Remove from heat and stir in heavy cream, chopped fresh parsley, and ground nutmeg.
8. Add cooked chicken breast and cooked linguine. Stir and then transfer it all to a casserole dish.
9. Sprinkle with shredded Parmesan and bake until heated through, 30-40 minutes. Garnish with chopped parsley.

# Chicken Parmesan from Frozen

You can make Chicken Parmesan with frozen chicken breasts, and thus save yourself having to defrost the chicken. This only works if the chicken breasts were frozen individually though. If you bought them already frozen in a bag, they're likely separate and are ready to go. If you bought them fresh and they came in a pack all squished together and you froze them like that, then you should defrost them before cooking them. But never fear, I've given instructions for using thawed chicken breasts too.

# Chicken Parmesan from Frozen

*Continued from previous page*

**Yield:** 4 servings

**Prep Time:** 5 minutes

**Cook Time:** 30 mintues

**Total Time:** 35 minutes

**Ingredients:**

1/3 cup panko breadcrumbs
Cooking oil
1/2 tsp. salt
1/4 tsp. pepper
1/4 tsp. garlic powder
1/4 cup grated Parmesan cheese
4 medium frozen boneless skinless chicken breasts that were frozen individually and are not attached to each other now
1/3 cup tomato sauce, divided
1/2 cup shredded mozzarella cheese

1. Preheat oven to 425°F. Lightly oil a baking sheet.

2. In a small bowl combine panko, 1 tablespoon cooking oil, salt, pepper, garlic powder, and Parmesan cheese.

3. Place chicken breasts on prepared pan and brush the top of each with about 1 teaspoon of tomato sauce. Top each with one quarter of the breadcrumbs.

4. Bake until cooked through to 165°F, as read on an instant-read thermometer, 30-40 minutes. (If using thawed chicken breasts, cook until cooked through to 165°F, or about 20-25 minutes).

5. Remove from oven and preheat broiler. Top each breast with 1 heaped tablespoon of tomato sauce and 2 tablespoons mozzarella. Broil until cheese is melted, 2-3 minutes.

# Chicken Marsala

*If you've never tried Marsala before, I urge you to get a bottle. You can find some very inexpensive ones at your local liquor store and they're just fine. I will say that I don't love to drink it on its own, not really at all. But it's really delicious to cook with. You can make it the star of the show, like in today's recipe, or you can add a splash of it to all kinds of things. It adds just a touch of sweetness and tons of flavor. It's great in soups and stews and in all kinds of gravies and sauces.*

**Yield:** 4 servings

**Prep Time:** 10 minutes

**Cook Time:** 15 minutes

**Total Time:** 25 minutes

**Ingredients:**
2 (6 oz.) boneless skinless chicken breasts
1/2 cup all-purpose flour
1/4 tsp. garlic powder
3 Tbsp. vegetable oil
8 oz. sliced mushrooms
1/2 cup sweet Marsala fortified wine
1/4 cup low-sodium chicken stock
Salt
Pepper

1. Pound chicken breasts out to equal 1/4-inch thickness then cut in half.
2. In a shallow bowl combine flour, garlic powder, 1/4 tsp. salt, and 1/4 teaspoon pepper. Dredge chicken in flour.
3. Add vegetable oil to large skillet and heat over medium until shimmering.
4. Add chicken and cook 2-3 minutes on each side. Remove to a paper-towel-lined plate.
5. Add mushrooms to pan and cook, stirring occasionally until well-browned, about 4 minutes.
6. Season mushrooms with 1/4 teaspoon salt and then add the Marsala wine, scraping the bottom of the pan to pick up any bits. Stir until the wine is thickened to a syrup.
7. To the pan, add chicken stock and simmer 2-3 minutes.
8. Return chicken to pan and heat through.
9. Transfer chicken to plates and spoon mushrooms and sauce over top.

# Chicken Piccata

*In Italy, piccata dishes are usually made from veal or swordfish. In North America, we tend to use chicken. We're a tad chicken-obsessed over here. Ha! Piccatas can vary in several ways but the main important ingredients are lemon and butter. It should be really tart and lemony and rich all at once.*

**Yield:** 4 servings

**Prep Time:** 8 minutes

**Cook Time:** 12 minutes

**Total Time:** 20 minutes

**Ingredients:**
2 boneless skinless chicken breasts
1/2 cup all-purpose flour
1/4 tsp. garlic powder
1/4 tsp. pepper
1/4 tsp. salt
2 Tbsp. olive oil
4 Tbsp. unsalted butter, divided
1/4 cup fresh lemon juice
1/2 cup low-sodium chicken stock
1/4 cup drained capers

1. Pound chicken breasts to an even 1/4-inch thickness. Cut each one in half to make 4 portions.

2. In a medium bowl mix together the flour, garlic powder, pepper, and salt.

3. Dredge chicken in the flour mixture so that it's dusted in white. Shake off excess.

4. Heat the olive oil and 2 tablespoons of the butter in a large skillet over medium-high heat. When hot, add chicken.

5. Cook chicken until brown on both sides, about 2-3 minutes per side. Transfer to a plate lined with paper towel.

6. To the pan add the lemon juice, chicken stock, and capers. Scrape the bottom of the pan and then bring to a boil.

7. Return chicken to the pan. Cook until chicken is hot and no longer pink inside, about 5 minutes.

8. Remove chicken to a large clean serving plate. Arrange in a single layer.

9. Remove pan from heat. Add the remaining 2 tablespoons of butter to the pan and whisk it vigorously. Taste. Season with salt and pepper to taste. Pour over chicken.

Photo: Allie Doran

# Chicken Cacciatore

*By Allie Doran*

*I like to use boneless, skinless chicken thighs for Cacciatore. But traditionally this is a "hunter's style" chicken (that's what cacciatore means), so you can use a whole chicken cut into pieces instead. It's a very versatile recipe that way. You'll just need about 2 pounds of chicken.*

# Chicken Cacciatore

*Continued from previous page*

**Yield:** 4-6 servings

**Prep Time:** 10 minutes

**Cook Time:** 35 mintues

**Total Time:** 40 minutes

**Ingredients:**
2 Tbsp. olive oil
2 lbs. boneless skinless chicken thighs
1 medium onion, chopped
1 green bell pepper, chopped
3 garlic cloves, minced
1 tsp. salt
1 tsp. Italian seasoning
1/4 tsp. pepper
1 (14 oz.) can diced tomatoes
1 (8 oz.) can tomato sauce
2 Tbsp. tomato paste

1. Heat the olive oil over medium heat in a large pot until hot.

2. Sear the chicken thighs until a nice brown crust is formed on each side. You may need to do this in batches so that it can brown instead of steaming. It will steam if it's too crowded in the pan. Once the chicken is seared, remove it from the pan and set aside on a plate.

3. Add the onion and bell pepper to the pot and sauté until softened and slightly brown, about 3-4 minutes.

4. Add the garlic, salt, Italian seasoning, and pepper. Cook for 2 more minutes.

5. Add the diced tomatoes, tomato sauce, and tomato paste. Stir to combine.

6. Add the chicken back into the pot and bring the mixture to a boil. Reduce the heat to a simmer, cover with a lid, and cook until chicken is cooked through to 165°F, about 20 minutes.

# Chicken Goulash

*In Hungary Goulash is typically a stew that is served in a bowl. However, I often see it mixed with pasta in North America. For this dish, I combined the two ideas. You make a rich and hearty paprika-flavored stew and then you serve it over egg noodles. This version is made with chicken instead of the more traditional beef.*

**Yield:** 4 servings

**Prep Time:** 10 minutes

**Cook Time:** 35 minutes

**Total Time:** 45 minutes

**Ingredients:**
1 Tbsp. olive oil
1 medium onion, chopped
2 carrots, peeled and chopped
1 green bell pepper, chopped
1 lb. boneless skinless chicken thighs, cut into 1/2-inch pieces
2 garlic cloves, minced
2 tsp. sweet paprika
1 tsp. salt
1/2 tsp. pepper
16 oz. tomato sauce
6 oz. tomato paste
1 cup low-sodium chicken stock
1 (12 oz.) bag of egg noodles
1/4 cup sour cream

1. Add the olive oil to a large pot over medium heat.

2. Once the oil is hot, add the onion, carrot, and green pepper. Cook for 5-7 minutes, or until the vegetables begin to soften.

3. Add the chicken and cook for 5 minutes stirring occasionally before adding the garlic, paprika, salt, and pepper.

4. Sauté for 3 additional minutes and then add the tomato sauce, tomato paste, and stock.

5. Bring the mixture to a boil over medium heat, cover and reduce to a simmer.

6. After the goulash has simmered for 20 minutes, boil a large pot of water for the egg noodles.

7. Cook the egg noodles according to the package directions and drain.

8. Remove the goulash from the heat and stir in the sour cream.

9. Serve the goulash over a bed of egg noodles. Top with more sour cream if desired.

Photo: Allie Doran

# Chicken Paprikash

*Chicken Paprikash is a traditional Hungarian dish that braises bone-in chicken in a paprika sauce and is traditionally served over egg noodles or dumplings.*

**Yield:** 4-6 servings

**Prep Time:** 10 minutes

**Cook Time:** 1 hour

**Total Time:** 1 hour, 10 minutes

**Ingredients:**
1 Tbsp. olive oil
1 Tbsp. unsalted butter
2 and 1/2 lbs. bone-in chicken thighs
1 medium onion, halved and thinly sliced
1 Tbsp. all-purpose flour
1 Tbsp. tomato paste
3 tsp. paprika
1 tsp. salt
1/4 tsp. pepper
1 and 1/2 cups low-sodium chicken stock
3/4 cup sour cream
16 oz. egg noodles, cooked according to package directions

1. Heat the olive oil and butter in a large pot over medium-high heat until hot.

2. Add the chicken thighs, in batches if your pot isn't big enough to give them each space, and sear until browned on all sides, 3-4 minutes per side. Remove the chicken thighs.

3. Turn the heat down to medium. Add the onion and sauté until soft and golden brown, about 4 minutes.

4. Add the flour, tomato paste, paprika, salt, and pepper and cook for 3 minutes.

5. Add the chicken stock and sour cream and stir until everything is well combined.

6. Bring the mixture to a boil. Add the chicken thighs back to the pan. Cover and turn the heat down to low.

7. Simmer for 15 minutes with the lid on. Then take the lid off and simmer until the chicken is cooked through to 165°F as read on an instant read thermometer, about another 15 minutes.

8. Serve over hot egg noodles.

# Chicken Cordon Bleu from Frozen

*We've talked about cooking chicken breasts from frozen a few times now in this book. That's because I'm pretty obsessed with it. The convenience of having chicken breasts in my freezer and knowing that I can immediately get dinner started by putting them straight into the oven has been revolutionary in my house. I hope you find the technique helpful also. But if you're not into it, I've given instructions for using thawed chicken breasts also.*

**Yield:** 4 servings

**Prep Time:** 5 minutes

**Cook Time:** 35 minutes

**Total Time:** 40 minutes

**Ingredients:**
1/3 cup panko breadcrumbs
1 Tbsp. olive oil
1/2 tsp. salt
1/4 tsp. pepper
1/4 tsp. garlic powder
1/4 tsp. dried thyme leaves
4 frozen boneless skinless chicken breasts that have been frozen individually
4 tsp. mustard (yellow or dijon)
4 slices black forest ham
4 slices of Swiss cheese

1. Preheat oven to 425°F. Lightly oil a baking sheet.

2. In a small bowl combine the breadcrumbs, oil, salt, pepper, garlic powder, and thyme.

3. Put the chicken breasts on the prepared baking sheet. Spread or brush 1 teaspoon of mustard onto each breast. Sprinkle with the breadcrumbs, pushing down to help them adhere to the mustard.

4. Bake until chicken is 165°F according to an instant read thermometer, 30-40 minutes. (If using thawed chicken breasts, cook until 165°F, about 20-25 minutes).

5. Remove chicken from oven. Top each breast with a slice of the ham, folded in half, and then a slice of the cheese, also folded in half. Return to the oven and bake until cheese is melted, about 5 minutes.

*Photo: Allie Doran*

# Panko Crusted Chicken Kiev

*By Allie Doran*

*Make sure you have a little bit of space in your freezer before starting this dish. That's because you'll need to freeze a log of flavored butter for a bit, and then later freeze the stuffed chicken breasts for a little while too. Why do the freezing? Freezing the butter makes it easier to slice and also to keep it in place when you wrapping the chicken around it. Freezing the stuffed raw chicken breasts helps them stay together and keep their shape for when you bread them and for the first bit of the cooking time.*

# Panko Crusted Chicken Kiev

*Continued from previous page*

**Yield:** 4-6 servings

**Prep Time:** 45 minutes

**Cook Time:** 35 mintues

**Total Time:** 1 hour, 20 minutes

**Ingredients:**
1/2 cup unsalted butter, softened
1/4 cup chopped parsley
2 garlic cloves, grated
1/2 tsp. dried oregano
1/2 tsp. salt
1/4 tsp. pepper
2 lbs. boneless skinless chicken breasts
1/4 cup all-purpose flour
1 tsp. salt, divided
1 egg
1 Tbsp. water
3/4 cup panko breadcrumbs
1/2 tsp. garlic powder
1/4 tsp. paprika
1/4 cup olive oil

1. To make the filling, mix together the softened butter, parsley, grated garlic, oregano, salt, and pepper in a bowl.
2. Scoop the mixture out onto a piece of plastic wrap and form into a log. Wrap tightly, and place in the freezer for at least 15 minutes.
3. Pound the chicken breasts out between two pieces of plastic wrap or parchment paper until they're an even thickness. Lay the chicken on a baking sheet lined with parchment paper.
4. Remove the butter filling from the freezer and cut into 4-6 strips, depending on how many chicken breasts you have.
5. Lay one strip on the wide edge of one of the chicken pieces. Roll the chicken up around the butter. If desired, secure with toothpicks. Repeat with each piece of chicken.
6. Place the parchment lined baking sheet with the chicken rolls into the freezer for 15 minutes.
7. Meanwhile, preheat the oven to 400°F and prepare the breading as follows.
8. Lay three bowls out on your counter. To one, add the flour and 1/2 teaspoon of the salt. To another, add the egg and water and whisk. To the third, add the remaining salt, panko, garlic powder, and paprika.
9. Once the chicken has chilled, heat a thick bottom skillet over medium-high heat.
10. Roll the chicken first in the flour, then the egg mixture, and finally the panko mixture, coating each chicken roll.
11. Once all of the chicken rolls are coated, measure the oil into the hot skillet and swirl it around. Add the chicken rolls and cook for about 3-5 minutes per side, or until the breading is golden brown.
12. Remove the chicken from the oil and place on an oven-safe rack set over a baking sheet. Place baking sheet, rack, and chicken in the oven and bake until an instant-read thermometer reads 165°F for the center of the chicken, about 15-18 minutes. Rest for 5 minutes before serving.

# Chicken Enchilada Casserole

*By Lauren Keating*

*Chicken Enchilada Casserole is quicker to make than regular enchiladas because you don't have to do all the work of filling and rolling individual tortillas.*

**Yield:** 8 servings

**Prep Time:** 15 minutes

**Cook Time:** 45 minutes

**Total Time:** 1 hour

**Ingredients:**
1 (28 oz.) can enchilada sauce, divided
1 Tbsp. olive oil
1 lb. boneless skinless chicken breasts, diced
1 green bell pepper, diced
1 (4 oz.) can diced green chili peppers
1 (15.5 oz.) can black beans, drained
1 cup frozen corn
8 soft corn tortillas
2 cups shredded Mexican blend cheese
Fresh cilantro

1. Preheat oven to 375°F.
2. Pour 1/4 cup enchilada sauce into a 9"x11" casserole dish and spread until the bottom of the dish is evenly coated.
3. Heat the oil in a skillet set over medium-high heat.
4. Add the chicken and cook until browned, 4-5 minutes.
5. Add the bell pepper and chilis and cook 5-6 minutes, until softened.
6. Stir in the beans, corn, and remaining enchilada sauce. Simmer 5 minutes, until slightly thickened.
7. Cut the tortillas in half. Arrange 8 tortilla pieces in a single layer covering the bottom of the casserole dish.
8. Cover with half of the chicken mixture and 1 cup cheese.
9. Repeat with another layer of tortillas, chicken, and cheese.
10. Cover the pan with foil and bake for 20 minutes.
11. Uncover and bake an additional 10 minutes, until cheese is bubbling.
12. Remove from the oven and garnish with cilantro.

# Chinese Garlic Chicken

*By Emily Dingmann*

*The garlic sauce looks pretty unassuming when you mix it up. But when it hits the hot pan, you'll see how it starts to get thick and sticky like a real Chinese chicken sauce. What's the secret? The cornstarch helps thicken it and gives it that classic consistency.*

**Yield:** 4 servings

**Prep Time:** 10 minutes

**Cook Time:** 10 minutes

**Total Time:** 20 minutes

**Ingredients:**
5 cloves garlic, minced
1/4 cup soy sauce
1 Tbsp. sesame oil
2 Tbsp. honey
1 Tbsp. cornstarch
1 Tbsp. vegetable oil
1 lb. boneless skinless chicken breast, cut into 1-inch pieces
1 tsp. toasted sesame seeds (optional)
1 green onion, chopped (optional)

1. Whisk together minced garlic, soy sauce, sesame oil, honey, and cornstarch until smooth.

2. Heat vegetable oil in a large skillet or wok over medium-high heat. Add chicken and garlic mixture to pan and stir fry, stirring frequently, until chicken is cooked through and sauce has thickened, about 5-7 minutes.

3. Garnish with sesame seeds and green onion, if desired.

# Leftover Chicken Faux Pho

Vietnamese Pho is a noodle soup with a rich broth that usually involves a lengthy process. This is a much faster faux Pho that is a great way to use up leftover chicken. If you don't have leftover chicken, don't worry. Thinly slice raw chicken and add it to the soup at the same time as instructed. You simply need to simmer the soup for longer, until all of the chicken slices are white all the way through, about 5 minutes. Finally, don't skip the fish sauce called for in this soup. It's a pungent liquid that you can store in your fridge and add anytime a soup, stew, or sauce lacks a bit of meatiness. A few drops of fish sauce won't make it taste like fish, or like anything, but it adds meaty depth. It's one of key ingredients in this soup.

# Leftover Chicken Faux Pho

*Continued from previous page*

**Yield:** 4-6 servings

**Prep Time:** 15 minutes

**Cook Time:** 15 mintues

**Total Time:** 30 minutes

**Ingredients:**
6 cups low-sodium chicken stock
2 Tbsp. vegetable oil, divided
2 cinnamon sticks
8 whole cloves
1 large onion, peeled and quartered
a 2-inch piece of unpeeled ginger root, cut into 4 pieces
6 oz. rice sticks (rice vermicelli)
1/2 cup fresh cilantro or basil leaves or both
2 cups bean sprouts
1 jalapeno, seeded and thinly slices
1 lime, cut into wedges
1/2 tsp. salt
1 lb. cooked chicken meat, cubed
1 Tbsp. fish sauce

1. Measure the chicken stock into a large microwave-safe bowl and put it in the microwave for 8 minutes.

2. While the stock heats, measure 1 tablespoon of the oil into a large pot over medium heat. Add the cinnamon sticks, cloves, onion, and ginger. Turn the heat to high and let everything cook and scorch a bit.

3. While the aromatics are scorching, put your kitchen faucet on for hot water. Put the rice sticks into a large bowl and top with about 12 cups of the hot tap water. Add the remaining tablespoon of oil and swirl it around.

4. Keep stirring the aromatics occasionally and letting them darken until the stock has finished heating. Until then, get the soup toppings ready. Arrange the cilantro, bean sprouts, jalapeno slices, and lime wedges on a serving plate.

5. Once the stock is finished heating, pour it over the scorched aromatics. Add the salt and stir. Cover and bring it to a boil. Reduce heat to low and simmer for 3-4 minutes.

6. Use a slotted spoon to remove and discard the aromatics from the stock.

7. Add the chicken to the pot along with the fish sauce. Let it simmer to heat through.

8. Drain the noodles. Divide them among 4-6 soup bowls. Ladle the chicken and broth over top. Serve the plateful of fresh toppings alongside for people to add as they'd like.

# Chicken Curry

*I like to use chicken thighs for this recipe, but if you are a dyed-in-the-wool chicken breast fan, you could substitute it for the thighs. Serve with hot cooked white rice and/or some naan bread. If you can't find naan at the grocery store, try using soft pita bread instead.*

**Yield:** 4 servings

**Prep Time:** 15 minutes

**Cook Time:** 15 minutes

**Total Time:** 30 minutes

**Ingredients:**
2 Tbsp. olive oil
1 medium onion, chopped
3 cloves garlic, minced
1 Tbsp. minced fresh ginger
1 and 1/2 tsp. garam masala
1 tsp. salt
1 tsp. ground cumin
1 tsp. ground turmeric
1/8 tsp. ground cayenne pepper
1 (15 oz.) can crushed tomatoes
1 and 1/2 cups low-sodium chicken broth
2 lbs. boneless skinless chicken breasts or thighs or a combination, cut into 1-inch pieces
1/2 cup plain yogurt, at room temperature
1/4 cup chopped cilantro for serving

1. In a large pot set over medium-high heat, heat oil. Add the onions and cook until soft, about 5 minutes.

2. Add the garlic and ginger. Cook until fragrant, about 2 minutes

3. Add garam masala, salt, turmeric, cumin, and cayenne stirring so that the onion mixture is coated. Cook until very fragrant, about 1 – 2 minutes.

4. Add the stock and tomatoes and bring to a simmer. Cook uncovered for 5 minutes.

5. Add chicken and simmer until cooked through to 165°F on an instant read thermometer pierced into a piece of chicken, 5-10 minutes.

6. Stir in the yogurt and heat through, about 2 minutes. Garnish with cilantro.

Photo: Leigh Olson

# Chicken Korma

*This recipe is timed so that you can get your ingredients prepped, simmering sauce made, spices toasted, and onions sautéed (the instructions through step #7), while the chicken is marinating. Once the simmering sauce has been poured over and the cover placed on the skillet, you can make a pot of rice and then have everything ready at the same time.*

**Yield:** 4 servings

**Prep Time:** 15 minutes

**Cook Time:** 20 mintues

**Total Time:** 35 minutes

**Ingredients:**
2 lbs. skin-on bone-in chicken thighs

*Marinade*
1/2 cup whole fat yogurt
4 cloves garlic, minced
2-inches fresh ginger, grated
2 tsp. garam masala
1 tsp. turmeric powder
1 tsp. salt

*Simmering Sauce*
1 cup whole fat yogurt
1/4 cup ground almonds, almond flour or almond meal
1/4 tsp. cayenne pepper

*For chicken*
1 Tbsp. vegetable oil or ghee
1 bay leaf
4 whole cloves
2-inches cinnamon stick
2 medium onions, grated
1/2 tsp. cardamom
2 tsp. ground coriander
1 tsp. garam masala
1/4 cup chopped cilantro for serving

1. Remove chicken from package and pat dry.
2. In a large mixing bowl, combine marinade ingredients.
3. Place the chicken in the bowl with the marinade and spoon marinade over chicken making sure that each piece is coated liberally. Allow to marinate for 20 minutes.
4. While the chicken is marinating, in a medium mixing bowl combine the simmering sauce ingredients. Set aside.
5. Heat a large skillet over medium-high heat and add oil.
6. Add the bay leaf, cloves, and cinnamon stick. Sauté until the spices become fragrant, about 1 minute.
7. Add the grated onion and cook until it just starts to brown.
8. Add the marinated chicken along with any extra marinade in the bowl and brown lightly on both sides, about 3 minutes per side.
9. Reduce the heat to low, add the simmering sauce, cardamom, coriander, and garam masala.
10. Cover the skillet and simmer for 20 minutes or until the chicken is cooked through. Garnish with cilantro.

# Chicken Vindaloo

*Chicken Vindaloo is not for the faint of heart. It's often described on menus in Indian restaurants as packed with flavor, spicy, and fiery. But don't let any of that scare you off from this recipe. Although it's packed with flavor, you can control the spiciness and fieriness of the recipe by reducing or increasing the amount of red pepper flakes to fit your spicy tolerance.*

**Yield:** 4 servings

**Prep Time:** 10 minutes + time to marinade

**Cook Time:** 35 minutes

**Total Time:** 45 minutes + time to marinate

**Ingredients:**
8 cloves garlic, minced
2 Tbsp. red pepper flakes, reduce to accommodate your spicy tolerance
1 Tbsp. paprika
1 Tbsp. minced fresh ginger
2 tsp. garam masala
1 tsp. ground mustard
1 tsp ground turmeric
1 tsp. brown sugar
3 Tbsp. rice vinegar
1 Tbsp. lemon juice
2 lbs. boneless skinless chicken thighs, cut into 1-inch pieces
2 Tbsp. olive oil
1 large onion, chopped
1 Tbsp. tomato paste
1/2 cup water or low-sodium chicken stock
1/4 cup cilantro

1. In a large bowl, combine the garlic, red pepper flakes, paprika, ginger, garam masala, ground mustard, turmeric, brown sugar, vinegar, and lemon juice. Stir to combine.

2. Add the chicken and stir making sure that all pieces are coated with the marinade. Cover and refrigerate for 4 hours or overnight.

3. Heat a large skillet over medium-high heat and add the olive oil. Add onions and cook until softened, 5-8 minutes.

4. Add the chicken and any marinade in the bowl and cook for 5 minutes.

5. Add the tomato paste and water or chicken stock, stir to combine. Reduce the heat and bring to a simmer. Cover and cook an additional 20 minutes or until the chicken is cooked through. Garnish with cilantro.

*Photo: Jill Silverman Hough*

# Chicken Tikka Masala

Tikka masala is basically a two-step process. Step one is the chicken—marinating it in a spicy yogurt sauce, then cooking it. A tandoor oven would be most authentic, but who has one of those? Luckily, grilling or broiling works fine. The idea is high enough heat to get some good browning or light charring. Step two is making the spiced tomato-cream sauce. Then you put the two together and serve the mixture over rice. And don't forget plenty of naan to sop up every drop.

# Chicken Tikka Masala
*Continued from previous page*

**Yield:** 4-6 servings

**Prep Time:** 30 minutes

**Cook Time:** 30 mintues

**Total Time:** 30 minutes, plus 5 hours to marinate

**Ingredients:**
4 cloves garlic, minced
4 tsp. grated fresh ginger
4 tsp. garam masala
1 and 1/2 tsp. ground coriander
1 and 1/2 tsp. ground cumin
1 tsp. turmeric
1 cup plain low-fat yogurt
1 and 1/2 tsp. salt, or more to taste
1 and 1/2 pounds boneless, skinless chicken breasts or thighs or a mixture, cut into 1 and 1/2-inch pieces
1 Tbsp. vegetable oil
1 large onion, chopped
1 and 1/2 tsp. chili powder
1/4 tsp. ground cardamom
1/4 tsp. ground cayenne pepper
1 (28 oz.) can crushed tomatoes
1 cup heavy cream
Chopped fresh cilantro or cilantro sprigs for garnish

1. Combine the garlic, ginger, garam masala, coriander, cumin, and turmeric.

2. Combine the yogurt, salt, and about half of the garlic-ginger mixture.

3. Put the chicken in a large resealable bag and add the yogurt mixture. Squeeze out as much as air as possible, seal the bag, and set aside in the refrigerator to marinate for at least 4 hours and as long as overnight.

4. Thread the chicken onto skewers (discard marinade).

5. Preheat a grill to high and lightly oil the grate (or preheat the broiler, position a rack about 5 inches from the heat, and lightly oil a rimmed baking sheet). Grill (or broil) the chicken, turning once or twice, until just cooked through and browned in spots, 12 to 15 minutes.

6. Meanwhile, in a large skillet over medium heat, warm the oil. Add the onion and cook, stirring occasionally, until tender and lightly browned, 6 to 8 minutes.

7. Add the chili powder, cardamom, cayenne, and remaining garlic-ginger mixture and cook, stirring occasionally, until fragrant, about 2 minutes.

8. Add the tomatoes and salt and bring to a boil. Reduce to a simmer and stir in the cream. Adjust the heat to maintain a gentle simmer and cook until the sauce is thickened to your liking, about 10 minutes. Add salt to taste.

9. Take the chicken off the skewers and add it to the sauce. Cook 2 to 3 minutes. Garnish with cilantro.

# Quick Moroccan Stew with Chickpeas and Chicken

*This Moroccan-inspired soup uses harissa as the main flavoring ingredient. Harissa is a delicious new item to add to your pantry. It's a red chili paste from northern Africa where it's used as a condiment. The heat varies based on the heat of the peppers. In addition to the chilies it usually contains garlic, cumin, and cinnamon, making it an interestingly flavorful hot sauce.*

**Yield:** 5-6 servings

**Prep Time:** 15 minutes

**Cook Time:** 15 minutes

**Total Time:** 30 minutes

**Ingredients:**
1 Tbsp. olive oil
1 cup carrot matchsticks (sometimes packaged as shredded carrots), roughly chopped
2 ribs of celery, chopped
1 small onion, chopped
1/2 tsp. cumin
1/2 tsp. cinnamon
1/4 tsp. ground coriander
1–2 Tbsp. harissa paste, to taste
1 (28 oz.) can petite diced tomatoes
4 cups low-sodium chicken stock
1/2 tsp. salt
1 lb. chicken breast cutlets, thinly sliced
1 (16 oz.) can reduced sodium chickpeas
1 lemon, zested and then juiced
a handful of flat-leaf parsley

1. Heat the olive oil in a large pot over medium-high heat. Add the carrot matchsticks, celery, and onion. Cook stirring until softened, 3-5 minutes.

2. Add cumin, cinnamon, and coriander. Stir and cook for 30 seconds. Add the harissa and stir it in. Then add the diced tomatoes, stock, and salt.

3. Cover and heat on high until it reaches a boil. Reduce heat to a simmer.

4. Once the soup is simmering, add the chicken and stir. Cook stirring occasionally until it is no longer pink inside, about 2 minutes. Add the chickpeas and heat through. Add the lemon juice and ladle into soup bowls. Garnish each portion with about 1/2 teaspoon of lemon zest and a few leaves of parsley.

# Colombian Crema de Aquacate (Cream of Avocado Soup) with Chicken

*This soup might sound strange to those who have never heard of it or tried it but you need to know that it's seriously delicious. The creaminess of the avocado is just plain sublime, and there are other wonderful flavors in there to go with it.*

**Yield:** 6 servings

**Prep Time:** 10 minutes

**Cook Time:** 20 minutes

**Total Time:** 30 minutes

**Ingredients:**
1 Tbsp. olive oil
1 small onion, chopped
1 clove garlic, minced
4 cups low-sodium chicken stock
2 tsp. lime juice
2 ripe avocados, peeled, cored and mashed
1/2 tsp. salt
1/4 tsp. cumin
1 pint half and half
3 cooked chicken thighs, shredded
6 sprigs cilantro (optional)

1. Heat a large pot over medium heat. Add onion and sauté until translucent. Add garlic and cook 30 seconds. Add chicken stock and lime juice. Stir. Add avocadoes, salt and cumin. Stir.

2. Increase heat to high and bring to a boil, stirring occasionally. Reduce to a simmer and cook 5 minutes.

3. Transfer to a blender (depending on the size of your blender, you may have to purée half of the mixture at a time). Purée until smooth.

4. Return avocado purée to the pot. Add the half and half and the chicken. Heat through over medium heat, stirring continuously. Ladle into soup bowls and garnish with cilantro, if desired.

Photo: Kelly Nardo

# Chinese Chicken Meatballs

*By Kelly Nardo*

*Chinese meatballs, usually called Lion's Head, are light, tender, and juicy meatballs with a savory flavor. They're usually made of ground pork which is part of why they're so juicy. Since we're using ground chicken, which can be drier, it was important to add some ingredients that have some extra moisture, like the water chestnuts, green onions, and ginger. The technique of steaming the meatballs also helps them to stay juicier. Serve the meatballs on their own in some of the cooking liquid or over rice.*

# Chinese Chicken Meatballs
*Continued from previous page*

**Yield:** 14 meatballs

**Prep Time:** 15 minutes

**Cook Time:** 35 mintues

**Total Time:** 50 minutes

**Ingredients:**
1 lb. ground chicken
1/2 cup water chestnuts, finely chopped
2 green onions, chopped
1 large egg
2 Tbsp. soy sauce
1 Tbsp. sesame oil
1 Tbsp. sugar
1–2 Tbsp. corn starch
1 tsp. grated ginger
1/2 tsp. salt
1–2 Tbsp. cooking oil, for frying
Low-sodium chicken stock for steaming

1. In a large mixing bowl add chicken, water chestnuts, green onions, egg, soy sauce, sesame oil, sugar, 1 tablespoon corn starch, ginger, and salt. Mix well until combined but don't overmix as that can make the meatballs tough. Mixture should be wet, but you should still be able to form into balls. If needed add more corn starch.

2. Cover and place in the refrigerator 5–10 minutes to firm up. Remove meat mixture from the refrigerator and use an ice cream scoop to form into large meatballs. Roll gently so they hold together.

3. Heat a large skillet over medium heat. Add 1 tablespoon of cooking oil and let it get hot.

4. Add some of the meatballs in a single layer, spreading out evenly, and cook for 3–5 minutes, flipping occasionally, until golden brown on the outside (they will still be raw on the inside).

5. Once browned, remove from pan and place on a plate lined wtih paper towel.

6. Cook remaining meatballs as instructed in steps 3-5.

7. In a large stockpot, add meatballs. Pour in chicken stock, just enough to cover the meatballs, and bring to a boil over high heat. Turn heat to low and simmer for 30 minutes or until meatballs are cooked through. Serve meatballs on their own or with some of the cooking stock.

# Italian Chicken Meatballs

*By Allie Doran*

*We make these meatballs on the larger side and use a blend of chicken and pork for optimal flavor. Ingredients such as Parmesan, fresh parsley, and breadcrumbs create the classicly delicious flavor profile. There's also milk in the mix. While you're free to use a lower fat milk, using whole milk gives them a richer flavor.*

**Yield:** 6 servings

**Prep Time:** 15 minutes

**Cook Time:** 20 minutes

**Total Time:** 35 minutes

**Ingredients:**
3 Tbsp. olive oil, divided
1 small onion, finely chopped
3 cloves garlic, minced
1 cup breadcrumbs
2 large eggs
1/2 cup whole milk
1/4 cup Parmesan cheese
1 Tbsp. chopped fresh parsley
1 Tbsp. Italian seasoning
1/2 tsp. garlic powder
1 and 1/2 tsp. salt
1/2 tsp. pepper
1 lb. ground chicken
1 lb. ground pork

1. Place a large skillet over medium heat. Add 1 tablespoon of the olive oil and allow it to heat.

2. Add the onion to the skillet and sauté until translucent, about 5 minutes. Add the garlic and cook for an additional 2 minutes.

3. In a bowl, mix the onions and garlic, breadcrumbs, eggs, whole milk, Parmesan cheese, parsley, Italian seasoning, garlic powder, salt, and pepper.

4. Add the chicken and pork and mix well with a fork or your hands, incorporating everything evenly but do not overmix (it makes the meat tough).

5. When everything is mixed together, take about 3 tablespoons of the meat and roll into large meatballs. Heat the remaining two tablespoons of olive oil in the skillet over medium heat.

6. Add the meatballs and turn the heat to medium-low. Sauté the meatballs for 15 to 20 minutes, flipping them over occasionally. When they're cooked through, remove from the heat.

# Chicken Albóndigas

*By Emily Dingmann*

*Spanish Albóndigas are meatballs that are cooked in a thick and spicy smoked paprika sauce.*

**Yield:** 30 meatballs

**Prep Time:** 10 minutes

**Cook Time:** 30 minutes

**Total Time:** 40 minutes

**Ingredients:**
1 egg
1 lb. ground chicken
3 cloves garlic, minced, divided
1/4 cup breadcrumbs
Salt
Pepper
2 tsp. smoked paprika, divided
2 Tbsp. olive oil, divided
1 cup finely chopped fresh tomatoes
1/2 cup tomato paste
1/4 cup red wine
1 tsp. red pepper flakes
1 Tbsp. honey
1/4 cup chopped fresh cilantro (optional)

1. In a medium bowl, whisk the egg until beaten. Add the chicken, one third of the garlic, and breadcrumbs. Season with 1/2 teaspoon of salt, 1/4 teaspoon of pepper and 1 teaspoon of the smoked paprika. Lightly mix together with hands until incorporated, but be careful not to over mix.

2. Roll into 3/4 to 1-inch balls – you should have about 30 of them.

3. Heat large pan over medium-high heat and add 1 tablespoon of olive oil to pan. Cooking in batches so you don't overcrowd pan, brown the meatballs for about 7 minutes, rotating frequently to brown on all sides.

4. Transfer browned meatballs to plate and set aside. Repeat with remaining meatballs. When meatballs are finished, wipe out grease with paper towel.

5. To the same pan, add the remaining teaspoon of smoked paprika, 1 tablespoon of olive oil, tomatoes, tomato paste, red wine, red pepper flakes, and honey.

6. Bring to a boil over medium-high heat stirring occasionally.

7. Turn heat to low. Add meatballs to pan and stir carefully to cover with sauce.

8. Cook, covered, stirring occasionally, until meatballs are cooked through, about 10 minutes. Season with salt and pepper to taste and garnish with chopped cilantro.

Photo: Tawnie Kroll

# Swedish Chicken Meatballs

*By Tawnie Kroll*

*Swedish meatballs are all about that creamy sauce and the touch of allspice mixed into the meat. They're decadent for sure, but worth it!*

# Swedish Chicken Meatballs
*Continued from previous page*

**Yield:** 28-30 meatballs

**Prep Time:** 20 minutes

**Cook Time:** 40 mintues

**Total Time:** 1 hour

**Ingredients:**
1/2 cup panko breadcrumbs
2 large eggs
2 Tbsp. milk
1 lb. ground chicken
1 lb. ground pork
1/2 tsp. white pepper
1/2 tsp. garlic powder
1/4 tsp. allspice
1 tsp. salt
3 Tbsp. unsalted butter, divided
3/4 cup low-sodium chicken stock, divided
2 Tbsp. all-purpose flour
1 and 1/2 cups heavy cream
Parsley, for garnish

1. Preheat oven to 200°F. In a medium mixing bowl, whisk together panko breadcrumbs with eggs and milk. Then mix in chicken, pork, white pepper, garlic, allspice, and salt. Mix well but don't overmix.

2. Roll into golf-ball-sized meatballs.

3. In a large frying pan over medium heat, melt 2 tablespoons of the butter and place half of the meatballs in the hot pan, about 1 inch apart from each other. Cook on one side for 3-4 minutes and then flip.

4. Cook until no longer pink in the middle, another 4-5 minutes, flipping occasionally to brown all sides.

5. Once the meatballs are cooked through, put them on a baking sheet in the oven to keep them warm while you cook the second batch of meatballs. After each batch, de-glaze your pan with 1/4 cup of the stock to clean the little bits of meat up. Reserve this liquid each time to use for your gravy in the next step.

6. When you have finished cooking the second batch of meatballs and deglazing the pan, melt the remaining 1 tablespoon of butter in the pan. Take it off of the heat. Add the flour and whisk to form a roux (a thick smooth paste).

7. While continuing to whisk, drizzle in the reserved deglazing liquid. Gradually pour heavy cream in, about 1/4 cup at a time, whisk until smooth before adding 1/4 cup more. Repeat until cream is gone. Then whisk in the remaining 1/4 cup of stock.

8. Return pan to heat and cook over medium until it comes to a simmer. Taste and add salt and pepper if needed. Combine meatballs and gravy. Garnish with parsley if desired.

# CHAPTER 10
# CHICKEN CLASSICS

Classic Fried Chicken
Oven Fried Chicken
Pickle Fried Chicken Sandwich
Homemade Shake in a Bag Chicken
Nashville Style Hot Chicken
Chicken and Kale Taco Salad
Chicken Salad
Avocado Chicken Salad
Chicken Fried Chicken
Spinach and Artichoke Pasta Bake
Chicken Burgers
Baked Chicken Parmesan
Chicken Meatloaf
Chicken Parmesan Baked Pasta
Chicken Shepherd's Pie
Chicken Pot Pie
Chicken Parmesan Sliders
Leftover Chicken Casserole
Cauliflower Rice Stuffed Peppers
Baked Chicken Meatballs
Chicken and Dumplings

Chicken and Cheese Stuffed Potatoes
Chicken and Waffles
Chicken, Broccoli, and Rice Casserole
Chicken and Wild Rice Casserole
Chicken and Collard Greens Stir Fry
Chicken and Cheese Quicke
Chicken and Spinach Scrambled Eggs Benedict
Taco Lettuce Wraps
40 Clove Garlic Chicken

Photo: Ilona Orzechowska

# Classic Fried Chicken

*By Ilona Orzechowska*

You can totally go the traditional route and buy a whole chicken for this recipe and then cut it up into 10 pieces — 2 wings, 2 thighs, 2 legs, and each breast gets cut in half for a total of 4 breast pieces. Or, you can save yourself the time and hassle and buy 4 pounds of whatever cut of chicken you want. For instance, you can get all chicken drumsticks, or all chicken thighs, or all bone-in breasts. Yes, this means that you can make a whole batch of your favorite pieces of fried chicken. You're the one making it so why not make it the way you like it best!

# Classic Fried Chicken
*Continued from previous page*

**Yield:** 10 pieces

**Prep Time:** 3 hours, 20 minutes

**Cook Time:** 25 mintues

**Total Time:** 3 hours 45 minutes

**Ingredients:**
1 (4 lb.) whole chicken, cut into 10 pieces with breasts cut in half
2 and 1/2 cups buttermilk
2 tsp. hot sauce
1 and 1/2 tsp. salt, divided
2 cups all-purpose flour
1 tsp. sweet paprika
1/2 tsp. garlic powder
1/8 tsp. pepper
1/8 tsp. nutmeg
3 to 4 cups vegetable oil

1. In a large container mix together buttermilk, hot sauce, and 1/2 teaspoon of salt. Place chicken pieces into the buttermilk and cover. Refrigerate and leave it for at least 3 hours or overnight.

2. Before frying, in a ziptop bag, mix flour with remaining 1 teaspoon of salt, sweet paprika, garlic powder, pepper, and nutmeg. Close and shake it well to mix.

3. Remove chicken pieces from buttermilk, letting the excess buttermilk drip off. Place 2 pieces in the bag and shake it well, until the chicken is thoroughly coated. Remove and place on a wire rack. Repeat for remaining pieces of chicken.

4. Get out a wide pot deep enough to fit the 4 cups of oil and have the same amount of space left over (for when you drop in the chicken and the oil level rises). Add oil and heat over medium heat until it reaches 350°F. Use a candy thermometer to monitor the temperature of the oil throughout.

5. Place chicken in the oil and fry for about 20-25 minutes, turning halfway through. Once the chicken is dropped into the oil the temperature will lower to 300°F to 325°F. Keep it at around that temperature, adjusting the heat of the stove to do so. Lower the heat if the exterior of the chicken seems to be cooking faster than the interior.

6. Chicken is done when internal temperature is 165°F or higher on an instant-read thermometer. Once it reaches the safe temperature, remove chicken pieces to a plate lined with paper towel to sop up extra oil. Sprinkle lightly with more salt, if desired.

# Oven Fried Chicken

*By Brittany Poulson*

*One of the secrets to this recipe is to mix the breadcrumbs with a bit of oil before adhering them to the chicken. This helps the crumbs brown and get crunchy all over. Our second secret is in how we bake it. Instead of baking the chicken right on the sheet pan, we put a wire rack between the two. This allows for nice, even baking on both sides of the chicken.*

**Yield:** 6 servings

**Prep Time:** 15 minutes

**Cook Time:** 20 minutes

**Total Time:** 35 minutes

**Ingredients:**
Cooking spray
2 egg whites
3/4 cup panko bread crumbs
1/3 cup finely shredded Parmesan cheese
1 tsp. Italian seasoning
1/2 tsp. salt
1/4 tsp. pepper
1 Tbsp. olive oil
2 lbs. boneless skinless chicken breasts or thighs or a mixture

1. Preheat oven to 400°F. Line a baking sheet with a silicone mat or parchment paper then set a wire rack on the sheet and spray with cooking spray.

2. In a medium bowl, whisk the egg whites together. In another medium bowl, combine the panko, Parmesan cheese, Italian seasoning, salt, and pepper. Add the olive oil and toss to moisten everything.

3. Dip chicken in the egg whites, then dredge each chicken tender in the panko cheese mixture, gently pressing it onto the chicken. Plate the breaded chicken onto the prepared wire rack.

4. Bake for 20-25 minutes or until the chicken reaches an internal temperature of 165°F on an instant-read thermometer. Remove from the oven and allow to rest 5 minutes before serving.

Photo: Sam Ellis

# Pickle Fried Chicken Sandwich

*By Sam Ellis*

*Why use pickle juice to marinate chicken? The pickle juice here acts simultaneously as a brine and as a marinade. The salt and vinegar in the pickle juice help create the perfect environment for two things. The first is an osmosis reaction where the flavors of the pickle juice are flowing into the chicken making sure each bite is moist and flavorful. The salt and vinegar also help break down the molecules in the protein to make it nice and tender.*

**Yield:** 8 servings

**Prep Time:** 1 hour, 30 minutes

**Cook Time:** 30 mintues

**Total Time:** 2 hours

**Ingredients:**
3 lbs. boneless skinless chicken breasts
1 (24 oz.) jar dill pickle slices
1 cup buttermilk
1 egg
1 and 1/2 cup all-purpose flour
1 tsp. paprika
1 tsp. salt
1/2 tsp. garlic powder
1/2 tsp. pepper
Peanut or vegetable oil
Hamburger buns

1. Butterfly the chicken breasts lengthwise. For larger pieces, cut the butterflied chicken piece in half.

2. Place in a gallon bag and pour in 1 cup pickle juice from the jar of pickle slices. Close the bag and let rest in a flat layer in the refrigerator for 1 hour, flipping halfway between.

3. While the chicken is resting, combine buttermilk and egg in one bowl, whisking until incorporated.

4. In another large bowl, mix together flour, paprika, salt, garlic powder, and pepper. Line a large plate with paper towels.

5. When the chicken is done in the brine, heat a 12" skillet with high edges over medium-high heat with oil filling the skillet about 1/2" full. Use a candy thermometer to determine when the oil reaches 350°F.

6. While the peanut oil is heating, dip chicken pieces in flour mixture, covering entirely, then the wet mixture and back into the flour mixture. Set these aside on another plate until ready to fry.

7. Carefully place chicken in the oil, not crowding the skillet. (You will likely need to fry the chicken in batches. If so, turn oven to 200F so that fried chicken can stay warm while subsequent batches are cooking.)

8. Check the temperature of the oil once the skillet is full and adjust temperature if needed.

9. Cook, flipping halfway through, until the internal temperature of the chicken reaches 165°F as read on an instant read thermometer, about 6-8 minutes total.

10. Remove from skillet and place on paper towel lined plate. Serve on hamburger buns with dill pickle slices.

# Homemade Shake in a Bag Chicken

*By Allie Doran*

*Shake in a bag is simply a mixture of breadcrumbs, herbs, seasonings, and oil that you probablly already have in your pantry. It's really fast to throw it together into a ziptop bag. You can make a big batch and store it sealed in the freezer. Just take some out and use it. Discard any mixture that comes into contact with chicken.*

**Yield:** 4-6 servings

**Prep Time:** 5 minutes

**Cook Time:** 25 minutes

**Total Time:** 30 minutes

**Ingredients:**
1 cup unseasoned, plain breadcrumbs
2 tsp. onion powder
2 tsp. dried parsley
2 tsp. dried basil
1 tsp. salt
1 tsp. paprika
1 tsp. garlic powder
1 tsp. sugar
1 Tbsp. vegetable oil
Cooking spray
1.5 to 2 lbs. skinless chicken pieces, with or without bone.

1. In a large ziptop bag, mix together the breadcrumbs, onion powder, parsley, basil, salt, paprika, garlic powder, and sugar.

2. Add the oil and mush everything around until all of the mixture is moistened.

3. Use right away, or seal bag and store in the freezer for up to 1 month until you're ready to use.

4. When ready to coat chicken, take breadcrumb mixture out of freezer and let it sit at room temperature for 10 minutes.

5. Preheat oven to 400°F. Line a baking sheet with aluminum foil and spray lightly with cooking spray.

6. Add chicken pieces to the breadcrumb mixture in the ziptop bag one piece at a time. Seal and shake bag until chicken piece is coated. Transfer to prepared baking sheet and repeat with other pieces.

7. Bake until internal temperature of chicken is at 165°F as read on an instant read thermometer inserted into thick part of chicken, not touching bone. This will be approximately 20-25 for boneless pieces (like boneless breasts and thighs) and 40-45 minutes for bone-in pieces (like bone-in breasts, thighs, drumsticks, leg quarters, or wings).

# Nashville Style Hot Chicken

*By Allie Doran*

*Nashville Hot Chicken takes classic, buttermilk marinated chicken and dredges it in a spicy flour mixture. The chicken is fried and then it gets brushed with a hot and tangy honey butter glaze. Get out some napkins and make sure you've got a nice cold beverage because the cayenne in here is gonna knock your tongue off! Ha!*

# Nashville Style Hot Chicken

*Continued from previous page*

**Yield:** 6 servings

**Prep Time:** 15 minutes, plus 8 hours marinating

**Cook Time:** 25 minutes

**Total Time:** 40 minutes, plus 8 hours marinating

**Ingredients:**
1 and 1/2 lbs. boneless skinless chicken breasts
1 cup buttermilk
1 Tbsp. and 2 tsp. cayenne pepper, divided
2 cups vegetable oil
1 cup all-purpose flour
1/2 tsp. garlic powder
1/2 tsp. salt
1/4 tsp. pepper
1 cup unsalted butter
2 Tbsp. honey
1 tsp. apple cider vinegar

1. Butterfly the chicken breasts by slicing them in half horizontally such that each breast is two thinner cutlets. Add them to a bowl or a large plastic bag.
2. Add the buttermilk and 1 teaspoon of cayenne to the chicken. Make sure everything is mixed up really well and the chicken is coated and is covered with the buttermilk. Marinate for 8 hours or overnight.
3. When you're ready to cook, remove the chicken from the fridge and let it come to room temperature for 20 minutes while you prepare the flour dredge and heat the oil.
4. Add the oil to a large pot over medium heat and heat to 300°F. Use a candy thermometer to gauge the temperature and to try to keep it at 300°F throughout.
5. Whisk together the flour, garlic powder, salt, pepper, and 1 teaspoon of the cayenne.
6. Shake excess buttermilk off of a piece of chicken. Dip it into the flour mixture on both sides, then back into the buttermilk on both sides, and then back into the flour mixture on both sides, shaking any excess flour off and making sure the entire piece of chicken is covered in the dredge. Repeat with each piece of chicken. Arrange coated chicken pieces in a single layer on a plate as you go.
7. Fry the chicken pieces, about 4-5 minutes per side until golden brown and the internal temperature reaches 165°F. You may need to do this in batches as you don't want to crowd the chicken – make sure the chicken pieces are not touching as they fry.
8. Remove the chicken and let it drain on a wire rack with a paper towel underneath.
9. While the chicken is frying, melt together the butter, honey, apple cider vinegar, and the remaining tablespoon of cayenne in a small pot. Stir occasionally.
10. When all the chicken has fried, brush the chicken liberally with the spicy honey butter glaze.

# Chicken and Kale Taco Salad

*When you use kale in a salad you need to massage the leaves a bit so that they're less tough. If you'd prefer to skip the massaging, use baby spinach or a spring mix instead.*

**Yield:** 4 servings

**Prep Time:** 15 minutes

**Total Time:** 15 minutes

**Ingredients:**
1/2 cup Greek yogurt
1 avocado, pitted and peeled
2 Tbsp. lime juice
1 Tbsp. sauce from a can of chipotles in adobo
1/2 tsp. chili powder
Salt
8 oz. chopped kale
2 Tbsp. olive oil
2 cups cooked cubed or shredded chicken
1 cup shredded cheddar cheese
1 (15 oz.) can low-sodium black beans, drained and rinsed
2 bell peppers, sliced
1 pint grape tomatoes, halved
2 green onions, chopped
1/2 cup tortilla strips

1. In a blender or food processor purée Greek yogurt, avocado, lime juice, adobo sauce, chili powder, and 1/2 teaspoon of salt until smooth.

2. Put kale in a large bowl. Drizzle with olive oil. Massage oil into leaves. Let rest 5 minutes. Add yogurt dressing and massage again. Add a pinch of salt. Stir.

3. Divide kale among 4 dinner plates. Top each serving with one quarter of the chicken, cheddar cheese, black beans, bell peppers, grape tomatoes, green onions, and tortilla strips.

# Chicken Salad

*This recipe has you poach chicken breasts or thighs to use in the chicken salad. However, you can use 4 cups of any leftover cooked and cubed chicken meat that you have. Note that everything other than the chicken, mayonnaise, salt, and pepper are listed as optional here. This is so that you can customize the chicken salad to your preference. For instance, I don't like sweet chicken salad so I would omit the grapes and almonds and just use the celery and green onions. However, if you like it sweet, you might only choose to include the grapes and almonds. All four (the celery, green onion, almonds, and grapes) also work well together if you like a sweet and savory mix.*

**Yield:** 6 servings

**Prep Time:** 20 minutes

**Cook Time:** 10 minutes

**Total Time:** 30 minutes

**Ingredients:**
1 and 1/2 lbs. boneless skinless chicken breasts or thighs or a mixture
1 and 1/2 tsp. salt, divided
1/2 to 1 cup mayonnaise
1/4 tsp. pepper
2 ribs celery, finely chopped (optional)
1 green onion, finely chopped (optional)
16 grapes, quartered (optional)
1/4 cup slivered almonds (optional)

1. Arrange the chicken in a pot large enough that they fit in a single layer. If they overlap a little bit, that's fine.

2. Sprinkle 1 teaspoon salt over chicken. Add enough cool tap water to cover the chicken by 1 inch.

3. Heat on the stove over high heat until it reaches a boil.

4. Reduce heat to low. Cover and simmer until chicken is cooked through to 165°F as read on an instant read thermometer placed in the middle of a breast, 9-14 minutes depending on the thickness of the chicken.

5. Remove chicken from poaching liquid. Discard liquid or save for another use. Let chicken rest for 5 minutes.

6. Cut chicken into 1/4 to 1/2-inch cubes. Put in a medium bowl and transfer to fridge to cool for 10 minutes.

7. To the chicken add 1/2 cup mayonnaise, the remaining 1/2 teaspoon salt, and the pepper. Add any or all or none of the celery, green onion, grapes, and almonds that you are using. Stir gently to combine.

8. If you like your chicken salad moister, add up to 1/2 cup more mayonnaise.

9. Taste and add more salt and pepper if desired.

# Avocado Chicken Salad

*Avocado is creamy, delicious, and healthy, which is why it's a great substitute for mayonnaise in chicken salad.*

# Avocado Chicken Salad
*Continued from previous page*

**Yield:** 2 servings

**Prep Time:** 5 minutes

**Total Time:** 5 hours

**Ingredients:**
1/2 avocado
1 and 1/4 cup finely chopped cooked chicken
1 rib celery, finely chopped
1 green onion, chopped
1/2 tsp. lemon juice
1/8 tsp. salt
1/8 tsp. garlic powder
1/8 tsp. pepper

1. In a medium bowl, mash the avocado with a fork until smooth.

2. Add the chicken, celery, green onion, lemon juice, salt, garlic powder, and pepper.

3. Stir until well combined.

# Chicken Fried Chicken

*By Emily Dingmann*

*Typically, chicken breasts are used for chicken fried chicken but we used thighs in this recipe for two reasons. Reason number one, the dark meat yields a juicier chicken – and it's also harder to over-cook and dry out. Reason number two, the uneven surface area of a chicken thigh means there are a lot more spots for the flour to stick to and that is a good thing. More flour = more crispy bites.*

**Yield:** 4 servings

**Prep Time:** 10 minutes, plus 4 hours marinating

**Cook Time:** 15 minutes

**Total Time:** 25 minutes, plus 4 hours marinating

**Ingredients:**

*Fried Chicken*
1 and 1/2 lbs. boneless skinless chicken thighs
1 cup buttermilk
Oil for frying (like canola, vegetable, or peanut)
3/4 cup all-purpose flour
1 tsp. paprika
1/4 tsp. cayenne pepper
1 tsp. salt + some for sprinkling

*Gravy*
1 cup whole milk
2 Tbsp. all-purpose flour
1 tsp. salt
1/2 tsp. pepper

**Fried Chicken**

1. Combine chicken and buttermilk together in a bowl. Let sit in refrigerator for at least four hours, or up to 24 hours.

2. Take chicken out of refrigerator at least a half hour before cooking.

3. Heat oil in a large cast iron skillet over medium-high heat. You want it to be about 1 inch deep.

4. Preheat oven to 250°F. Put a metal oven-safe rack on a baking sheet. Set aside.

5. In a clean large bowl, whisk together 3/4 cup of the flour, paprika, cayenne pepper, and 1 teaspoon of the salt.

6. Dredge a chicken piece through flour mixture so that it is lightly coated in flour. Shake off excess. Transfer to a plate. Repeat with all pieces of chicken.

7. Put some of the chicken pieces in the oil. Don't crowd the pan. Fry for about 4-5 minutes, then flip over and fry for another 4-5 minutes, or until it reaches an internal temperature of 165°F. (Larger pieces will take longer.)

8. Remove chicken from oil and rest on the metal rack. Sprinkle lightly with salt. Transfer rack with baking sheet below it to the warm oven for the chicken to stay warm while frying remaining chicken in batches.

# Chicken Fried Chicken

*Continued from previous page*

9. When done frying chicken, keep it warm in the oven while making the gravy.

**Gravy**

1. Scoop out 2 tablespoons of the frying oil and put it in a small sauce pan. Whisk in 2 tablespoons of flour. Put over medium heat.

2. Whisk together until smooth and golden in color. Pour in milk slowly while continuously whisking.

3. Bring to a boil, then lower heat. Let thicken, about 1-2 minutes, and remove from heat.

4. Season with salt and pepper. Taste and add more if desired but note that it will taste a little bland on its own, but is perfect on the chicken so be careful to not over-salt.

5. Arrange chicken on plates and top with gravy.

# Spinach and Artichoke Pasta Bake

*This pasta dish originated because there was a tub of spinach artichoke dip in the fridge that was about to reach its expiration date. I added it to a baked pasta dinner. It was sooooo good. I decided that I just had to recreate that but I didn't want to have to buy several tubs of pre-made dip to do it. Instead, I created a recipe that uses cream cheese, mayonnaise, frozen spinach, and canned artichoke hearts to get that spinach and artichoke dip flavor. There's also some mozzarella, and some chicken in there too, of course!*

**Yield:** 6 servings

**Prep Time:** 15 minutes

**Cook Time:** 30 minutes

**Total Time:** 45 minutes

**Ingredients:**

12 oz. uncooked penne pasta
2 (10 oz.) boxes of frozen spinach
8 oz. cream cheese
1/2 cup mayonnaise
1 tsp. garlic powder
1/2 tsp. salt
1/4 tsp. pepper
1 and 1/2 cup shredded mozzarella cheese, divided
3 cups finely chopped cooked chicken
2 (14 oz.) cans baby artichoke hearts, drained
1/4 cup shredded Parmesan cheese

1. Cook penne pasta according to package directions. Drain and set aside. Preheat oven to 350°F.

2. Meanwhile, put spinach in a large microwave-safe bowl and defrost in the microwave.

3. Add cream cheese and warm in the microwave for 30 seconds. Stir. Heat for another 30 seconds. Stir until smoothly combined with the spinach.

4. Add mayonnaise, garlic powder, salt, and pepper.

5. Return drained pasta to pot along with spinach sauce, 1 cup of the mozzarella, chicken, and baby artichoke hearts. Stir until all the pasta is coated. Spoon into a 13"x9" pan.

6. Top with the remaining 1/2 cup mozzarella and with the Parmesan cheese.

7. Bake until heated through and browned a bit on top, about 30 minutes.

Photo: Jill Silverman Hough

# Chicken Burgers

Chicken burgers can be a little dry because they have less fat than beef, but also because, unlike beef, they have to be cooked through and through (no rare chicken, please!). So what do we do? One egg added to the mix adds quite a bit of moisture. Some Worcestershire sauce also adds moisture and some rich meaty flavor. The Worcestershire combined with the chili powder also lend a little color, which makes the burgers look more appetizing.

**Yield:** 4 servings

**Prep Time:** 1 hour, 15 minutes

**Cook Time:** 10 minutes

**Total Time:** 1 hour, 25 minutes

**Ingredients:**
1 large egg
1 Tbsp. Worcestershire sauce
3/4 tsp. salt
1/2 tsp. chili powder
1/2 tsp. garlic powder
1/2 tsp. onion powder
1/2 tsp. pepper
1 lb. ground chicken
Cooking oil
Hamburger buns
Lettuce, tomatoes, condiments, and other toppings of your choice

1. In a large bowl whisk together the egg, Worcestershire, salt, chili powder, garlic powder, onion powder, and pepper.

2. Add the chicken and combine. Handle the mixture as gently and sparingly as possible (overmixing can make the burger tough).

3. Divide the mixture into 4 equal portions. Shape each into a ball, then flatten the balls into discs, about 4 inches in diameter. Make them thinner in the center.

4. Arrange the patties on a plate or platter, cover with plastic wrap, and refrigerate for at least an hour. Alternatively, you can put them in the freezer for 20 minutes.

5. Heat a skillet or grill to medium-high and lightly oil the skillet or grate. Cook the patties until the internal temperature is 165°F, 3-4 minutes per side.

6. Arrange the patties on the buns and serve with your favorite toppings.

# Baked Chicken Parmesan

*I love making baked versions of foods that are usually fried. They're usually healthier than the original, and popping a pan of something into an oven is always less work than standing over a fryer or frying pan.*

**Yield:** 4 servings

**Prep Time:** 10 minutes

**Cook Time:** 25 minutes

**Total Time:** 35 minutes

**Ingredients:**
4 (6 oz.) boneless skinless chicken breasts
1 and 1/4 cups breadcrumbs
1/4 cup grated Parmesan cheese, plus more for garnish
2 Tbsp. vegetable oil
1 tsp. dried thyme
1/2 tsp. salt
1/4 tsp. pepper
2 egg whites
2 tsp. Dijon mustard
1 cup tomato sauce
1 cup shredded mozzarella cheese

1. Preheat oven to 400°F.
2. Cut chicken breasts in half and pound to equal 1/4-inch thickness.
3. In small shallow bowl or pie plate, combine breadcrumbs, Parmesan cheese, vegetable oil, thyme, salt, and ground pepper.
4. In another shallow bowl combine egg whites and Dijon mustard.
5. Dredge chicken in egg mixture then the breadcrumb mixture.
6. Place chicken on a wire rack set on a baking sheet.
7. Repeat with remaining chicken and then bake until cooked through, about 20 minutes.
8. Top each with 1/4 cup tomato sauce and 1/4 cup mozzarella cheese. Bake until cheese is melted and sauce is heated through, 5-7 minutes.
9. Garnish with more Parmesan cheese.

# Chicken Meatloaf

*By Georgina Walker*

*This is a moist chicken meatloaf recipe requiring just one bowl and one pan.*

**Yield:** 6 servings

**Prep Time:** 10 minutes

**Cook Time:** 1 hour

**Total Time:** 1 hour, 10 minutes

**Ingredients:**
Cooking spray
2 lbs. ground chicken
1 cup panko breadcrumbs
1 medium onion, finely chopped
1 egg
1 garlic clove, minced
1/2 cup plus 4 Tbsp. ketchup, divided
3 Tbsp. Worcestershire sauce, divided
1 tsp. dried thyme
1 tsp. dried oregano
1 Tbsp. brown sugar
1 Tbsp. red wine vinegar

1. Preheat oven to 350°F. Grease a loaf pan with cooking spray.

2. Combine ground chicken, panko, onion, egg, garlic, 4 tablespoons of the ketchup, 2 tablespoons of the Worcestershire sauce, thyme, and oregano in a large bowl. Mix with your hands until well combined but don't overmix as that can make it tough. Shape into a loaf.

3. Transfer to greased loaf pan and smooth out the edges so the top is flat and the surface is even.

4. In a small bowl, combine the remaining 1/2 cup ketchup, brown sugar, red wine vinegar, and remaining tablespoon of Worcestershire. Pour half over top of the meatloaf. Bake for 45 minutes.

5. Remove the meatloaf from the oven and pour the remaining glaze over it. Increase the oven temperature to 400°F. Bake for another 15 minutes. Remove from the oven to cool to help it set for 10 minutes.

6. Turn onto a long plate and slice.

*Photo: Jamie Silva*

# Chicken Parmesan Baked Pasta

*By Jamie Silva*

All you really need is pasta, marinara sauce, cheese (lots of cheese!), and leftover cooked chicken to make this delicious dinner. If you have some breadcrumbs and fresh basil, bonus!

**Yield:** 6-8 servings

**Prep Time:** 15 minutes

**Cook Time:** 30 minutes

**Total Time:** 45 minutes

**Ingredients:**
1 (16 oz.) box rigatoni pasta
2 cups cooked chicken, shredded
1 (24 oz.) jar of marinara sauce, divided
1/2 cup shredded mozzarella cheese, plus more for topping
1/2 cup grated Parmesan cheese
1/2 cup Italian breadcrumbs
Cooking spray

1. Preheat oven at 375°F.
2. Cook pasta according to package instructions. Drain.
3. Pour 2 tablespoons of the marinara sauce into the bottom of a baking dish. Spread it around. Set aside.
4. Add pasta to a large bowl. Toss with chicken, remaining marinara sauce, mozzarella, and Parmesan.
5. Transfer pasta mixture to prepared baking dish. Smooth it out and then top with more mozzarella and then the breadcrumbs. Spray breadcrumbs lightly with cooking spray.
6. Bake in the oven until heated through and cheese is melted, 25-30 minutes.

# Chicken Shepherd's Pie

*In the UK shepherd's pie is made with ground lamb. If you make the same thing with ground beef, as Americans typically do, Brits call it cottage pie. I have zero idea what they'd call this version though since it's made with ground chicken. Let's just call it Chicken Shepherd's Pie, agree that it's delicious, and then dig in!*

**Yield:** 6 servings

**Prep Time:** 25 minutes

**Cook Time:** 25 minutes

**Total Time:** 50 minutes

**Ingredients:**

*For the Filling:*
1 Tbsp. vegetable oil
1 small onion, finely chopped
2 carrots, peeled and finely chopped
2 cloves garlic, minced
2 sprigs thyme or 1 tsp. dried thyme
1 and 1/2 lbs. ground chicken
1 tsp. salt
1/2 tsp. pepper
2 Tbsp. all-purpose flour
1 Tbsp. tomato paste
1 cup low-sodium chicken stock
2 tsp. Worcestershire sauce
3/4 cup frozen corn, defrosted
3/4 cup frozen peas, defrosted

*For the Mashed Potatoes:*
2 and 1/2 lbs. Russet potatoes, peeled and cut into 1/2 to 3/4-inch cubes
1 Tbsp. salt
2 Tbsp. unsalted butter
1/4 cup milk, heated
1 egg yolk

**For the Filling:**

1. Heat the oil in a medium sauté pan over medium-high heat. Add the onions and carrots and cook until softened, about 5-6 minutes. Add garlic and thyme and stir.

2. Add the chicken, salt, and pepper. Stir occasionally until meat is cooked through, about 5-7 minutes. Drain off excess fat, if any.

3. To chicken add flour and tomato paste. Stir until incorporated. Cook for 1-2 minutes. Stir in the stock and Worcestershire sauce.

4. Bring mixture to a boil, then reduce heat to a simmer, stirring occasionally until very thick, 2-3 minutes. Remove thyme sprigs.

5. Add defrosted corn and peas. Taste and season with salt and pepper, if needed.

**For the Mashed Potatoes:**

1. Place cut potatoes in pot filled with cold water. Add salt. Turn heat to high and cover slightly. Once boiling uncover and drop heat to medium. Cook until you can pierce potatoes easily with a fork, about 10-15 minutes. Drain potatoes.

2. Add butter and then mash the potatoes. Once mashed stir in heated milk.

3. Quickly stir potatoes while adding egg yolk, moving quickly to prevent egg from cooking in chunks. Taste and season with salt, if desired.

# Chicken Shepherd's Pie

*Continued from previous page*

**Assembly:**

1. Preheat oven to 425°F.

2. In 11"x7" pan add chicken mixture and spread evenly. Top with mashed potatoes starting at the corners working around the edge. This should seal in the meat for better chance of avoiding boil-overs.

3. Scrape a fork lightly all over top of potatoes to create ridges. Bake until tops of potato ridges are browned, 20-25 minutes.

# Chicken Pot Pie

*By Allie Doran*

*This recipe has a convenient version and a homemade version hidden in it. You can do the crust as directed, made from scratch, or you can buy frozen puff pastry or even crescent roll sheets. As to the filling, you can use homemade Cream of Chicken Soup, like from the recipe in Chapter 6 or thin out the condensed soup recipe from Chapter 1, or you can get store-bought canned soup. Or you can use canned soup and make your own crust, or use homemade soup with puff pastry. So many options to get dinner on the table in whatever way you prefer.*

**Yield:** 4-6 servings

**Prep Time:** 35 minutes

**Cook Time:** 35 minutes

**Total Time:** 1 hour, 10 minutes

**Ingredients:**
*For the crust:*
1 and 1/2 cups all-purpose flour
1/2 tsp. salt
a pinch pepper
1 stick (1/2 cup) cold unsalted butter, cubed
4–5 Tbsp. ice water

*For the filling:*
2 Tbsp. unsalted butter
1 medium onion, chopped
1 and 1/2 cups celery, chopped
1 lb. boneless, skinless chicken breast or thighs, in 1/2-inch pieces
2 garlic cloves, minced
2 Tbsp. all-purpose flour
1 tsp. salt
1/2 tsp. pepper
1/4 tsp. fresh thyme
1/8 tsp. paprika
1 cup frozen mixed vegetables
2 cups cream of chicken soup (Note: this is cream of chicken soup NOT condensed)
1 egg
1 Tbsp. water

1. Make the pastry by adding the flour, salt, pepper, and butter to a food process or bowl. Work the butter into the flour with the processor or a pastry cutter until the mixture looks like coarse crumbs.

2. Add the water gradually until the dough pulls together. Shape the dough into a disc and wrap in plastic wrap. Let the dough rest in the fridge for 30 minutes while you prepare the filling.

3. Preheat the oven to 350°F.

4. Heat the butter in a large pot over medium heat until bubbly.

5. Add the onion and celery and cook for 3 minutes to soften. Add the chicken.

6. Cook stirring occasionally until chicken is browned and cooked through, about 10 minutes.

7. Add the garlic, flour, salt, pepper, paprika, and thyme and cook for 3 minutes. Then add the frozen vegetables and cream of chicken soup.

8. Bring the mixture to a slow boil, scraping the bottom of the pan to get all of the flavor bits up. Reduce the heat to low and simmer for 5 minutes until thick and bubbly.

9. Pour the filling into a pie plate.

# Chicken Pot Pie

*Continued from previous page*

10. Roll the dough out to a circle that's about 10 inches in diameter. Lay the crust on top of the pie plate and the filling.

11. Whisk the egg and tablespoon of water together and brush all over the crust. Pierce the crust with a fork or knife to create vent holes.

12. Bake until the crust is golden and filling is bubbly, about 35 minutes. Let rest for 5-10 minutes before cutting.

Photo: Allie Doran

# Chicken Parmesan Sliders

*By Allie Doran*

**When chicken parm and a bun love each other very much ... delicious sliders are born.**

# Chicken Parmesan Sliders
*Continued from previous page*

**Yield:** 6 sliders

**Prep Time:** 15 minutes

**Cook Time:** 30 minutes

**Total Time:** 45 minutes

**Ingredients:**
1 large chicken breast
1/2 cup all-purpose flour
1 egg
1 cup panko breadcrumbs
1 tsp. garlic powder
2 tsp. oregano, divided
1/2 tsp. salt
3 Tbsp. olive oil
6 potato slider buns
6 slices of mozzarella cheese
1/2 cup pizza sauce
4 Tbsp. unsalted butter
2 Tbsp. grated Parmesan cheese
1 clove garlic, minced

1. Preheat oven to 375°F.

2. Cut chicken breast in half, butterflying it, and then cut each half into thirds, yielding 6 pieces of chicken.

3. Measure flour into a bowl, crack and whisk an egg into a second bowl, and combine breadcrumbs, garlic powder, 1 teaspoon of oregano and salt in a third bowl.

4. Heat a large frying pan on medium-high heat.

5. Bread the chicken by dipping first into the flour, then into the egg, and finally into the seasoned breadcrumbs.

6. Once all of the chicken is coated, add olive oil to the hot pan and swirl it until it shimmers. Add chicken and cook for 5-7 minutes on each side, or until it has a golden crust and is cooked all the way through. Once cooked, transfer the chicken to a plate.

7. Line a baking pan with parchment paper and lay the bottom half of the rolls into the pan. On each bun put 1/2 slice of cheese, 1 tablespoon of pizza sauce, a piece of chicken, an additional teaspoon of pizza sauce, and the remaining 1/2 of a cheese slice. Add the top of the bun.

8. Melt the butter and stir in the Parmesan cheese, minced garlic, and the remaining 1 teaspoon of oregano. Drizzle that on top of the sliders, cover with foil, and place into the oven for 10 minutes. Remove from oven, uncover and bake for an additional 8 minutes. Let rest 5 minutes.

# Leftover Chicken Casserole

*By Ilona Orzechowska*

*For this casserole you can use leftover rice or store-bought cooked rice. If you want to make rice specifically for this, start with 3/4 cup of dry rice and cook according to package directions.*

**Yield:** 4 servings

**Prep Time:** 15 minutes

**Cook Time:** 25 minutes

**Total Time:** 40 minutes

**Ingredients:**
Cooking spray
2 cups cooked white long grain rice
2 cups cubed or shredded cooked chicken
1/2 cup frozen peas, defrosted
1 (10.75 oz.) can condensed chicken soup or homemade (see Chapter 1)
1/4 cup milk
1/4 tsp. salt
1/4 tsp. poultry seasoning
1 cup shredded cheddar cheese
1/2 cup panko breadcrumbs
1/2 tsp. olive oil

1. Preheat oven to 350°F and spray a 9"x9" baking dish with cooking spray.

2. In a large bowl combine cooked white rice, chicken, peas, condensed chicken soup, milk, salt, and poultry seasoning.

3. Transfer mixture to the prepared baking dish.

4. In a small bowl mix shredded cheddar cheese, panko breadcrumbs, and olive oil. Sprinkle over the casserole.

5. Bake until heated through and bubbling, and topping is browned, for 30-35 minutes.

# Cauliflower Rice Stuffed Peppers

*By Tawnie Kroll*

*Since riced cauliflower cooks quickly, you don't need it to be fully cooked through and softened before adding it to the peppers. It'll soften easily in the oven. This saves a lot of time over tranditional stuffed peppers where you have to cook the rice before making the stuffing and filling the peppers. Gotta love those tasty, healthy time-savers, right?*

**Yield:** 5 servings

**Prep Time:** 10 minutes

**Cook Time:** 35 minutes

**Total Time:** 45 minutes

**Ingredients:**
1 Tbsp. olive oil
1 small onion, chopped
2 cups cooked shredded chicken
1/2 tsp. salt
1/2 tsp. oregano
1/2 tsp. pepper
3 cloves garlic, minced
3 cups cauliflower rice
1 (15 oz.) can tomato sauce
5 large bell peppers
2 cups shredded mozzarella cheese

1. Preheat oven to 350°F.

2. Heat olive oil over medium heat in a large skillet. Add the onion and cook, stirring occasionally until softened, about 3-4 minutes. Add in shredded chicken, salt, oregano, pepper, and garlic. Stir to combine. Then stir in cauliflower rice and can of tomato sauce.

3. Slice off the tops of each bell pepper, about 1/2 inch. Remove the seeds and membrane. Pepper should be able to stand up straight, if not — cut a thin slice off of the bottom.

4. Stuff bell peppers with cauliflower mixture and place in a 9"×13" inch baking dish. Bake until peppers and cauliflower are soft, about 30 minutes. Add cheese on top and bake for another 3-5 minutes.

*Photo: Allie Doran*

# Baked Chicken Meatballs

*By Allie Doran*

The beauty of this recipe (or any meatball recipe, really) is that you can make a double batch, cook them all, and then throw one in the freezer for another night. Who doesn't love having dinner in the freezer ready to heat on a super busy weeknight?

# Baked Chicken Meatballs
*Continued from previous page*

**Yield:** 4 servings

**Prep Time:** 15 minutes

**Cook Time:** 25 minutes

**Total Time:** 40 minutes

**Ingredients:**
2 and 1/2 Tbsp. olive oil, divided
1/2 small onion, finely chopped
2 garlic cloves, minced
1/2 cup breadcrumbs
1 large egg
1 Tbsp. whole milk
1 tsp. Italian seasoning
1 tsp. salt
1/2 tsp. pepper
1 lb. ground chicken

1. Preheat the oven to 400°F. Place a large skillet over medium heat. Add 1/2 tablespoon of the olive oil and allow it to heat.

2. Add the onion to the skillet and sauté until translucent, about 5 minutes. Add the garlic, and cook for an additional 2 minutes.

3. In a bowl, mix together the cooked onions and garlic, breadcrumbs, egg, milk, Italian seasoning, salt, and pepper.

4. Add the chicken and mix well with your hands, but don't overmix as that can make the meatballs tough.

5. Line a baking sheet with parchment paper or silicone mat.

6. Take about 2 tablespoons of the mixture and roll into a meatball. Place on the prepared baking sheet. Repeat with remaining meat.

7. Place baking sheet in the oven for 20-25 minutes until the meatballs are cooked through. Turn on the broiler and broil for 2-3 minutes to brown more, if desired.

# Chicken and Dumplings

*By Leigh Olson*

*There are many different kinds of dumplings in the world and from my experience, they're all delicious. But, I particularly like the ones in this dish. They're light and fluffy because of the baking powder, and have some richness because of the butter.*

**Yield:** 6 servings

**Prep Time:** 15 minutes

**Cook Time:** 40 minutes

**Total Time:** 55 minutes

**Ingredients:**
2 lbs. boneless skinless chicken thighs or breasts, cut into 1-inch pieces
1 tsp. salt
1/2 tsp. pepper
4 Tbsp. olive oil, divided
1 medium onion, chopped
1 cup sliced carrots
1/2 cup chopped celery
3 cloves garlic, minced
1 Tbsp. chopped fresh thyme or 1/2 tsp. dried
1 Tbsp. chopped fresh rosemary or 1/2 tsp. dried
1/4 cup all-purpose flour
2 Tbsp. unsalted butter
6 cups low-sodium chicken stock
1/2 cup white wine
3/4 cup heavy cream

*Dumplings*
1 and 1/2 cups all purpose flour
1 Tbsp. baking powder
1/2 tsp. salt
1/3 cup milk
1 Tbsp. unsalted butter, melted
1/4 cup chopped parsley

1. Season the chicken with salt and pepper.

2. Heat a large pot over medium-high heat, and add 2 tablespoons of the oil. Working in batches, brown the chicken on all sides. Remove from pan.

3. Add the remaining 2 tablespoons of oil to the pot. Add onions, carrots, and celery. Sauté until the onion becomes translucent, 5 – 7 minutes. Add the garlic, thyme, and rosemary. Cook for another minute.

4. Add the flour and butter, stirring until the butter has melted completely and the flour has been distributed.

5. Gradually add the stock, stirring constantly.

6. Add the wine and cream. Return the chicken to the pan. Bring to a boil. Reduce the heat, and simmer for 15 – 20 minutes.

7. To make the dumplings, in a large bowl, mix together the flour, baking powder, and salt.

8. Pour the milk and butter into the flour mixture and stir until just combined. Don't over mix.

9. Drop spoonfuls of the dumpling mixture on to the top of the gently simmering stew. Cover and cook until a toothpick inserted in the center of the dumplings comes out clean, about 12 – 15 minutes.

10. Garnish with parsley.

# Chicken and Cheese Stuffed Potatoes

*Microwaving potatoes and then stuffing them is a great way to get a hearty, and fun, dinner onto the table quickly. Once you know the technique, you can use all kinds of different fillings and toppings.*

**Yield:** 4 servings

**Prep Time:** 5 minutes

**Cook Time:** 25 minutes

**Total Time:** 30 minutes

**Ingredients:**
2 large russet potatoes
1 Tbsp. oil
1 lb. ground chicken
3/4 tsp. salt, divided
1/4 tsp. pepper
1/4 tsp. garlic powder
1 Tbsp. all-purpose flour
1/2 cup low-sodium chicken stock
1 tsp. Worcestershire sauce
1/2 cup frozen peas, defrosted
1 Tbsp. unsalted butter
3/4 cup shredded cheddar cheese, divided
2 Tbsp. milk

1. Preheat broiler.

2. Stab each potato in a few places with fork. Put them on a plate and in the microwave. Cook on high 5 minutes. To test if they're done, poke on both sides of each potato with a fork. If it goes in easily, potatoes are done. If not, flip and cook for an addition 1-2 minutes.

3. In medium skillet, heat oil over medium heat. Add ground chicken and stir to break up. Add 1/2 teaspoon salt, pepper, and garlic powder. Cook stirring occasionally until cooked through, about 7-8 minutes. Drain off fat if needed.

4. Sprinkle chicken with flour and stir in. Slowly stir in stock and Worcestershire sauce and stir to combine.

5. Stir occasionally until it reaches a boil. Reduce heat and simmer until thickened, about 2-3 minutes. Stir in peas.

6. Cut potatoes in half and scoop out middle, keeping a 1/2-inch edge all around. Place potato filling in bowl.

7. To the potato add butter, 1/2 cup of the shredded cheese, 1/4 teaspoon salt, and milk. Mash.

8. Fill hollowed out potatoes with chicken filling. Top with mashed potatoes. Sprinkle with remaining cheese.

9. Place on baking sheet and broil until the cheese is melted, about 3-4 minutes.

*Photo: Sam Ellis*

# Chicken and Waffles

*By Sam Ellis*

*This recipe is a little tricky to make by yourself because you want to have hot, freshly cooked waffles AND hot, freshly fried chicken ready at the same time. If you're doing this on your own, the best thing to do is to have the oven stay warm at about 250°F and then either start with the waffles or with the chicken and keep the first warm on an uncovered baking sheet while you do the other. If you have a second set of hands available, have one person make the waffles while the other makes the chicken. You still want the oven set to 250°F though in case one of you finishes before the other.*

# Chicken and Waffles
*Continued from previous page*

**Yield:** 8 servings

**Prep Time:** 30 minutes

**Cook Time:** 30 minutes

**Total Time:** 1 hour

**Ingredients:**
*Waffles:*
2 cups all-purpose flour
2 Tbsp. sugar
4 tsp. baking powder
1/2 tsp. salt
2 eggs
1 and 1/2 cups milk
1/2 cup vegetable oil
1 tsp. vanilla extract
Cooking spray

*Chicken:*
3 lbs. boneless skinless chicken breasts
1 cup buttermilk
1 egg
1 and 1/2 cups all-purpose flour
1 tsp. paprika
1 tsp. salt
1/2 tsp. garlic powder
1/2 tsp. pepper
Vegetable oil
Maple syrup

**Waffles:**

1. Sift together flour, sugar, baking powder, and salt in a bowl.

2. Separate egg whites and yolks. Put egg whites in a small bowl and egg yolks in a large bowl.

3. In bowl with the egg yolks, mix milk, vegetable oil, and vanilla extract.

4. Using a hand mixer or stand mixer with a whisk attachment, beat egg white into stiff peaks.

5. Slowly fold the dry ingredients into the yolk and milk mixture. Once combined, gently fold in the egg whites.

6. Preheat oven to 250°F.

7. Heat a waffle iron over medium heat. Once heated, spray with cooking spray and add in about 1 cup of the mixture depending on the size of the iron and cook through according to waffle iron. When waffle is cooked, transfer it to a sheet pan and put it in the warm oven to stay warm. Continue until batter is gone.

**Chicken:**

1. Butterfly the chicken breasts horizontally. Cut into long 1" wide strips.

2. Combine buttermilk and egg in one bowl, whisking until incorporated.

3. In another large bowl, sift together flour, paprika, salt, garlic powder, and pepper.

4. Heat a 12" skillet with high edges over medium high heat

with vegetable oil filling the skillet about 1/2" full. Use a candy thermometer to determine when the oil reaches 350°F.

5. While the vegetable oil is heating, dip chicken pieces in dry mixture, covering entirely, then the wet mixture and back into the dry mixture. Set these aside in a single layer on a large plate until ready to fry.

6. Carefully place chicken in the vegetable oil, not crowding the skillet. Check the temperature of the oil once the skillet is full and adjust temperature if needed. Cook on both sides about 5-6 minutes each side or until the internal temperature of the chicken reaches 165°F. Remove from skillet and place on paper towel lined plate.

7. Serve chicken pieces on waffles and top with maple syrup.

# Chicken, Broccoli, and Rice Casserole

*By Ilona Orzechowska*

*You might wonder if you can skip sautéing the onion before mixing it into the casserole. You don't want to do that because it may not fully soften in the oven. Plus, sautéing the chopped onion with butter adds so much flavor to the casserole. After the onions have softened, add frozen broccoli and cook it a bit so it becomes softer and cooks off some of the extra liquid.*

**Yield:** 8 servings

**Prep Time:** 15 minutes

**Cook Time:** 30 minutes

**Total Time:** 45 minutes

**Ingredients:**

- 1 Tbsp. unsalted butter
- 1/2 small onion, chopped
- 5 cups frozen broccoli, defrosted
- 1 (10.75 oz.) can condensed chicken soup or homemade from Chapter 1
- 1 cup pasteurized processed cheese (ex. Cheez Whiz or Velveeta)
- 1/2 cup milk
- 1/4 tsp. salt (optional)
- 3 cups cooked white long grain rice
- 2 cups cubed cooked chicken
- 1/2 cup shredded cheddar cheese

1. Preheat oven to 350°F. Grease 9" x 9" baking dish.

2. In a large pan over low heat melt the butter. Add onion and sauté on medium until softened, 3-5 minutes. Add broccoli and cook for another 5 minutes.

3. Add condensed chicken soup, pasteurized processed cheese, and milk while stirring to make a sauce. Cook for 5 minutes stirring occasionally. Taste and season with salt if needed.

4. Add rice and chicken to the sauce and mix well.

5. Pour rice mixture into the baking dish. Add shredded cheddar cheese on top.

6. Bake until heated through and cheese is melted, 30-35 minutes.

# Chicken and Wild Rice Casserole

*By Sam Ellis*

*Feel free to skip the almonds if you'd like but they definitely add texture and flavor. If you do use them, make sure you buy sliced or slivered almonds. Whole almonds are too big. You want that nutty crunch without overpowering the dish.*

**Yield:** 6 servings

**Prep Time:** 20 minutes

**Cook Time:** 35 minutes

**Total Time:** 55 minutes

**Ingredients:**
1/3 cup unsalted butter
1 small onion, chopped
8 oz. button mushrooms, sliced
2 Tbsp. all-purpose flour
1 and 1/2 cups low-sodium chicken stock
1 cup heavy cream
3 cups cubed cooked chicken
4 cups cooked wild rice
1 (4 oz.) jar diced pimentos, drained
1/3 cup slivered almonds

1. Preheat oven to 350°F.

2. Over medium heat in a medium sauté pan, add butter and let melt. Add in onion and mushrooms and stir to coat. Cook until softened, about 5 minutes.

3. Add flour and stir to coat. Slowly stir in chicken stock. Bring it to a simmer so it thickens.

4. Remove from heat and stir in heavy cream.

5. Add in chicken, cooked rice, and pimentos. Stir so everything is incorporated.

6. Pour into a 3-quart casserole dish.

7. Add sliced almonds on top and bake until heated through and bubbling, 30-35 minutes.

# Chicken and Collard Greens Stir Fry

*I like buying those big bags of chopped dark greens, like collards, kale, and mustard greens. I throw them into soups and stews, tear them into salads, or, I stir fry them!*

**Yield:** 4 servings

**Prep Time:** 5 minutes

**Cook Time:** 10 minutes

**Total Time:** 30 minutes

**Ingredients:**
2 Tbsp. honey
2 Tbsp. soy sauce
1 Tbsp. + 1 tsp. vegetable oil, divided
1/2 tsp. sesame oil
2 boneless skinless chicken breasts, thinly sliced
1 red bell pepper, sliced
2 cloves garlic, thinly sliced
1 tsp. sesame seeds
10 oz. collard greens, chopped and washed
1 green onion, chopped

1. In a small bowl, whisk together honey and soy sauce until well combined. Set aside.

2. In a large skillet or wok, heat 1 tablespoon of the vegetable oil and the sesame oil over medium-high heat until very hot.

3. Add the chicken. Stir often until cooked through, 4-6 minutes. Transfer to a plate.

4. Add the remaining 1 teaspoon of oil to the skillet and then add the bell pepper, garlic, and sesame seeds.

5. Stir and cook until pepper is al dente, 2-3 minutes.

6. Add the greens. Cook stirring continuously until wilted, 3 minutes.

7. Return the chicken to the skillet and add the honey mixture. Stir to heat through. Serve garnished with the green onion.

# Chicken and Cheese Quiche

*Making quiche involves mixing together some ingredients with some eggs, pouring it into a pie crust (go with store-bought to simplify, or make your own), and then baking it. Give it a try for brunch this weekend, or use it for a special Breakfast-for-Dinner weeknight meal.*

**Yield:** 8 servings

**Prep Time:** 10 minutes

**Cook Time:** 40 minutes

**Total Time:** 50 minutes

**Ingredients:**
1 (9-inch) pie crust
4 large eggs
1 and 1/2 cups whole milk
1/4 tsp. salt
1/8 tsp. pepper
1 cup shredded sharp cheddar cheese
1 cup chopped cooked chicken (or cooked chicken sausage or smoked chicken breast lunchmeat)

1. Preheat oven to 350°F.

2. Remove pie crust from refrigerator. If store-bought, soften according to package instructions.

3. Crack eggs into a medium bowl. Whisk with a fork until no clear streaks of egg whites remain.

4. Add milk, salt, and pepper. Stir until fully combined.

5. Put pie crust into a 9-inch pie plate.

6. Sprinkle pie crust with cheese. Top with chicken.

7. Pour egg mixture over cheese and chicken.

8. Bake quiche on the lowest rack of the oven until it's mostly set but slightly jiggly in the middle, 35-45 minutes. If the pastry is browning too much around the edges, cover the edges with aluminum foil.

9. Let quiche cool to warm (at least 15 minutes) before slicing and serving. Or allow it to cool completely and then cover and refrigerate to serve cold within the following 2 days.

10. Reheat quiche by covering with aluminum foil and baking at 325°F until warmed through, about 15 minutes. Or slice it and microwave slices individually on the defrost setting for 30 seconds at a time until heated through. Or reheat slices in the air fryer set at 350°F for 4-6 minutes.

# Chicken and Spinach Scrambled Eggs Benedict

*Poaching eggs can be a pain so when I make eggs benedict I tend to scramble the eggs instead. And if I'm scrambling them, I might as well add some tasty ingredients like chicken sausage and spinach. As to the hollandaise sauce, this recipe is life-changing. You make it in the blender, no whisking required, and it's ready in minutes. I know you're going to be making this one all the time now.*

**Yield:** 6 servings

**Prep Time:** 25 minutes

**Cook Time:** 0 minutes

**Total Time:** 25 minutes

**Ingredients:**
8 eggs
2 Tbsp. milk
1 tsp. vegetable oil
8 links fully-cooked chicken breakfast sausage, sliced
2 cups spinach leaves
1/4 tsp. salt
1/4 tsp. pepper
4 English muffins, split open

*Hollandaise Sauce:*
6 egg yolks
2 Tbsp. lemon juice
1/2 tsp. salt
a pinch of cayenne pepper
1 cup (2 sticks) unsalted butter

1. Whisk the 8 eggs and milk together in a medium bowl. Set aside.
2. Heat a large skillet over medium heat. Add the oil.
3. Add the sausage and cook until lightly browned in places.
4. Add the spinach and stir for a minute.
5. Add the whisked eggs, salt, and pepper, and stir often until fully set. Remove from heat. Cover skillet with foil to keep eggs warm.
6. Meanwhile, toast the English muffins and make the Hollandaise sauce.
7. To assemble, arrange two English muffin halves, cut side up, on a dinner plate. Top with one-sixth of the egg mixture and a couple tablespoons of hollandaise.

**Hollandaise Sauce:**

1. Put the egg yolks, lemon juice, salt, and cayenne in the blender. Pulse a few times to mix. Scrape down sides of blender.
2. Melt the butter in the microwave or in a small pot over low heat until melted and steaming. You want it really warm.
3. With the blender running at medium speed, slowly drizzle the butter into the egg yolks. It should thicken by the time you've added all the butter. Continue to blend for an additional 30 seconds to thicken further.

Photo: Georgina Walker

# Taco Lettuce Wraps

*By Georgina Walker*

Taco Lettuce Wraps are basically tacos without the shell. You use a leaf of lettuce instead of the taco. Not only are they healthier but they're so delicious and fun to eat too!

**Yield:** 4 servings

**Prep Time:** 15 minutes

**Cook Time:** 10 minutes

**Total Time:** 25 minutes

**Ingredients:**
1 Tbsp. olive oil
1 lb. ground chicken
1 (1 oz.) packet of taco seasoning
1/2 cup tomato salsa
8 leaves of lettuce (green leaf, hydroponic butter, or romaine)
1 small tomato, finely chopped
1 avocado, chopped
1/2 cup shredded cheddar cheese
1/2 cup sour cream
2 green onions, chopped

1. Heat olive oil in a skillet over medium-high heat. Add chicken and cook, stirring occasionally, until cooked through, 5-6 minutes.
2. Stir in taco seasoning and cook for one minute.
3. Add salsa and stir until combined.
4. Spoon chicken onto lettuce leaves.
5. Top with tomato, avocado, cheese, sour cream, and green onions.
6. To eat, tuck lettuce leaves around filling and pick up and eat, as though the lettuce is a soft taco.

# 40 Clove Garlic Chicken

*By Tawnie Kroll*

*Don't let the 40 cloves of garlic intimidate you. Once you roast garlic, the garlic actually takes on a more buttery and mild flavor compared to raw garlic. And if you're worried about dreaded garlic breath, don't be. Roasting garlic helps with that too! Note that you really can't use chicken breasts for this recipe. The reason is that they would cook more quickly than the time the garlic needs to soften and roast. So either the chicken would be dry or the garlic would be undercooked. If you really want to use breasts, roast the garlic in the pan for 15 minutes first and then add the seared chicken breasts and bake until cooked through to 165°F, about 20 minutes.*

**Yield:** 4 servings

**Prep Time:** 10 minutes

**Cook Time:** 30 minutes

**Total Time:** 40 minutes

**Ingredients:**
8 boneless skinless chicken thighs
1/2 tsp. salt
1/2 tsp. pepper
3 Tbsp. olive oil, divided
2 Tbsp. unsalted butter
40 cloves of garlic, peeled
3/4 cup low-sodium chicken stock
1/3 cup white wine
3 sprigs fresh thyme
2 sprigs fresh rosemary

1. Preheat oven to 350°F. Season the chicken with salt and pepper.

2. In an oven-safe sauté pan over medium heat, heat 2 tablespoons of the olive oil and the butter together. Once the oil is hot, add the chicken and cook until brown underneath, about 4-5 minutes. Flip and brown on the other side. Transfer chicken to a plate and set aside.

3. Add the remaining tablespoon of oil and the garlic cloves to the same pan and cook stirring occasionally until slightly softened, 3-4 minutes.

4. Add the garlic cloves to the plate with the chicken.

5. Add the stock and wine to the pan you browned the chicken in and let the liquid simmer for 2 minutes. While it simmers, use a wooden spoon to scrape up any bits stuck to the pan.

6. Add the chicken and garlic back to the pan. Top chicken with fresh thyme and rosemary sprigs (break up sprigs if needed to get some on each piece of chicken).

7. Bake until chicken is cooked through to 165°F as read on an instant read thermometer, about 30 minutes.

8. Transfer chicken and garlic to a serving plate. Stir the juices in the pan and taste them. Add salt and pepper if desired. If the juices taste good, pour them over the chicken and garlic before serving, or put them in a gravy boat to serve alongside.

9. Serve chicken with roasted garlic cloves on the side.

# About the Author

Christine Pittman is a Canadian living in Florida with her two kids and two cats. She has two websties, COOKtheSTORY.com and TheCookful.com, with a combined readership of over 2 million visitors per month. She focuses on helping cooks of all levels improve their skills by learning the why behind the steps in her recipes. When she's not in the kitchen or at her computer, Christine is likely walking in the woods, swimming in the pool, or dancing in the club.

# Acknowledgements

This book couldn't have been made without the reminders and gentle proddings from my business manager, Heather McCurdy, nor without the graphic design skills of Beth Brombosz. I'm also forever grateful for the inspiration and motivation that my mastermind group brings to me. Casey, Jill, and Leigh – "You guys are awesome and I love you."

Thank you to the cooks who have taught me, most notably my mom (Phyllis Pittman) and my Baba (Etta Melnyk). And, thank you to those who have instilled such a strong work ethic and entrepreneurial spirit in me. Dad (Barry Pittman), that's you. And mom too!

I'm also very thankful to the team of recipe developers, photographers, writers, and bloggers who contribute to my websites, some of whom have contributions in this book. The recipes and pictures in this cookbook are all by me unless otherwise noted. In which case, they're by the talented individuals listed on the next page.

Finally, a huge thank you to those that I cook for, both in person and to the readers who visit my sites and read and try my recipes. I couldn't do this without the love and support that you all continue to bring to me every day.

Thank you!

–Christine xoxo

# Contributors

Meghan Basset – cakenknife.com
Sara Blackburn – realbalanced.com
Lyndsay Burginger – wideopeneats.com
Rebecca Clyde – nourishnutritionblog.com
Traci Devito – petitechefblog.com
Emily Dingmann – myeverydaytable.com
Allie Doran – missallieskitchen.com
Amanda Dorich – oldhousetonewhome.net
Sam Ellis – theculinarycompass.com
Amy Getman – happyhealthyrd.com
Lauren Keating – healthy-delicious.com
Tawnie Kroll – krollskorner.com
Jess Larson – playswellwithbutter.com
Stephanie Manley – copykat.com
Kelly Nardo – eatthegains.com
Ellie O'Brien – hungrybynature.com
Leigh Olson – theheritagecookbookproject.com
Ilona Orzechowska – ilonaspassion.com
Brittany Poulson – yourchoicenutrition.com
Lauren Sharifi – biteofhealthnutrition.com
Jamie Silva – asassyspoon.com
Jill Silverman Hough – jillhough.com
Georgina Walker – thehomecookskitchen.com

*All recipes and pictures in this book are by Christine Pittman unless otherwise noted.*

Made in the USA
Columbia, SC
20 May 2020